D1524196

The 'Incumberances'

Nob Kishen's Nautch Party, watercolour illustration by
Sir Charles D'Oyly for his satirical poem 'Tom Raw, the Griffin'.
© *Victoria and Albert Museum, London.*

The 'Incumberances'

British Women in India
1615-1856

JOAN MICKELSON GAUGHAN

OXFORD
UNIVERSITY PRESS

OXFORD
UNIVERSITY PRESS

Oxford University Press is a department of the University of Oxford.
It furthers the University's objective of excellence in research, scholarship,
and education by publishing worldwide. Oxford is a registered trademark of
Oxford University Press in the UK and in certain other countries

Published in India by
Oxford University Press
YMCA Library Building, 1 Jai Singh Road, New Delhi 110 001, India

ISBN-13: 978-0-19-809214-8
ISBN-10: 0-19-809214-8

Typeset in Bell MT Std 10.5/13
by The Graphics Solution, New Delhi 110 092
Printed in India by Akash Press, New Delhi 110 020

In memory of Dr Gerald Brown
wise mentor and gentle friend

contents

Contents

preface

IT ONCE WAS CUSTOMARY TO THINK of all the British women who
ever went out to India as 'memsahibs'—a single, colourless group,
pitiful and self-pitying, bored and boring, decorative, redundant,
plagued with prickly heat, gossipy, whiny, scrambling for 'place' in
a social order that became increasingly rigid especially after the
1857 Mutiny, sweating about in clothes completely incongruous
with India's climate, fitfully trying to create little Englands in their
pathetic bungalows, flitting through the 'hot weather' at a hill station and then mouldering on the plains through the monsoons. In
the late 1880s, Wilfrid Scaven Blunt thought the memsahibs were
responsible for half the bitter feelings between the races. Richard
Burton thought they were contemptible, and Rudyard Kipling's
vicious Mrs Hauksbee became the prototype for the entire group.

A major justification for empire was the chance to redeem fallen
'natives', to pick up the 'white man's burden' and to seize the chance
to 'do good'. Thus, another 'type' that has survived is the woman who
embraced the imperial burden and went to India to teach, nurse, or
to operate orphanages. Such women were often dismissed as tedious
and boring, ridiculed for having 'gone native' and not quite fitting
into the social patterns of Anglo-India. Often, they were missionaries themselves or came out to India as wives of missionaries. Many
others, however, came out singly to educate and to heal Indians,

particularly Indian women. Indeed, the history of the British presence in India is not complete without mention of the work of women such as Annette Akroyd Beveridge and Mary Carpenter on behalf of female education in India, or the remarkable Margaret Noble who not only opened schools for Hindu girls but converted to Hinduism herself and became known as Sister Nivedita.

That bifurcated perception of the place of British women in India is nearly as old as the East India Company's presence there. In 1615, the Court of Directors also saw only two roles that women might play—either they would get in the way or they could be spiritual or emotional supports for the men to whom they were attached. It might be argued (albeit with perhaps more than one caveat) that both the nineteenth-century memsahib and the bearer of burden stereotypes derived from that dichotomous view. Recently there has been a trend, particularly among feminist historians, to do what the Directors did in 1615, that is, to overlook the complexity of the experience British women had in India and to 'type' them, to view their presence as symbolically representing something, or to give them a role, or roles, of which the women themselves seem not to have been aware. Thus, another type that has emerged is the model of British women not only as embodiments of the domestic values—industriousness, moral purity, devotion to duty, and so on—that justified or underlay the Raj, but also as full partners in embodying the masculinity by which the British ruled the 'effeminate' races of India.

The British were in India for almost two centuries before there was any empire for or about which to bear a burden, or in which to be a memsahib, a doer of good, or a symbolic representation of a racial or imperial set of values. Like their male counterparts, the roles of the English women who came to India in the seventeenth and eighteenth centuries were defined largely by the policies and purposes of the East India Company, or, in the early nineteenth, by the government. And, like their male counterparts, many of these women played out those roles—and just as many ignored them and created new and unique roles for themselves.

It is important to remember that British women—and men—occupied two very different worlds in India. The first was the Anglo-Indian world whose values, behaviours, and tastes they shaped and were shaped by. That world was not simply a transplanted England.

First, and most obvious, it was hot, hotter than any place in Britain or, for that matter, in all of Europe. The climate required physical and often psychological adjustments. One did not, could not, act in India as one would in England for the simple reason that one did not feel the same as one might in England. Second, social hierarchy mattered in Anglo-India as much as in Britain but there was far more fluidity as commerce in the seventeenth and eighteenth centuries, and military and civilian service in the nineteenth replaced birth as the determinants of social status. Third, for much of the period, Britain was essentially rural, sparsely populated, and homogenous. The Anglo-Indian world, on the other hand, was cosmopolitan, racially and religiously heterogeneous, and immensely populous. There were lots of people, especially servants bustling about, and their notions of proper social conventions were not at all what an English man or woman would have been accustomed to. Privacy was an extremely rare commodity. Everybody knew everybody else, as well as their children, servants, latest diseases, family histories, and personal habits. One could not possess an eccentricity, engage in an illicit affair, have an unruly child, abuse a subordinate, or fail to receive a coveted commission without one's compatriots thousands of miles away knowing about it.

Finally, like Britain itself, Anglo-India was a world in flux. The English men and women who came to India in the seventeenth century were essentially 'on the make', viewing India as a place in which to get very, very rich, and then to live long enough to enjoy their riches. Their religious views, if they had any, were usually sufficiently Protestant to be orthodox. The religious and political upheavals in England were fairly remote in India where Antinomianism mattered far less than making a profit. These people were not inclined to study Hinduism, Islam, or any other religion with any great zeal, and often worried more about Catholic influences upon their community than about Hinduism. They acknowledged racial differences but, on the whole, they were not very good racists nor were they interested in India's history. A woman was something upon which a man spawned progeny. Like her Indian sisters, she had few legal rights, and the ordinary man was not particularly interested in investing her with any more than she might personally demand of him.

By the nineteenth century, the Industrial Revolution, the Enlightenment, military victories both in Europe and in India, and the emotional intensity of both Romanticism and Evangelicalism had given the English man an entirely different set of values through which he viewed his fellow creatures, male or female, European or Indian. He was still a Protestant but Protestantism itself had changed. To the core Christian belief in One Saving God and a general nod in the direction of the Ten Commandments of Moses and the two great commandments of Love ordained by Jesus, had been added a list of hitherto rather unchristian values—industry, thrift, feminine delicacy, and, in the late eighteenth century with the help of John Wesley, the notion that cleanliness was next to godliness. By then, too, the status of women at home had begun to change, if ever so slightly, and the share they would take in formulating and articulating Christian and, in particular, British Christian values, had been enlarged. Those same influences, however, had not affected India. Thus, the cultural gap which had been fairly narrow in the seventeenth century would have widened in the nineteenth even without the reality of empire.

The second world was India itself, where memories of the cruelties of the Portuguese along the Malabar Coast in the early sixteenth century when the Inquisition had been freely employed to discourage new converts to Christianity from relapsing were still fresh. In addition to that lingering onus, both Hinduism and Islam were closed systems; whatever was outside them was, to use Edward Said's term, 'Other'. To the Hindu, the European was outside caste, one in outer darkness; to the Muslim, he was an infidel; and both communities had distinct and ancient notions of the role women should occupy which were unlikely to be influenced by anything from Europe. A few years before the Mutiny, Martha Weitbrecht was on a morning walk towards wells where Indian women came to draw water when she encountered a group of three or four women, standing with their *ghurras*, or earthen vessels, lying on the ground. One of the women thought Mrs Weitbrecht's foot had touched a neighbour's ghurra and exclaimed, 'See, she has polluted it; you must break your ghurra', but the other woman protested that, though near, Mrs Weitbrecht had not touched it. Thus, the pot was saved.[1] Clearly, any woman or man who sought to breach the cultural barrier, as so many did, had to face the possibility of a rebuff, not from his compatriots but from India itself.

Although India is home to a variety of religious expressions, Hinduism cannot be separated from India in the way that, say, Protestantism can be separated from Britain. A Protestant does not necessarily have to be British to be Protestant and vice versa. Underlying the fabric of Hindu civilization are three assumptions that, with the best of intentions, a European could not have penetrated. The first is the sense of time. Since the appearance of Saint Augustine's *City of God* in the fifth century, the West has viewed time in a linear fashion. It is going from somewhere, the City of Earth, to somewhere else, the Heavenly City. History thus shows an upward progression; things get better spiritually as well as materially. The Hindu view of time is cyclical, and there are cycles within cycles. There is then no progression to a 'better' and it is foolish then to think in terms of 'progress' of any kind.

The second assumption has to do with karma. Every action, whether mental or physical, of necessity produces an appropriate result. A good action produces good fruit; a bad action, bad fruit. But neither good nor evil has anything to do with a deity. Thus, there is no divine reward for the one and divine punishment for the other. Since ethical behaviour has nothing to do with a deity, to the European, Indian gods would appear as absurdities. On the other hand, since karma is linked with the notion of rebirth/reincarnation, the European might have found common ground in the ancient Greek notion of metempsychosis.

The third assumption, somewhat resembling European notions of class and related to the ancient notion of a Great Chain of Being, has to do with dharma, that is, the conduct that is expected of one within the context of one's social class. It is from this structuring of social relationships that caste derives. No man can perform another's duties or obligations. What is right for one man is wrong for another. Behaviour inconsistent with one's caste (or class, in Europe) upsets an order that is ancient, irrevocable, and iron-clad.

Finally, in both Islam and Christianity, truth is one, unified, and revealed by God. In Hinduism, however, although all truths ultimately are one, there are many levels of that truth, none of which has anything to do with a deity. The truth for one man may be quite different from the truth of another man. This is not 'toleration' nor is it the 'deviousness' Indians were so often accused of so much as the fact that, to a Hindu, all truths, all social practices, can be encapsulated within a society, as long as there is willingness to accept the premise on which this encapsulation is based.[2]

Racial distance notwithstanding, even in the nineteenth century, at the apogee of imperialism, there was always a remarkable fluidity of reactions among British women to both India and the Anglo-Indian community in which they lived. What is far more significant than the chasm that characterized racial relationships after 1857 and in the two or three decades before that is that, despite the deep cultural differences, for the greater bulk of the time the British were in India, those differences were so often and so completely bridged by men and women on both sides of the racial divide. For British women, however, far more than for British men, the penetration of India presented formidable obstacles. Yet, despite those obstacles, many women did engage India and they did so in a variety of ways.

It is misleading to speak of a feminist or specifically feminine gaze as if it were a unified, monolithic thing. The reasons for which women went to India in the seventeenth century and their reactions to India once they arrived were very different from those of their granddaughters and great granddaughters in the eighteenth and early nineteenth centuries. Even among contemporaries, their expressions were immensely varied, highly individual, and unique, coloured by personal, social, religious, and cultural backgrounds. Some of the women who came out to India were desperately poor and viewed India as a place to advance economically and socially. Others were socially quite secure at home. Some were quite religious, others a bit amoral. Some grew in India, others languished. Some explored as much of India as they possibly could, learned her languages, and collected her arts, learned to appreciate her music, poetry, and religions, and developed deep friendships with her people; others hated everything about her and withered. For some, India was a home; for others, it was an exile, a land of regrets. Few changed India very much but very few left unchanged by her.

To fully understand the roles British women played in India, one must look at India not only through the expectations men, and often some women themselves, had, but also through the multifarious ways in which the women themselves experienced India in light of those expectations. And when one does that, one is confronted not with a mirror but with a prism.

This study is divided into three parts: the first, the Age of the Factory, covers the period from the initial decision of the East India Company's directors about women in 1615 to the Battle of Plassey in 1757. The second part, the Age of the Nabobs, goes from Plassey to 1805, when Richard Wellesley, having defeated the most formidable threat to British dominance in India, Tipu Sultan in 1799, and having moulded the government of India into roughly the framework it would have until 1947, returned home. The third period, the Age of Improvement, ending on the eve of the Mutiny, were decades when English women found opportunities to encounter India and to shoulder responsibilities that had hitherto been unavailable to them.

notes

1 Martha Weitbrecht, *Women of India and Christian Work in the Zenana* (London: James Nisbet & Co., 1875), 122.

2 Ainslee Embree, 'Tradition and Modernization in India: Synthesis or Encapsulation?' Presented at the International Symposium on Science and Society in South Asia, Rockefeller University, 5 May 1966.

part one

The factory, 1615–1757

BY THE MIDDLE OF THE SEVENTEENTH CENTURY, the East India Company had lifted its initial prohibition against women going out to the Indies when it became clear that the Company might lose valuable servants unless wives were allowed to accompany their husbands to their posts. Single women, however, did not go until after the Restoration when the Company sent out the first 'fishing fleets' carrying young women who, it was hoped, would soften the manners of its factors and encourage Protestant progeny.

Those were the expectations of the Company. The expectations of the women themselves were often slightly different. They seem to have little intention of softening manners and, in fact, according to some sources, became as 'debauched' as the male factors. They did marry and produce children that would be raised Protestant but, largely because of their low salaries and the monastic character of the factories, the simple presence of English women did not assure that the factors would marry them rather than Catholic Portuguese women or, more likely, cohabit with Indian concubines.

Once the prohibition was relaxed, almost all of the women who came out to India were wives or daughters of the merchants, chaplains, surgeons, and soldiers attached either to the Company or to the numerous interlopers also engaged in the Indies trade. And the fact that they were attached—or expected to be attached—to men who were not imperial administrators meant that, to the extent that they could engage in commerce as some of them did, they could share the Company's purposes in India. As many women found, India could provide economic opportunities which, while not as lucrative as those available to men, gave them a chance at real financial independence.

Despite the Company's hopes that the mere presence of English women would promote settled family life, the world of the factory was vastly indifferent, indeed hostile, to the presence of an English wife and family, but it was neither the quarrelsomeness nor the drinking—to both of which women would contribute substantially when they did arrive—nor the presence of concubines that lay at the root of that unwelcoming environment. Rather, it was the fundamental nature of the factory itself—an intensely masculine, semi-monastic, Christian citadel of commerce that presented the greatest difficulty.

1

an 'extreamlie unkind' decision

ANCHORED JUST OFF SANDWICH IN MID-FEBRUARY 1615, William Keeling stood on the deck of his ship watching the tiny craft carrying his wife back to shore recede in the distance. Anticipating that the East India Company might deny her license to travel to the Indies, Anne Keeling had stowed away in William's cabin. She had been discovered and the Company's Directors had faced William with an ultimatum—despite the dozens of letters he had written them protesting his great love for Anne, if he wished to go to the Indies as their servant, it would have to be without his wife. At least for the moment, Keeling had chosen the Indies, but he would refer to the order which had put Anne on that boat as 'that extreamlie unkind l[ette]er fro. Sr Tho. Smith, never obliviable'.[1] Weeks later from the Cape, Keeling was still begging the Directors to send Anne out to him.

Sir Thomas Smith was the first governor of the East India Company's twenty-four member Court of Directors, and the 'extreamlie unkind' decision he and the other Directors had taken had not been reached easily or lightly. Nor was it at all a reflection of simple misogyny. Three times they had debated whether or not Anne, or for that matter, any wife, should be allowed to join her husband. Some of the Directors had felt it was a good thing for a wife to go with her husband 'as very fitting for the quiet of his mind and the good of his soul, as a curse befalleth those that keep man and wife asunder'.[2] On the other hand, women were thought to be both physically and emotionally unfit to be at sea. They were believed to encourage vice among the seamen and, worse, they were thought to bring bad luck.

Keeling was a valuable, albeit flamboyant man. The tusk of an African elephant that he had killed on an earlier voyage hung in the cabin in which Anne had hidden. The first performance of a Shakespearean play on the African coast had come when Keeling, in order 'to keepe my people from idleness and unlawfull games or sleepe',[3] had ordered his crew to sew costumes and memorize lines in order to perform *Richard the Second* and *Hamlet*. In his mid-twenties, he had acquitted himself so well in command of one of the ships on the Company's Second Voyage in 1604 (each fleet, separately funded, was called a Voyage) that he had been given command of the entire Third Voyage in 1607. That Third Voyage had been critical.

When Queen Elizabeth had signed the East India Company's original charter on 31 December 1600, it had not been India but the spices of the Malay Archipelago that had been the target of the Company's trade. Besides the pepper of the 'Spice Islands' which would be a staple of the East India Company trade until well into the nineteenth century, other spices were valued not only for their obvious culinary worth but also for medicinal purposes, particularly in the treatment of gastrointestinal ailments. Nutmeg and mace were used to treat rheumatism, cloves were useful for toothache and to relieve nausea and vomiting, especially in pregnancy, and they as well as many others were thought to be effective as aphrodisiacs.

It had not been until the Third Voyage that a serious interest in India had begun to be established. It was during that voyage that the factors at Bantam and in the Moluccas told the Directors that cloths imported from Cambay on India's Malabar Coast were in great demand, and if the factories could be furnished with them they could be profitably exchanged for spices. Trade should therefore be attempted with Cambay and at the city of Surat which lay at the mouth of the Gulf of Cambay.

Sailing from England on 1 April 1607, Keeling had had three vessels under his command, the *Dragon*, the *Hector*, and the *Consent*. He had also carried William Hawkins, a relative of the illustrious Elizabethan 'sea dog' of the same name, and an employee of the Company who was possibly even more colourful than Keeling himself. It had been Hawkins' task to establish the Company's first factory at Surat.

Keeling had returned to England in December 1608 with the most lucrative cargo hitherto loaded in the Malay Archipelago. The *Consent* alone came back with a cargo of cloves whose original cost was £2,948.15s. It sold for £36,287, a profit of 234 per cent.[4] The success of the Third Voyage allowed the Company to ask for and receive from James I a charter to trade exclusively and, unlike the original charter which had been valid for fifteen years, in perpetuity. The only caveat was that the Crown could revoke the charter with a three years' notice.

It was precisely because he had been so successful on the Third Voyage that Keeling had been given command of this, the Company's Twelfth Voyage in 1615. He had £26,660 in money and £26,065 in goods, a fleet of six vessels,[5] and for a short time, the company of his beloved Anne.

That the Directors even debated whether to allow Anne Keeling or any woman—or even men—to travel to the Indies may fill even the sturdiest soul with some alarm. Indeed, it might be wondered why Keeling or any other captain would visit such a trial upon someone he loved. The journey out was terrifying. On a voyage in tiny, wooden, creaking vessels that could last from two to six months, there was no part that was either safe or comfortable. If they survived the fierce currents and winds of the Strait of Gibraltar which still claim lives, winds off the coast of Africa could and often did sweep ships as far as the coast of Brazil. After being scorched by heat at the equator, passengers shivered with cold at the Cape of Good Hope, and at almost any point in the voyage there might be no wind at all and the ship would sit becalmed for weeks. William Keeling, of course, was well aware of the perils and discomforts of the voyage. In fact, it had been on that Third Voyage that his troubles had been so great that he finally gave up enumerating them and, after several days of 'muche winde and bad weather', he simply wrote in his journal of 'a storme'.[6]

Weather, however, was not the only or perhaps even the worst threat to one's life, limb, and comfort. Since the journeys of Saint

Paul, prayers for the ransom of captives had been a common theme in Christian liturgies. In the seventeenth century, those prayers were no less urgent as scores of unfortunates fell into the hands of the pirates who roamed the Mediterranean Sea and the Atlantic and Indian Oceans. Between 1610 and the 1630s, Cornwall and Devon, both sea-going counties heavily involved in trade with southern Europe, would lose a full fifth of their shipping to North African corsairs. Tales of torture, of harsh and prolonged confinements in ghastly prisons, the rape of female captives, and forced conversions to Islam filled sermons as well as the arena of public discourse. In addition to prayers, parish, community, and often government resources were required to ransom captives.[7] The Company was in business to make a profit. The expense of ransoming captives could be high.

Pirates may have been the most frightening of the human perils at sea, but there were others as well. In 1604, the success of the Company's Second Voyage under Sir Henry Middleton had led several independent merchants who were understandably jealous of the Company's monopoly on the Eastern trade to petition James I for the right to trade in the Indies. In a direct violation of the exclusive privileges granted the East India Company by Elizabeth, the king had granted a license to Sir Edward Michelborne and several others to also engage in the East Indian trade. Besides competing in the Indies trade, these 'interlopers', as they were called, continued to prey upon the Company's fleets as with at least as much enterprise as any pirate. Some simply ignored the Company's monopoly, and the Company's furious lobbying in England to stop them merely led to the use of vessels sailing under a foreign flag. Attempts to intercept them at sea were time-consuming as well as dangerous, and trying to get local officials to deal with them rarely met with much success. The solution ultimately became the union of the interlopers or 'New' Company with the original 'Old' Company in 1709, an act which effectively created a new corporation, the United Company of Merchants of England trading to the East Indies.

Other European contenders for the East Indian trade, particularly the Dutch and Portuguese, had already proven themselves to be treacherous as well. The Portuguese had been in the Spice Islands since 1514; the Dutch had arrived there about the same time the

English had, in 1605. As the Company had already learned, it was often hard put to defend its own factors who, unlike women, presumably had at least some chance of defending themselves. On India's Malabar Coast, the Portuguese were as menacing as the Dutch were in the Malay Archipelago. When William Hawkins arrived at Surat in 1608, he discovered almost immediately that he 'could not peepe out of doors for fear of the Portugals, who in troops lay lurking in by-wayes, to give me assault to murther me'.[8]

Weather, pirates, and interlopers, however, did not take as many lives as disease did. The Scientific Revolution had brought advances in medicine but it was still in a rather frightening state of underdevelopment. *If* one survived the voyage out, the diseases contracted by the Europeans in the East were puzzling, infinitely varied, and catastrophic. In addition to familiar enemies such as typhoid or enteric fever, cholera, dysentery, and small pox, India provided poisonous insects, vermin, and a wide variety of viruses to which Europeans had little or no immunity. However, although medical science still revolved around the four humours, there had been some progress. Fresh fruit was by then known to be an antidote to scurvy, but crews were still plagued by the disease. The First Voyage to Acheen in Sumatra had been commanded by Sir James Lancaster who had carried lemon juice. His other captains, however, decided not to bring any. Thus, Lancaster's men got all the way to the Cape with all or most of their teeth intact; the others arrived quite toothless. Lancaster's sailors were also fortunate in not having careful medical attention. The cures for the maladies with which Europeans were familiar can quite terrify one. Practised with more exuberance than efficacy, medical procedures involved a variety of emetics, purgatives, and bleeding both as therapies and preventives. The upper classes who could, unfortunately, afford the best medical care were the most vulnerable. When Charles II was on his deathbed, he was tortured with over fifty ferocious drugs while red hot irons were applied to his shaven head and naked feet.

Finally, the voyage out was simply uncomfortable. The accommodations were cramped and dirty; a bucket of salt water sufficed for a bath tub; another bucket was a toilet. At the start of the voyage there might be fresh meat because cows and sheep were carried aboard, but that could run out and the preserved meat was saltier and tougher.

Water could turn the color of tea with a nasty odor and a worse taste. As late as 1854, Harriet Tytler had to hold her nose tightly to get down a meal in her cabin.[9] Captains who could be paragons of gallantry on land might become insolent, overbearing tyrants once on board their ships. A woman could expect to be in the company of sailors whose notions of civility were usually limited, at best. She would have little or no privacy from either them or the ship's rats. Women who could afford it had cabins above decks; otherwise, they were housed below in stuffy little cubby holes with canvas walls.

Besides the dangers of the voyage, the Directors' decision in the Keeling matter may also have been influenced by Sir Thomas Roe who would be going on this voyage to the court of the Moghul emperor, Jehangir, who had succeeded his father, the great Akbar, a decade earlier. An Esquire of the Body to Queen Elizabeth and knighted by James I, Roe seems to have been proposed for the embassy by Sir Thomas Smith himself. Tall, with a commanding presence, a gentleman 'of a pregnant understanding, well-spoken, learned, industrious, and of a comelie personage', he was by his own definition, a 'man of qualitye'.[10] In contrast to swashbucklers such as Keeling and Hawkins, Roe appears rather priggish, but what he thought about the conduct of his mission mattered greatly. Although he had been married only seven weeks, Roe intended to leave his new bride in the care of one of her uncles. Besides fearing for the safety and the possible negative effect that the influence of a wife might have, the expense of maintaining and defending a person who could contribute nothing to the Company's coffers would also have been a consideration.

Assuming that something in England did not make remaining at home a fate worse than India —an assumption, incidentally, that one makes with some trepidation—Anne Keeling raises three major questions about British women in India in the seventeenth century. First, the Directors did change their minds about women being in India. Why and when? What did they expect of the women whom they first allowed and then actually encouraged to go to India? Did those expectations change as the activities of the Company itself changed? Later, in the late eighteenth and nineteenth centuries, the Company's commercial purposes would be subordinated to imperial goals, and its servants would be not only trading, conquering, and governing India but also studying, exploring, mapping, drawing, proselytizing, 'improving', and even trying to Anglicize India. What role or roles did the Company expect women to play in those activities and did the ladies fulfil those expectations?

Second, given the extreme difficulties and hazards of the voyage out and of conditions in India itself, why would any woman want to go to India? What did India offer a woman that she could not have found either by staying in England or going somewhere else, America perhaps, or some other country in Europe? By the end of the seventeenth century, women were clearly making India their home. The conditions that had made the voyage so treacherous and unpleasant in the first part of century had not changed; indeed, in the political breakdown following the death of the Emperor Aurangzeb in 1707, India had, if anything, become even more hazardous. Yet, instead of a massive exodus of women and children back to England, the population lists show a significant and growing, albeit still small number of English women residing in India.

Related to that question is the third: What was life like for the women who did go out in the seventeenth, eighteenth, and early nineteenth centuries? That question must be answered on two levels: first, how did the Company's purposes affect their behaviour within the Anglo-Indian community itself and second, to the limited extent that they could encounter India, how did they engage it?

To the first question, why the Directors changed their minds about admitting women to India, the answer lies in the original debate about Anne Keeling. As the Directors discovered in 1615, the curse that could befall those who kept a husband and wife apart could be financial. Because he had been so successful on the Third Voyage in 1607, the Directors ordered Keeling not to return with the fleet but to assume over-all command of the Company's East Indian affairs from either Bantam or Djakarta. Faced with the prospect of another long separation from home, Keeling understandably would want Anne with him. When the Directors reached their 'extreamlie unkind' decision, Keeling consented to command the Twelfth Voyage but then refused to remain in the East. Thus, the Company deprived itself of what would have been an extraordinarily capable agent in what then promised to be a very lucrative market. The lesson was not lost on them. Because of—and despite—the dangers, if there was to be any permanency at all about the East Indian trade, settled family life with the promise of a progeny that would not only be Christian but Protestant would require a reconsideration of the 1615 decision.

To the second question, why a woman would brave dangers, disease, distance from England, and all that was familiar to go to India, the answer is a bit elusive. Filial or conjugal fidelity such as Anne Keeling's is part of the reason. Moreover, throughout the first two centuries of Britain's involvement with the subcontinent, when marriage was an economic necessity for women, financial security might explain the journeys of many, if not most, of the English women who went to India. Still, why not wait in the relative safety of England for the return of a husband as many wives did? If a husband did not return, if he died or was killed before his return, what would any wife hope to gain by being with him except to share his fate? Indeed, something like that had already happened. Two years earlier, Sir Thomas Powell and his wife had accompanied Sir Robert Sherley to Persia where Sherley had served as Shah Abbas' ambassador. The party had then traveled east and Powell had died at Karachi. Shortly thereafter, his wife gave birth to their child, the first English child to be born in India, but neither she nor the child lived more than a few days.

We know little of Anne Keeling, Lady Powell, or, for that matter, any of the women who went to India in the seventeenth and early eighteenth centuries. In an age of massive female—and male—illiteracy, it is not surprising that neither Anne Keeling nor any other woman has left a diary, a journal, or letters that would reveal their intentions. The little we do know has to be gleaned from what others said about them, and those others were men whose interests spared little time or energy for women. What is quite obvious, however, is that these women had to have been almost insanely adventurous, and strong enough both mentally and physically to endure what they knew would be a notoriously dangerous environment for an indefinite period of time.

What their purposes were not is perhaps easier to understand. They were not missionaries, nurses, or educators as some nineteenth- and twentieth-century women were to be—women who might be tempted to see something 'deficient' in Indian culture and be interested in changing things. They did not seek or expect to find something illuminating in Hinduism or something romantic or spiritually fulfilling. Nor were they tourists. There had been European tourists in India as early as the sixteenth century. They had been men, not women. India was, frankly, too dangerous for any European to travel about in search of oddities. Nor, unlike many of their contemporaries who journeyed to North America, did they come seeking a refuge from the political and religious upheavals of the seventeenth century.

To third question, what was life like in India for the women who came to India, the answer lies in the footnotes in many of the sources which detail marriages of daughters, sisters, nieces, and widows who clearly were quite content to remain in India. Widows did not return to England, daughters married in India, and by the end of the century, there is a recurrence of family names—Fowke, Powney, Pigot, Pitt, Gyfford, Munro, Wynch, and Russell. British women had become proprietors of businesses and owned houses in their own right and, despite its dangers, they clearly viewed India not as an exile, as many Victorians would, but as a home and a very comfortable one at that.

After the Twelfth Voyage, Keeling never returned to the East. He came home in 1617, a very wealthy man. The first person to greet him at the Downs was Anne. Their joy of each other was, however, relatively short-lived. William died on the Isle of Wight in October 1620 at the age of forty-two, shortly after the birth of his second son, also named William. His epitaph announces that he was 'a merchant fortunate, a captain bould, a courtier gracious, but (alas) not old'.[11] The following April, Anne remarried. Her second husband, John Hobson, was described as a gentleman of Ningwood, in the parish of Shalfleet. Anne herself would bear—and bury—three more children before her own death in 1631.[12]

For several years, the Directors continued to meet in Sir Thomas Smith's house, then in the houses of various city merchants until, in 1648, the Company acquired the mansion in Leadenhall Street that, for the rest of its history, would be its home.

Meanwhile, three other women had already arrived in India who would give the Directors good reason to believe that the 'extreamlie unkind' decision they had made in the Keeling case might have been rather prudent, after all.

notes

1 Michael Strachen and Penrose Boies, eds, *The East India Company Journals of Captain William Keeling and Master Thomas Bonner, 1615–1617* (hereafter *Keeling/Bonner Journal*) (Minneapolis: University of Minnesota Press, 1971), 58.

2 Cited from Great Britain, Public Record Office, in ibid., 5.

3 Cited in Beckles Willson, *Ledger and Sword, or The Honourable Company of Merchants of England Trading to the East Indies: 1599–1874*, 2 vols (London, New York, and Bombay: Longmans, Green, 1903), I, 68.

4 John Bruce, *Annals of the Honorable East India Company from Their Establishment by the Charter of Queen Elizabeth: 1600 to the Union of the London and English East India Companies, 1707–8*, 3 vols (London, Black, Perry, and King, 1810 [Republished at Farnborough: Gregg Press Limited, 1968]), I, 155.

5 Ibid., 166.

6 Strachen and Boies, *Keeling/Bonner Journal*, 179.

7 For a thorough account of piracy in the early modern period, the reader is referred to Linda Colley, *Captives: Britain, Empire and the World: 1600–1850* (London: Jonathan Cape, 2002).

8 Clements R. Markham, ed., 'The Journals of Captain William Hawkins' in *The Hawkins' Voyages during the Reigns of Henry VIII, Queen Elizabeth and James I* (London: Printed for the Hakluyt Society, 1878), 395.

9 Harriet Tytler, *An Englishwoman in India: The Memoirs of Harriet Tytler, 1828–1858*, ed., Anthony Sattin (Oxford University Press, 1986), 96.

10 Sir William Foster, ed., *The Embassy of Sir Thomas Roe to the Court of the Great Moghul, 1615–1619, as Narrated in His Journal and Correspondence*, 2 vols., second series (London, Printed for the Hakluyt Society, 1899), I, iv, from Court Minutes, 7 September 1614.

11 Strachen and Boies, *Keeling/Bonner Journals*, 8.

12 Letter in author's possession from Richard Smout, archivist, Isle of Wight.

2

the 'incumberances'

SWALLY, OR SUALLY, HOLE—PERHAPS AS UNPREPOSSESSING an utterance on English-speaking tongues in 1615 as it is now. And a rather unprepossessing place. Little tidal creeks flowing out of the low-lying mangrove swamps at the edge of Gujarat's warm, fertile plain emptied muddy sludge into the Gulf of Cambay. However, had one been standing on the quay at Swally Hole in the early seventeenth century, one would have seen the masts of scores of ocean-going ships—red-sailed Arab dhows, junks from China, Moghul vessels carrying pilgrims from Mecca, and perhaps a few European vessels as well, flying flags from the Netherlands, Portugal, and England. From the great ships, goods and people were loaded into flat-bottomed boats which then carried them about seven miles up the Tapti River to the city of Surat, the leading Moghul seaport and the commercial heart of western India. A centre for inlaid work and the manufacture of carpets, textiles, gold and silver thread, soap, and paper, Surat was also renowned for traffic in precious cloths, including rich silks, taffetas, satins, and calicoes. From the Persian Gulf came all kinds of precious gems—pearls, agates, dia-monds, rubies, sapphires, topazes, and other stones—and from the

Spice Islands, Dutch merchants brought pepper, nutmeg, cinnamon, cloves, and mace.

Surat's narrow streets were so thronged, especially near the bazaar, that it was no very easy task to pass through the crowds of fakirs, jugglers, holy men, money-changers, *munshee*s (translators), facto-tums, and merchants from Agra and Broach, Delhi, and Ahmedabad as well as the scores of Turks, Arabs, Chinese, Armenians, and Persians who would stand with their silks and stuffs in their hands or upon their heads to invite passersby to come and buy them. In the middle of the city was a spacious, vacant place called the Castle Green (because of its nearness to the castle) on which were laid all sorts of goods in the open air, except during monsoon.[1]

It had been the Third Voyage, commanded by William Keeling, that had landed William Hawkins and a companion, William Finch, at Surat in August 1608. His cargo had consisted of broadcloths, lead, iron, and quicksilver which he intended to exchange in Surat for cloths and other goods that could then be used to purchase pep-per and spices at Acheen in the Spice Islands. He also had some pres-ents (he and Thomas Roe both called them 'toys') intended for the emperor, Jehangir, from whom he hoped to get a *firman*, or license, for the Company to trade.

As soon as he landed, Hawkins was immediately confronted with a reality that later employees of the Company were to discover, often quite painfully—that, despite firmans, it was not always the emperor who controlled their lives and fortunes but local magnates who were an even graver and more constant threat to their trade, their liberty, and sometimes their very lives. And in the event that a firman could be extracted from a prince, there was no certainty that he, any more than the Moghul, would honour it. Even if he did, his subordinates might ignore it or demand extortionate payments for honouring it.

Upon his arrival, Hawkins' entire cargo was impounded by a local official named Mukhreb Khan who, in collusion with the Portuguese, dominated the trade on the entire Malabar Coast.[2] Mukhreb Khan did allow him to land, but then employed his own coachman to kill Hawkins either while he slept or to poison his food. He managed to escape the attempts to 'murther' him, but then a second part of his mission to Jehangir became soliciting his assistance in recovering his goods from 'that dogge Mukhreb Khan'.[3] Two and a half months after leaving Finch in charge of their goods at Surat, on 16 April 1609, Hawkins reached Agra, the Moghul capital, a little over six hundred miles from Surat.[4]

Although Agra then lacked the Taj Mahal and other monuments that are now well known, it did have the Pearl Mosque and the extensive fort with high red sandstone walls built in 1565 by Jehangir's father, the great emperor, Akbar.[5] It also possessed the Ram Bagh, the oldest Moghul garden in India, built by the founder of the dynasty, Babur, in 1528. In apartments adjacent to the palace lived the ladies of Jehangir's harem, the most powerful of whom was Nur Jehan, Jehangir's favourite wife, whose influence over her husband was so great that, as Roe would later note, she 'wholly governeth him'.[6]

To obtain the firman, Hawkins had to negotiate with a power far more formidable than the Hapsburgs, Stuarts, and Bourbons combined. Like his father, whom he had succeeded three years earlier, Jehangir kept an eclectic court where Hindu *yogis*, Muslim Sufis, Armenian Christians, and Portuguese Jesuits were as welcome as the English Protestant Hawkins. Jehangir was particularly delighted by Hawkins, however, partly because of Hawkins' ability to converse with him in Turkish (the Moghul family language, as opposed to the court language, Persian) and also apparently because of his ability to keep up with him in his regular drinking bouts. Hawkins arrived in state and rapidly advanced from honour to honour. Jehangir not only offered him a license for the factory at Surat plus a personal allowance of £3,200 a year but also the command of 400 horses. Hawkins accepted Jehangir's favours, believing, as he told the Directors, 'I should feather my nest and doe you service.'[7]

Nonetheless, after three years, Hawkins still lacked the firman. The reason had less to do with either Hawkins or his employers than with the machinations of the Portuguese who opposed any attempt to interfere with their monopoly of the Indian trade, and who could use (and be used by) factions at Jehangir's own court. Indeed, part of Hawkins' difficulty at court came from his nemesis, Mukhreb Khan. When Jehangir ordered him to reimburse Hawkins, Mukhreb Khan undervalued the cargo he had taken and then represented Hawkins' refusal to accept payment on the valuation as an act of disobedience to the emperor. To make matters worse, a crowd of 'unrulie'

Englishmen at Surat had gotten drunk and 'made themselves beasts and soe fell to lewd women', an offense for which they paid dearly in that, as it was quaintly put, 'in a shorte time manie fell sicke'. One of them, Thomas Tucker, had butchered a calf and was saved from a lynch mob only when the English themselves were sent to whip Tucker into insensibility.[8]

Although Hawkins' star waned at the court, the emperor gave him an Armenian Christian girl as a wife. She was the daughter of Mubarik Khan who had held high office under Akbar. Mubarik Khan had died suddenly leaving his daughter with 'only a few jewels'. Lacking an ordained clergyman, they were married by Hawkins' English servant, Nicholas Ufflet. Then, sometime later, the two were married again by a preacher who came out to India with Sir Henry Middleton, and 'for ever after I lived content and without feare', he wrote, 'she being willing to go where I went and live as I lived'.[9]

While she may have been willing to go where he went and live as he lived, her relatives had other ideas. Unable to embark for home from Surat and unable also to travel through 'Turkie, especially with a woman', Hawkins was forced to curry favour with the Jesuits in order to get a safe conduct from the viceroy at Goa to go through Portugal and from thence to England. When he reached Goa, however, his wife's mother and relatives, suspecting that they would never see her—or her husband's wealth—again, made him promise that she would go no further than Goa so that they might come and visit her there. If he intended to take her to Portugal, then he was to 'leave her that portion, that the custom of Portugall is, to leave to their Wives when they dye'. Faced with that bit of extortion, Hawkins was forced to obtain two securities from the hated Jesuits before he was finally able to leave India with his wife.[10] Whatever joy he did or did not have of his bride, however, was short-lived for he died en route to England in 1612. The new widow soon married again. The second time was to Gabriel Towerson, captain of the *Hector*.

As disappointed as Hawkins may have been in not securing the firman, an English toehold was soon established. On 29 November 1612, about the same time that Hawkins died, Captain Thomas Best repulsed a superior Portuguese force at Swally Hole. That victory was critical because it diminished the Portuguese influence at Jehangir's court, and the coveted firman arrived in December, allowing the

English Company the right to establish factories not only at Surat but also at Ahmedabad, the capital of Gujarat, at Ajmere, and at Cambay. Consequently, Best then ordered the establishment of a factory at Surat under Thomas Aldworth who, after the fashion of the Dutch, was referred to as a 'president'.

Surat thus became the Company's first presidency in India. In 1613–14, the object of agents in India was still not the Indian trade itself so much as to establish exchanges between the Malabar Coast and Bantam in the Spice Islands. Aldworth had noted on a journey to Ahmedabad that cotton yarn and baftees could be got more cheaply from the manufacturers in the cities of Broach and Baroda[11] than at Surat, and that he could buy indigo at Ahmedabad at a very low rate. It would, however, require that a stock should be placed in the hands of a factor at Ahmedabad, where the Dutch also had a factory, and that a resident should be at the emperor's court at Agra to get the protection of Jehangir and/or his ministers. Happily, a second naval victory, in 1614, again over superior Portuguese forces, had given the English Company a decisive diplomatic edge over its main European competitor, and paved the way for Thomas Roe's mission to Jehangir's court in 1615. The two naval encounters had also shown that, however the Company might wish otherwise, trade could not be conducted without military involvement.

Roe's mission was a formidable, and a formative, one—he was to obtain a firman to trade *anywhere* in India. Thus, rather than the simple firman sought by Hawkins, what Roe was to achieve would be a commercial treaty between sovereign powers. He would approach Jehangir's court, not as the representative of a company of merchants, but as the envoy of a fellow monarch.[12] Roe thereby embodied a fundamental transition in the Company's very nature from a purely commercial to a political entity. He was also the first in a long line of ambassadors, governors, and other officials with no prior experience or knowledge of India who would represent the Company and/or the Crown at an Indian court.

Roe landed at Surat at the end of 1615, and, like Hawkins, almost immediately collided with the local government, this time in the person of Zulfikar Khan. After Roe put forth his requests as demands, however, Zulfikar Khan then made a humble appeal for

Roe's friendship. Roe had little difficulty securing a safe conduct from Jehangir but before he set out for Jehangir's court, he met three women who were to convince him and the Company that, although a wife might quiet her husband's mind, she could also send the enterprises of other men badly awry, and that his uneasiness about his own wife, Anne Keeling, or any woman accompanying a husband to the Indies had not been misplaced.

Despite the difficulties her relatives had caused William Hawkins, the Company had allowed the new Mrs Gabriel Towerson to accompany her husband when he returned to the Indies, but Mrs Towerson had one critical advantage that Anne Keeling had lacked. Because of her numerous connections at the Agra court, Towerson had had every reason to think that his new wife could improve his personal fortunes and perhaps those of his employers as well. The Company apparently agreed.

Thus, by the time Roe reached Surat, Mrs Hawkins/Towerson had already returned to India and befriended an Indian widow who had also married an Englishman, a Mrs Hudson. Mrs Hudson had a maid, Frances Webbe, who, either before the voyage out or during it, had become pregnant and married a man named Richard Steele who had gone to Aleppo to collect a debt.[13] Because the debtor had fled to Persia, Steele had pursued him there and had become fluent in Persian, the Moghul court's official language. By the time he reached Surat, Steele had not only become convinced of the great advantages to be gained from trade with Persia, particularly in silk—an enterprise that Roe vehemently opposed—but he also lost no time in giving Roe a very bad impression of his character, an impression not helped by Steele's association with Sir Robert Sherley.

A year earlier, Roe had met Sherley at Hampton Court where Sherley's Catholicism and his Christian Circassian wife probably alarmed Roe less than his schemes to involve the Company in Persia's silk trade, a royal monopoly. The silk would have been carried either from a Persian port or from the island of Ormuz, held by the Portuguese. Sherley's willingness to negotiate with both Catholic Spain and Portugal, England's key competitors in the Indies trade—that is, to put his own personal interests before those of England—had led Roe to conclude that Sherley was 'as he is dishonest so is he subtile'.[14]

Trouble with the Steeles started before Roe left Surat, but Steele's proximity to Sherley's silk scheme was only a part of the difficulty. From Jehangir's son and eventual successor, Prince Khurram, Roe learned that Steele was giving out that he was the equal of the ambassador. Always conscious of his 'dignitie', Roe could not tolerate that slight to his prestige. Both he and his employers understood exactly how precarious the position of any group of merchants was and how much that 'dignitie' mattered. However, Roe was in no position either to simply dismiss Steele since he needed his linguistic skills in the negotiations with Jehangir. As if to deliberately irritate Roe even further, Steele also insisted upon bringing his wife '[which] secretly I mislike...' and he ordered Steele to leave her behind in Surat. On no account was she to be allowed to accompany her husband to court, but Thomas Kerridge, the chief factor at Surat, was ordered to treat her with charity and courtesy. Mrs Towerson, however, would accompany them since her friendship with Empress Nur Jehan might prove useful.

Despite Roe's objections, all three ladies—Mrs Steele, Mrs Hudson, and Mrs Towerson—embarked on the journey to the English factory at Ahmedabad, en route to Agra, in the company of a preacher named Gouldinge who had apparently developed an infatuation for one of the ladies, possibly the widow, Mrs Hudson. Gouldinge had been denied permission to accompany the women and had, in fact, been ordered to return to his ship. Instead, he had disguised himself in 'Moor's apparel' and surreptitiously boarded the ship in which the women were sailing. Gouldinge's shenanigans earned him a sharp reprimand from Roe who sent him packing back to Surat dressed in proper apparel.[15]

Roe's progress towards Ahmedabad was further hampered by a fever that he picked up at Ajmere. As if that were not enough, when he finally did reach Ahmedabad, he found Thomas Aldworth so sick of dysentery that he 'was more like an anatomy than like a man'.[16] Then, once he did arrive at court in Agra, he was not able to get an audience with Jehangir until 10 January 1616.

Although Roe was a very different sort from Hawkins, Jehangir seems to have been well disposed towards him. That was helpful, but Roe still had to deal with the hostility of Prince Khurram who was in alliance with Asaf Khan, the powerful prime minister and brother of Nur Jehan. Steele perhaps had little to do with court intrigues, but he had something of an agenda of his own with the emperor. He had conceived the idea of diverting the waters of the Jumna to pass through lead pipes to the different parts of the city. He got the idea from a similar scheme of diverting the Thames through pipes to houses in London at the end of the sixteenth century. Although it was perhaps not a bad idea, it was two centuries too early in India. When Roe heard of the project, he dismissed it as impracticable, but Steele managed to get an audience with Jehangir who was also not impressed with Steele's project. Steele's own court patrons, fickle as ever, then deserted him.

Nonetheless, according to Roe, Steele continued to present problems since he 'would deliver his owne tales and not a word what I commanded'.[17] Part of the tension between the two men reflects the opposition between Roe and the factors at Surat who, like Sherley and Steele, were interested in the Persian silk trade. But Roe also blamed his difficulties on Frances Steele. Richard Steele also 'hath gotten up his wife as a servant to Mistris Towerson, as her servant, and vowed to mee shee should live in her house'. Roe agreed to this arrangement but Steele immediately broke the agreement and 'carried her to a house of his owne, where hee lives with Coach, Palinke,[18] 7 horses, and ten servants' and then admitted to Roe that he had 'consented to the Covenants to deceive mee and to gett his wife into his own Power. The excuse of all is affection'.[19]

While the grand style in which Frances Steele was living was an annoyance to Roe, it must have been an even greater surprise to Mrs Steele herself. Even more surprising perhaps was that she was soon befriended by Jehangir's hostess, the widow of his older brother and the daughter of his *khan-khanae*,[20] who invited her to her own house. Frances Steele thereby became the first English woman not only to visit a *zenana*—with all the puzzles and intricacies that could involve—but one belonging to a very influential woman, a matter which did not go unnoticed by Thomas Roe. Mrs Steele was fetched in a chariot drawn by white oxen and attended by eunuchs, and brought into an open court in the middle of which was an open tank or well. Around this on a carpet-covered floor, sat the richly dressed female slaves of the khan-khanae's daughter. According to the description that later came to the attention of Samuel Purchas, they were 'of divers Nations and complexions: some blacke, exceeding lovely and comely of person notwithstanding…some browne, of Indian complexion; others very white, but pale, and not ruddy….' When the lady herself made her entrance they all did her reverence 'with their faces to the ground'. Apparently Mrs Hawkins/Towerson had coached Mrs Steele in the proper courtesies, for she made three curtsies 'after the English fashion' and gave her a present 'without which there is no visitation of great persons'. The lady ordered Mrs Steele to sit beside her and 'after discourse, entertained her with a Banket [banquet?]'. Nor was that one visit the end of it. There were many more visits and exchanges of gifts of women's clothing, some of which were garments—apparently saris—of thin calico, so delicate that they were 'like a smoke', and also of men's clothing, for the khan-khanae ordered his tailor to make a cloak of cloth of gold for Mr Steele 'after the English fashion very comely'.[21]

There is no direct record of what Frances Steele thought of the lives of her hostess and her companions. Given Roe's unflattering portrait of the couple, one might not be amiss if one assumes a bit of self-gratification in the short narrative. But something else is also missing. Later generations of English women would find the lives of Indian women of the upper classes to be materially rich but intellectually and emotionally empty. If Frances Steele found her hostess' life empty, she apparently did not express that. Again, Purchas might have omitted such an observation but it is more likely that a woman who had begun her career in India as a lady's maid and had been married under a bush was simply flattered in being the guest of a very important Indian lady.

And what of poor Thomas Roe? While Richard Steele strutted about Agra in a gold cloak and his wife was enjoying the company of one of the more influential women at court, Roe's own 'dignitie' was being undermined. Finally, it was Frances Steele's behavior that led him, in exasperation, to declare, 'I desier noe weomens company, but labour to leave such incumberances behynd'.[22] So untrustworthy did Roe find Steele that he finally warned the Directors to 'neither trust him with your goods nor pay him any wages until I have meanes to send him home'.[23]

The Steeles returned home with Roe in 1619 and, as might be expected, Steele's reception at home was cold. He was condemned for his 'unworthie carriage abroad', for having 'wronged my Lord Embassador by a false and surmised contestation and arrogating a higher title and place to himself then ever was intended' but also because he 'hath brought home a great private trade, [and] put the Company to an extraordinarye charge by a wife and children'.[24] Clearly, had it not been for Frances Steele, her husband would not have been introduced to the court where he could almost single-handedly unhinge Roe's delicate negotiations. But she and her children had committed a misdeed that was equally grave—they had been an expense to the Company for which there had been no return.

Mrs Towerson ultimately became a burden on the Company as well. When Towerson returned home in 1619, she elected to remain behind with her numerous relatives. Apparently, Towerson had no intention of ever rejoining her because in 1620, he applied for and was granted the post of principal factor for the Moluccas, a post that proved terribly unlucky in that he was among those tortured and murdered at Amboyna three years later. His widow then plagued the factors at Agra, which by then had an English factory, with regular requests for loans of money 'until her husband's return'.[25] It is quite doubtful that, with her horde of avaricious relatives, Towerson's death ended his wife's requests for loans, but Mrs Towerson was only the first among hundreds of widows who would insist on being sustained by the Company following the deaths of husbands whose prosperity it was very easy to overestimate.

Mrs Hudson herself was also an 'incumberance'. After living for five months in India at the Company's expense, she returned to England with a considerable cargo of goods, and apparently without the company of the troublesome preacher, Gouldinge. At the intercession of some friends, she was allowed to keep the cargo on the payment of £30 for freight.[26] How she had managed to acquire her goods—whether it was from her late husband or in her own private trade (as opposed to the 'country trade' for the Company)—is not known. In either case, one rather suspects that if she were able to accumulate a cargo worth such a substantial duty, she must have been a very enterprising lady. She had, however, done nothing to enrich the Company.

Mrs Hudson is, in fact, the first in a very long line of women who would come out to India for any number of personal reasons and

British Women in India

then, once there, manage businesses such as taverns, millinery shops, schools and, most importantly, the estates they had inherited from deceased spouses. The Company's problem with Mrs Hudson was not that she had gotten her cargo by private trade but that she had gotten it at the Company's expense while returning not a farthing to the Company's coffers.

By 1620, the debate in the Keeling case had by no means been resolved. It might be a sin to separate a man from his wife, but their stockholders expected the Company to see a profit. Women meant families and settlements, costly colonial responsibilities which neither the Company nor the Crown were yet prepared to embrace. They were capable of engaging in financial manoeuvres which the Company could not control, and worse, as Mrs Steele had shown, they could undermine the delicate diplomacy often required for the Company to do business in India. Quite simply, for the Company's Directors to change their minds about women going to India, they would need a very compelling reason to counteract the unhappy experiences they had had with Mrs Hudson, Mrs Steele, and Mrs Hawkins/Towerson. And, while no woman in England was likely to have known of the three ladies who had so plagued Roe, the question of why a woman would have wanted to go to India had been answered: Mrs Hudson and Mrs Hawkins/Towerson had shown that India represented economic opportunities, and Mrs Steele had seen a kind of feminine lifestyle that she could never have imagined for herself or anyone she probably ever would have known in England.

notes

1 John Ovington, *A Voyage to Surat in the Year 1689*, ed., H.G. Rawlinson (London: Humphrey Milford, Oxford University Press, 1929), 130.

2 By the Treaty of Tordesillas in 1494, Pope Alexander VI had awarded India to Portugal who had then established a post at Goa in 1510.

3 Clements R. Markham, ed., 'The Journals of Captain William Hawkins', in *The Hawkins' Voyages during the Reigns of Henry VIII, Queen Elizabeth and James I* (London: Printed for the Hakluyt Society, 1878), 394 ff.

4 Ibid., 399. The imperial court was not moved to Delhi until the reign of Jehangir's son and successor, Shah Jehan (1627–1658).

5 Nicholas Withington who was in Agra about this time described it as 'noe cittye, but a towne; yet the biggest that ever I saw'. Except for

the castle and some noblemen's houses by the river, Withington found the rest of town 'very ruinous'. See William Foster, ed., *Early Travels in India. 1583–1619* (London: Humphrey Milford, Oxford University Press, 1921), 226.

6 William Foster, ed., *Embassy of Sir Tomas Roe to the Court of the Great Mogul, 1615–1619 as Narrated in His Journal and Correspondence*, 2 vols (London: Printed for the Hakluyt Society, 1926), I, 111.

7 Markham, 'Hawkins Journals', 402.

8 Cited in John Keay, *The Honourable Company: A History of the English East India Company* (New York: Macmillan, 1991), 79.

9 Markham, 'Hawkins Journals', 404.

10 Ibid., 412–13.

11 All these cities would have been within fairly easy reach of Surat. Broach (Bharuch) is about forty-five miles from Surat; Baroda, about fifty miles beyond that; and Ahmedabad is roughly another fifty-five miles beyond Baroda.

12 It would not be until Sir William Norris' mission to the court of Aurangzeb in 1701 that the Moghul court would receive another representative of the Company. For a discussion of the two missions, Roe's and Norris', see Sanjay Subrahmanyam, 'Frank Submissions', in H.V. Bowen, Margarette Lincoln, and Nigel Rigby, eds, *The Worlds of the East India Company* (Woodbridge, Suffolk: The Boydell Press, 2002), 69.

13 Apparently, the marriage took place at the Cape under a bush. See Foster, *Roe Embassy*, II, 500.

14 Cited in Foster, *Roe Embassy*, I, xlvii, footnote.

15 See Arnold Wright, *Early English Adventurers in the East* (London: Andrew Melrose, Ltd., 1917), 129.

16 Footnote in Foster, *Roe Embassy*, I, 69.

17 Ibid., II, 484.

18 Palankin or palanquin. A sedan-chair carried by several bearers.

19 Ibid., 483.

20 The title translates literally as the head of the household. This powerful official seems to have been something like a modern chief of staff.

21 J. Talboys Wheeler, ed., 'Purchas's Pilgrimage' in *Early Travels in India (16th & 17th Centuries)* (Delhi: Deep Publications, 1974), 73.

22 Foster, *Roe Embassy*, II, 484.

23 Ibid.

24 From *Court Minutes*, 17 September 1619, cited also in Foster, *Roe Embassy*, II, 518.

25 Cited in ibid.

26 Note in ibid.

3

'a college, monasterie ... a house under religious orders'

FOR ALMOST TWO GENERATIONS , THE DIRECTORS remained steadfast in their assessment that wives were 'incumberances'. Then, in 1650, Aaron Baker threatened to refuse the governor's post at Bantam unless his wife, Elizabeth, could accompany him. He had been in England only one out of the past seventeen years, he argued, and would undertake that appointment only if his wife and two or three of her women servants could accompany him. At the same time, Captain Jeremy Blackman, whom the Company had chosen as the president of the Surat factory, also was contemplating bringing his wife out. After a long debate, it was decided to allow the women to go to the Indies, 'though this has never been allowed before'.[1] Unfortunately, before she could reach India, Elizabeth Baker died.

Interestingly, there is no evidence in the written record that anything was said at that time of the 'curse that befalleth those that keep man and wife asunder'. The 'curse' was obvious. Like William Keeling, Baker, described as 'an able and experienced merchant well fitted for the post',[2] was too valuable to lose. Quite simply, it was the value of a particular servant that determined whether a wife could accompany her husband. A decade earlier, in 1640, when Mary

Muschampe had petitioned to join her husband, George, at Bantam, she had been refused 'not only in respect of the charge, but because such a licence (which has never been granted before) would be an ill precedent', and she was advised to have patience until her husband's return. There may have been more than 'ill precedent' involved in their refusal, however. George Muschampe was not as valuable as Baker, and his involvement in private trade had not pleased the Directors. Moreover, by the time Mary appealed to the Court for sums from his estate following his death in the East, she had five children,[3] presumably all of whom were Muschampe's, and for all of whom the Company was bound to make provision.

Had Elizabeth Baker reached India, what would she have found? What would her life have been like? How would she have lived? What would she have thought of her surroundings?

In a very real sense, she would not have entered 'India' at all, nor would the factory that would be her home remind her very much of anything she might have left behind in England. Anglo-India was a world unto itself with unique manners, customs, architecture, and even articles of dress in accommodation to the climate. The commercial heart of the factory was the 'godown' or warehouse where goods purchased from the surrounding area would be stored until ships arrived from home to transport them, and goods from the home port could be unloaded for sale in the Indian market. In the larger factories, this was separate from a roomy building that contained offices and served as a residence for the factors whose sleeping apartments surrounded a common room which also served as a dining room, council chamber, and until the community could afford to build a church, also as a chapel. Despite Thomas Roe's caution to avoid military entanglements—a caution that the Directors dearly longed to honour even when it was perilous to do so—there also was often a barracks for the soldiers stationed there to defend the factors and their goods.

By the end of the seventeenth century, the Company would hold about two dozen factories in India, most of which were quite small.[4] Whatever the size, however, upon entering the factory one would immediately have been aware of the tremendous bustle, 'a continual hurley-burley, …a meer [sic] Billingsgate; for if you make not a Noise, they hardly think you intent on what you are doing'.[5]

For the most part, the 'continual hurley-burley' had to do with textiles rather than the spices which had been the original objective of the Indies trade. By the early 1620s, the English wardrobe and language had been enriched by vocabulary that included calicoes, ginghams, muslin, dungarees, bandanas, seersuckers, taffetas, and cambrics. Surat traded mainly calicoes, cottons, carpets, and 'Guinea cloths', a blue check cloth that became popular in West Africa and the West Indies. From the Coromandel Coast came chintzes that were ideal for wall hangings, bedcovers, and carpets and were cheap enough to be afforded by England's emerging middle classes. From Bengal came silks and muslins.[6]

Most trade was conducted through *banians* or *dubashes*. In official capacities, they acted as interpreters and liaisons between the indigenous merchants, and the civil and military servants of the Company. In households, they were at the head of the servant hierarchy and served the same purpose as in their official capacity—that is, they mediated between the English and the Indian worlds. Ultimately, no servants were more indispensable and more hated than banians. Although acting nominally on behalf of their masters, they could also trade on their own account and become quite rich as a result. Later, many distinguished native families like the Tagores in Bengal could trace the source of their wealth to their ancestors' occupations as banians. In addition to the banians, a rather large number of other servants was normally retained in the compound, partly for show, but also because the religious and caste restrictions of the Indians themselves made a large number of servants necessary.

The world of the factory was, however, not simply busy. One writer in the 1670s lamented 'the horrid swearing and profanation of the name of God, the woful [*sic*] and abominable drunkenness and uncleanness that so much reign and rage among the soldiery; and these not secretly or covertly, but as it were in the sight of the sun, and men refuse therein to be ashamed, neither can they blush'.[7]

The writer was a clergyman but his was only one in a very large chorus of complaints about morals in the factories—a chorus that would continue with multiple variations until 1947. One can quite sympathize with the Directors who, like perplexed parents reproving recalcitrant children, saw so many of their repeated exhortations so enthusiastically ignored. Despite threats of fines and imprisonment, they forbade swearing and the factors swore. They forbade duelling and the factors duelled. They ordered regular prayers but 'the worship of God . . . is exceedingly neglected by all, notwithstanding your orders to the contrary'.[8] They forbade dicing, but gambling, according to one source, 'seems to have been not an uncommon vice'.[9]

The Directors forbade drinking and their employees drank prodigiously. Claret, madeira, European and Shiraz wines, and English beers were shipped out in large quantities, but the favourite drink was arrack punch, a potent brew made of rose water, brandy, citron juice, tea, and sugar.[10] Soldiers were reputed to be the heaviest drinkers, but apparently it was difficult to find anyone who thought the virtue of abstinence was worth cultivating. Drinking was not merely a social misfortune. It was, after all, one shared heartily by English people at home as well as in the North American colonies where a tavern was often the first building erected after (and sometimes before) a church. The difference was that, in India, it could be fatal. A number of writers mention a disease they call 'barbiers', a kind of paralysis of the extremities, somewhat resembling beriberi, that apparently resulted from sleeping in the open air while inebriated.

The worst difficulty by far—and one no doubt exacerbated by the drinking—was the enormous amount of dissension within the factories. Brawling was frequent, violent, often deadly, and not confined to the barracks and taverns. The pages of the consultation books are filled quarrels between sailors and landsmen, merchants and soldiers, interlopers and private traders not licensed by the Company, and governors and members of their councils. The factors quarrelled with each other and with their Indian contacts, newcomers became embroiled with older residents and with each other. 'Good, honest' Job Charnock, the founder of Calcutta (modern Kolkata), was an irascible, hot-headed, and thoroughly competent man whose quarrel with William Hedges, an equally competent and hot-headed personality, reached Leadenhall Street.

Apart from the heat generated by parliamentary and religious questions, English society at home was notoriously cantankerous. Indeed, one author points out that 'the times were as lawless in [India] as they were in Covent Garden or the Strand'.[11] Nonetheless, as contentious as society might have been at home, the truculence of Anglo-India was so noticeable that Shaista Khan, the governor of

Bengal from 1664 to 1688, observed, 'The English are a company of base, quarrelling people, and foul dealers'.[12]

Part of the reason for the dissension was that people who were socially and usually geographically very distant from one another at home became, in India, near neighbours, and each compound was small. There might be as many as eight or ten factors or as few as two or three with only each other's company for years on end. They were also very young—the majority of them entered the Company's employ in their early or mid teens—and there was very little privacy, very little recreation available, and everyone knew everybody else extremely well. Unlike their compatriots in North America who could simply pick up their tools, horses, and wagons and move out into the wilderness when they found each other's company distasteful, the residents of a factory in India were rather 'stuck' with each other.

The hierarchy among the factors also generated conflict. British society at home had its ranks and orders, varying degrees of subordination and authority that were rarely questioned since good order was assumed to be the foundation of 'politeness' as well as of peace. While the order at home was based on birth, in India, birth mattered but not as much as one's place in the Company's service. Generally, the Company's civilian servants were divided into three ranks: in ascending order, there were writers, junior and senior factors, and junior and senior merchants. From among the factors was chosen the chief of the factory.[13] Advancement was usually based on seniority and at every promotion there was an increase in salary and new privileges.

There was, however, also a parallel order having to do with governance. By the end of the century, three factories would have become presidencies, all resembling the earliest factory at Surat in that each had a four-person Council, consisting of a president, accountant, warehouse-keeper, and purser-marine. There was also a secretary who did not sit on the Council but was a candidate for the first vacancy that opened upon it.[14]

By the time John Ovington arrived in the late 1680s, annual salaries ranged from £120 for the president down to £7 for apprentices.[15] What real salaries were, however, is impossible to say since, in addition to their diet, lodgings, and wages, the Company from the beginning of its existence had been forced to condone private or 'country' trade because no one could have been induced otherwise to take the enormous risks involved in the Indies trade for the meager wage the Company would insist on paying. This private trade was allowed in eastern ports but not, except in rare cases, in European ports, and ships' commanders regularly kept a large space for their own and others' private cargos.

While their private trade often occupied the factors as much as the Company's investment, it also provided enormous opportunities not only for considerable embezzlement but also for competition and jealousies as well. Moreover, what was legitimate private trade, what trade was not allowed, and the trade belonging to the Company often depended on how creatively one's accounts could be kept. Quite simply, not all the Company's servants found feathering one's own nest and doing the Company's service as compatible as they had been for William Hawkins, and one's nest often took precedence over the Company's service.

It was this private trade that made the social order in a factory so fluid. Until roughly the middle of the seventeenth century, the majority of the factors came from mercantile families and some were fairly well-educated. After the Restoration, however, men with ties to noble families also came out, but it was entirely possible for an apprentice to actually earn as much wealth as the most senior merchant, nobly born or not.

Besides the frictions that could arise from private trade, there was also a question that would persist well into the nineteenth century—how did civil rank compare with military rank? Did a captain rank as high as a junior merchant, for example? The civilian/military breach lay at the root of many of the quarrels, but the opportunities, dangers, and competitive nature of the trade itself as well as the distance from the restraining influences of society at home also contributed much to the general turbulence.

Dr John Fryer also suggested another reason for the truculence. Although the Company seldom named an undeserving man for the presidency of a factory, he said, 'yet they keep that Power to themselves, none assuming that Dignity till confirmed by them ...'[16] Thus, the president of any factory could see his authority overridden by a simple appeal to London from a subordinate. When an outstanding

British Women in India

figure did emerge and win widespread respect, it was often despite the Company, not because of it, or as Beckles Willson puts it, the great barrier between the Company and its servants was that 'the former did not know India and the latter did not know Leadenhall Street'.[17]

Shaista Khan's observation notwithstanding, the threat of Indian magnates and European rivals required vigilance, discipline, and some level of efficiency. Although every settlement had factions and fights, intrigues and feuds, it must be noted, too, that corruption and patronage were as much a part of the political system at home as they were in India. On the other hand, John Ovington noticed that 'the whole Business and Concern of all is zealously to promote the Honour and Interest of the Companies Affairs, in maintaining their Reputation, and vending their Commodities at as high Rates, and buying for them others at as low as they can'.[18] That zeal for the honour and interest of the Company had, well before it was a century old, made it the most powerful corporation in England.

The world Elizabeth Baker or any English woman would have encountered was vastly indifferent, indeed hostile, to the presence of an English wife and family, but it was neither the quarrelsomeness nor the drinking—to both of which women would contribute substantially when they did arrive—that lay at the root of that unwelcoming environment. Rather, it was the fundamental nature of the factory itself. As one person observed, the factory was 'more like unto [sic] a Colledge, Monasterie, or a house under Religious orders then [sic] any other, for we have much more Discourse of Religion, Philosophie, the government of the Passions and affections, and sometimes of history, then of trade and getting Mony for ourselves, though that allsoe be in noe manner neglected on the Company's behalfe...'[19]

Indeed, the ideal of an intensely masculine, Christian citadel of commerce for which the British were later criticized had its roots in these earliest factories. As the Keeling case illustrated, the Directors were a God-fearing set of men who placed great value upon the observance of religious duty both among themselves and among those they employed.[20] Carefully selected chaplains were provided for each factory and the minister was obligated to deliver a sermon once and public prayers three times on Sundays and to read prayers each morning and evening in the factory's chapel.

The Directors' care in choosing them could not guarantee upright conduct once they arrived in India; consequently, most of the chaplains who went to India at any time were probably no more nor no less devout than most of their flocks. The pages of Reverend Frank Penny's history of the church in Madras are replete with stories of chaplains whose genuine care for the virtue of their flocks was exemplary. There were exceptions. When one of the first chaplains, Reverend William Leske, did not get on well with his flock at Surat, he was sent home in 1617 on charges of drunkenness and licentiousness.[21] Chaplains were paid £100 a year (the same as the Judge Advocate) plus a house, but at least one observer wondered, 'How they manage it is a mystery to me, for they are not allowed to trade openly.' Nevertheless, like the Company's secular servants, the clergy too engaged in private trade, for the same writer also observed that they were frequently able to lay up several thousand pounds; he knew one who had hoarded enough money to purchase a bishopric and a seat in the House of Lords upon his return.[22]

Apart from the care taken in choosing chaplains, until well into the nineteenth century, correspondence from the Directors illustrates a paternalism and moralism that reached into the minute details of the factors' daily lives. At certain times every year, a time was to be set apart to enquire into the behaviour of the factors and 'let them know the account you have of them and as they deserve either admonish or commend them'. If through pride or idleness they had been neglectful of their duties 'or immoral in their life', they were to be given fair warning and if they then did not mind, they were to be dismissed.[23] To divert the men, following William Keeling's example, plays were recommended, especially Shakespeare.

Besides the obvious religious purpose, that care to obey God in all things had the more worldly motive of preventing the factors from becoming involved in frictions that would be dangerous and costly to themselves and also endanger their own and the Company's trade. Removed from whatever social constraints there might have been at home and under the seductive influence of the East—and the possibility of making a large personal fortune—the factors followed a regimen that strongly resembled that of a medieval guild apprenticeship. In short, the factory was part a noisy, showy bazaar and part a public school.

A typical day began at 6 a.m. with prayers, followed by the *chota hazri* or 'little breakfast'. Eventually, to avoid the heat of the day, the more active rode around 5 a.m., and then took a chota hazri of tea and biscuits, followed by a more substantial breakfast of devilled kidneys, stews, hashes, and brains, around 10. Work was from 9 to noon, then, in the earlier days, at midday, there was a substantial dinner followed by a more frugal meal in the evening. However, because the large midday dinner made work for the rest of the day difficult, the noon meal became the smaller 'tiffin' and the main meal migrated to the evening. At nine o'clock, the gates of the factory were closed.[24] Youth who stayed out after the gate was shut had to pay a fine. No one could live outside the factory unless given permission nor was anyone permitted to leave the factory without the president's permission.[25] If there were accommodations, unmarried young men were required to lodge at the factory; if accommodations were lacking, they were to 'make them—and not lie up and down in the town'.[26]

The collegial nature of the factory assured that maintaining anything like a family life was difficult at best. A complaint to the Company in August 1674 argued that

> the said inconveniencies are now much increased, all your servants in Councell being married and children coming on apace, so that ... it is next to impossible for them, as much more for their wives (who for want of room have all been faine to procure houses out of the Fort) to be absent from their families at those times so necessary to the well-ordering thereof, and for their own comfort ...[27]

The focus of the complaints ultimately was the obligation to be present at the main meal each day at the public, or General Table. The purpose of the Table was to maintain 'friendly correspondence', discuss the Company's business, and perhaps most important of all, to 'prevent all Jealousies and Animosities which might obstruct the publick Affairs from that Progress'.[28] The Court of Directors believed that the General Table kept their young servants from licentiousness and debauchery and kept them in a regular and virtuous course of living. Whatever its benefits, however, when more English women did come to India, the General Table became a point of increasing contention between the Directors in London and the factories in India.

In that very masculine world, an unmarried woman expecting to find available bachelors clamouring to undo her single status was likely to be disappointed, but the collegial nature of the factory was not the only reason. Only a very few senior merchants in the Company's service could actually afford to marry and maintain a wife, let alone a family. Although the Company expected its servants to supplement their low salaries with private trade, the enterprise that had so lucratively engaged Mrs Hudson was precarious at best. The distance between great wealth and great poverty was enormous and very, very fluid. Sometimes, a factor indeed could be enormously successful. In 1675, when Charles Bendysh died in Bombay, his enormous estate included a diamond ring, a pendant with gemstones and pearls, several Italian books, two guns, and a superbly furnished wardrobe.[29] Other factors also left formidable estates, which included looking glasses, books, jewellery, Bibles, and various fabrics. More typical, however, was the near poverty of poor Francis Forbes who left only 'a buckle belt with stones' and 'a cott: bed and curtains'. Or Benjamin Stacey who left an old belt, a pot of saffron, two wigs, and some ribbon. John Courtney died with little more than his clothes. He left only a pair of gloves, a coat, and 'briches'.[30] Thus, most of the men who left England single simply stayed that way for many years in India, loyally toasting their king and their wives if they had any back home—but not necessarily doing much more for them than that. In 1673, for instance, Agnes Spurin's husband, a soldier at Bombay, had to actually be ordered to pay part of his wages for the maintenance of his wife and family.[31] While such cases do not occur frequently in the records, quite clearly, the distress of being absent from one's family could be allayed by a variety of comforts in India.

And India could provide substantial comforts indeed. Quite simply, even if the Company's servants had received larger salaries and even if the factory ideal had not been monastic, it would have been extremely difficult for the 'plain, honest' English women that the Company eventually did allow to go to India to compete with the seductive beauty of professional Indian concubines. In many compounds, there was a bibi-khanae, a house of women. This was hardly a brothel. The term *bibi* in Hindustani, means 'high-class woman'[32] and indeed, these women were nothing at all like the whores one might have encountered on a London street. As a start, they were

British Women in India

clean. In an age where bathing was so singular an occurrence that Samuel Pepys mentions the rare occasions in his diary, that must have been refreshing. Two centuries later, Samuel Sneade Brown thought that 'those who have lived with native women for any length of time never marry a European; they are so amusingly playful, so anxious to oblige and please'.[33]

Throughout the seventeenth century, when neither the Sun King nor England's own Charles II troubled to conceal their extramarital activities, one searches in vain for directives from London against adultery, fornication, or homosexual activity. Indeed, the Directors were more concerned about dicing, drinking, duelling, and the like—activities which might have had direct or indirect economic consequences—than they were about mistresses, Indian, Portuguese, or otherwise. As Ronald Hyam has pointed out, expansion into Asia was not only a matter of Christianity and commerce, it was also a matter of copulation—with members of both sexes—and concubinage.[34] Although no figures are available to substantiate it, an argument might be made that the majority of the heterosexual liaisons during the entire history of the British involvement with India were between English men and Indian women.

By the end of the seventeenth century, a number of 'black women' are included on the passenger lists going from Britain to India as 'servants' to both British men and women.[35] While one perhaps might speculate on the kinds of services required of women such as these, the interesting thing is that they were returning *to* India *from* England, thus indicating a relationship that, while it was doubtless not sacramentalized, nonetheless, seems to have been as permanent and, more importantly perhaps, as socially acceptable as if it had been.

The very real affection that often developed between an Englishman and his concubine(s) carried over into the treatment given to children of mixed unions. Indeed, throughout the seventeenth and eighteenth centuries, wills not providing for the illegitimate children of such unions are rare, and institutions for the care of orphans were being founded and publicly funded well before the end of the seventeenth century.

Marriage was another matter entirely, however. While marrying and maintaining an English wife was extremely difficult for a factor and almost impossible on a sailor's or soldier's salary, legal/sacramental marriage to an Indian woman was likely to be completely out of the question. No Indian of the upper castes would have allowed his daughter or sister to marry a European since they were outside caste and thereby unclean. It is interesting to note that when Jehangir wanted to award a wife to William Hawkins, it was not a Hindu woman that he chose but an Armenian.

Sacramental marriage to a European woman was more feasible. These were likely to be Portuguese since, unlike either the English or the Dutch, the Portuguese had encouraged families since their initial entrance into India. Interestingly, in the lists of inhabitants which Madras began to keep fairly early in that factory's history, there are invariably categories for Portuguese Catholic women called *castees*, and women of mixed Indian-Portuguese descent called *mustees*[36] but never any for Indian wives. But that raised a complex problem. The Directors were perfectly willing to extend toleration to wives of Portuguese birth and assumed it was only natural that a Portuguese child would be Catholic, but it seemed equally natural that the child of an Englishman should be raised in the faith of his or her father. Religion is rarely simply a matter of creed; it is also a social and political matter. Rightly or wrongly, often rightly, Catholics in India were regarded as people not merely exercising their religion according to the dictates of their conscience but as persons bent on subverting political and religious liberty. And the Portuguese priests, primarily Jesuits, who earnestly tried to proselytize any soul within reach—Indian or European—did little to offset that perception.

It was in the Company's second presidency, Madras, that the issue of interfaith marriage would be resolved and, in the process, give the Company yet another reason to reverse its decision in the Anne Keeling case.

notes

1 Court of Committees, *Court Book*, vol. xx, 486, 20 February 1650, in Ethel Sainsbury, *A Calendar of the Court Minutes, etc. of the East India Company, 1650–1654* (Oxford: Clarendon Press, 1932), 21.

2 27 January 1641 in *Court Book*, vol. xvii, 394 in Ethel Sainsbury, *A Calendar of the Court Minutes, etc. of the East India Company, 1640–1643* (Oxford: Clarendon Press, 1909), 132.

3 See Court of Committees, 4 March 1642, *Court Book*, vol. xviii, 126 in Sainsbury, *Calendar, 1640–1643*, 235.

4 By the time of the union of the Old and New Companies, the following factories existed: Dependent on the presidency of Bombay were Surat, Agra, Swally, Broach, Ahmedabad, and Lucknow; on the Malabar Coast, were Carwar, Tellicherry, Anjengo, and Calicut; and in Persia, Isfahan, Gombroon (modern Bandar Abbas), and Shiraz.

Dependent on the presidency of Fort St George were Madras, Fort St David, Cuddalore, Portonovo, Pettipolee, Masulipatnam, Madapollam, and Vizagapatam, and also the Sumatra settlements of York Fort, Bencoolen, Indrapore, Tryamong, Sillabar, plus the factory of Tonquin in Cochin China.

Dependent on Fort William were Chuttanuttee, Ballasore, Cossimbazar, Decca, Hugli, Malda, Rajahmahal, Patna, and, more recently, Bantam.

The New Company's factories were at Surat, Masulipatnam, and Madapollam, and Pulo Kondor off the southern coast of Vietnam which would become famous later as a penal colony.

See Beckles Willson, *Ledger and Sword or The Honourable Company of Merchants of England Trading to the East Indies, 1599–1874*, 2 vols (London, New York, and Bombay: Longmans, Green, 1903), II, 39.

5 John Fryer, *A New Account of East India and Persia Being Nine Years' Travels, 1672–1681*, ed., William Crooke, 3 vols (London: Printed for the Hakluyt Society, 1909), I, 215.

6 Anthony Wild, *The East India Company: Trade and Conquest from 1600* (New York: Lyons Press, 2000), 24.

7 Rev. Patrick Warner's letter to the Court of Directors, 31 January 1676 in J. Talboys Wheeler, *Annals of the Madras Presidency*, 3 vols (Delhi: B.R. Publishing Corporation, 1985), I, 47.

8 Ibid., 48.

9 Willson, *Ledger and Sword*, I, 217.

10 The root of the word 'punch' is 'panj' or five referring either to the five ingredients or to the five flavours—sweet, sour, bitter, weak, and alcoholic—of which the drink is concocted. The word 'panj', incidentally, also gives Punjab its name from the five rivers that flow through it.

11 Wheeler, *Annals*, 45.

12 Cited in John Keay, *The Honourable Company: A History of the English East India Company* (New York: Macmillan, 1991), 153. Shaista Khan's opinion of the quarrelsome English merchants as opposed to those of the well-regulated Dutch factories led him to ban the Company from the Bengal trade, thus providing a spark for the hostilities that erupted between him and the Company in 1686.

13 Fryer, *New Account*, I, 215–16. After 1660, the rank of apprentice was added. Normally, apprenticeships were served for seven years.

14 Ibid.

15 John Ovington, A *Voyage to Surat in the Year 1689*, ed. H.G. Rawlinson (London: Humphrey Milford, Oxford University Press, 1929), 229. A bit more detail is provided by a Court Minute of 1674 where the salaries are listed at £10 for writers, £20 for merchants, £30 for junior factors and £40 for senior factors. See Sainsbury, *Calendar, 1674–76*, xxv–xxvi.

16 Fryer, *New Account*, I, 217.

17 B. Willson, *Ledger and Sword*, I, 357.

18 Ovington, *Voyage to Surat*, 228.

19 Colonel Henry Yule, ed., 'Miscellaneous Papers', in *The Diary of William Hedges, Esq. during His Agency in Bengal; as well as on His Voyage Out and Return Overland (1681–1687).* 3 vols (London: Printed for the Hakluyt Society, 1687–89), II, cccvi.

20 Reverend Frank Penny, *The Church in Madras: Being the History of the Ecclesiastical and Missionary Action of the East India Company in the Presidency of Madras in the Seventeenth and Eighteenth Centuries.* 2 vols (London: Smith, Elder, & Co, 1904), I, 1.

21 Cited in Michael Strachen and Penrose Boies, eds, *The East India Company Journals of Captain William Keeling and Master Thomas Bonner, 1615–1617* (Minneapolis: University of Minnesota Press, 1971), footnote, 54.

22 Cited in Henry Davison Love, *Vestiges of Old Madras, 1640–1800.* 3 vols, Indian Records Series (London: John Murray, 1913), II, 77, from Thomas Salmon.

23 Charles R. Wilson, ed., *The Early Annals of the English in Bengal, Being the Bengal Public Consultations for the First Half of the Eighteenth Century*, 3 vols (London: W. Thacker & Co., and Calcutta: Thacker, Spink & Co., 1900), lxv–vi.

24 Arnold Wright, *Early English Adventures in the East* (London: A. Melrose, Ltd., 1917), 310–12.

25 Ovington, *Voyage to Surat*, 229.

26 Cited in Wilson, *Annals*, lxv–lxvi.

27 Cited in Love, *Vestiges*, I, 396.

28 Ovington, *Voyage to Surat*, 230.

29 Old Wills. 1618–1720, G/40/23 in OIOC.

30 Ibid.

31 Court of Committees, May 16, 1673, *Court Book*, vol. xxviii, 239, in Sainsbury, *Calendar, 1671–1673*, 237.

32 Before the term 'memsahib' came into use in the nineteenth century, the term 'bibi' was also used to refer to English women. See, for example, Sydney Grier, ed., *The Letters of Warren Hastings to His Wife* (Edinburgh and

London: William Blackwood and Sons, 1905), 70, wherein Warren Hastings refers to the wife of a friend as 'Bibby Motte'.

33 Samuel Sneade Brown, *Home Letters Written from India between the Years 1828 and 1841* (London: Printed for Private Circulation by C.F. Roworth, 1878), 17.

34 Ronald Hyam, *Empire and Sexuality* (Manchester: University Press, 1991).

35 See, for example, Wilson, *Annals*, II, part 1, 341–2. The term 'black' was used rather indiscriminately to indicate any person of non-European origin.

36 *Mustee* is related to the nearly identical term used by the Portuguese to refer to people of mixed American Indian and Portuguese descent.

4

a saint and a 'mistris' at madras

THE DERISIVE TERM 'FISHING FLEET' WAS USED in the eighteenth and nineteenth centuries to refer to shiploads of young—and not so young—women who came out to India in search of husbands. The prize then was to secure 'three hundred pounds a year, dead or alive', namely, the income of a husband living or his pension when dead, provided he were a member of the civil service. The very first fishing fleets, however, carried women who came not entirely on their own initiative, but on that of the Company itself. They came in the 1670s and for a very simple reason—to populate the colonies with Protestant progeny. According to John Ovington who visited India in the late 1680s, the Company allowed 'Liberty to young Women to pass thither to gain Husbands, and raise their Fortunes' because 'so very few of their Children live, and of those that do, so many of them are sent for England, that fresh Colonies from thence are very necessary for supporting the Government and Affairs of the Island'.[1]

They arrived at the Company's second and third presidencies in India, Madras and Bombay, but it was in Madras that the tension between Protestant orthodoxy and full religious toleration was worked out. The struggle between Anglican England's Saint George and Catholic Portugal's Saint Thomas was much more serious than smaller matters such as precedence at the General Table, but it was worked through with far less spleen.

Unlike the rather swashbuckling adventures of the first merchants in Surat who found Portuguese, Indians, and occasionally their own countrymen willing to 'murther' them, the story of the establishment of Madras, modern Chennai, has a touch of romance about it and, in a wonderful twist of historic irony, the Portuguese threat changed from wanting to murder Englishmen to wanting to marry them.

By the end of the 1630s, in addition to Surat and subsidiary factories on the Malabar Coast, the Company had established several factories on the Coromandel Coast, all of which were subordinate to Bantam in the Spice Islands. Because of famine, competition from the Dutch who had come to the area more than a century before, and frequent wars between Golconda and its neighbours, the Indian headquarters had see-sawed between Armagon and Masulipatnam.[2] In March 1639, Francis Day, the agent at Armagon, sailed down the Coromandel Coast and called at a Portuguese fort named San Thomé. Built in 1522, San Thomé contained a few pure-blooded Portuguese as well as a large number of persons of mixed blood, all zealously attached to Catholicism. He then travelled north and at a fishing village called Madraspatnam (the patnam was later dropped) about four miles from San Thomé, he negotiated with the local *naik*, or ruler, for a building plot about one square mile upon which he proposed to build a fort to which the Armagon agency would remove.[3] He chose the site, he said, so that he could be close to his 'mistris'. Nothing is known about her, but the fact that San Thomé was less than half a day's march away suggests that the woman may have been Portuguese. Despite agreements with Portugal in 1630 and 1635,[4] the Portuguese could still bedevil English interests in India, a matter which seems to have interested him less than the lady. The not unimportant fact that cotton could be had there for a lower price than at Armagon no doubt also influenced him.

Apart from competition from the Dutch and the Portuguese, however, the flat, featureless, surf-swept beach had nothing at all that would seem to recommend it either for commerce or defense. Ocean-going vessels were required to drop anchor about a mile from the beach to avoid a reef of sand that runs parallel to the beach. They would immediately be surrounded by a fleet of catamarans or rickety boats that were simply bunches of planks lashed together with coconut-fiber twine. 'Crossing the bar', that is, making the harrowing trip through the breakers where men, women, merchandise, and furniture were tossed about like baubles became the stuff of many Englishmen's first stories of India. Spills were common, disasters frequent.

Whether it was the passion for his 'mistris' or his uncommon shrewdness about the cotton market—or a combination of the two—Day was willing to pledge his salary for the entire length of his service in the Company that cottons there would prove 15 per cent cheaper than at Armagon.[5] He threatened to resign if his plan was not adopted, and volunteered to meet all interest charges on money raised to build the necessary fort out of his own pocket. (He reneged on this offer.) Under the impression that the naik himself would build the fort—an impression that Day took no pains to dispel—the factors removed from Armagon. Once there, the Company's hand was forced and they had to build the fort—but not without some angst. Given the rising political tensions at home, their displeasure is understandable. A fort represented an expense that would not return an immediate profit and may have invited armed conflict with local native powers, something the Company was at great pains at all times to avoid.

Several writers arrived in February 1640 and, under the direction of Andrew Cogan, Day's superior at Masulipatam, soon began building Fort St George, so named for England's patron saint. Although at first opposed to Day and Cogan's policy, the Directors soon saw the wisdom of fortification. A garrison consisting of about thirty-five English and a number of native soldiers soon proved the Company's misgivings groundless and they approved the project. It took about fourteen years to complete the fort.[6] By the time it was finished, an enclave called White Town that for all practical purposes was synonymous with Fort St George had evolved.

From its foundation, Madras' White Town was essentially an English settlement rather than a compound in an Indian city. Nonetheless, although decidedly English, Madras was also wonderfully eclectic, both racially and religiously. Long before the arrival of the English, San Thomé itself, built on the site where legend had

it that the Apostle Thomas had been martyred, had been a collection of Muslims, Hindus, Portuguese, and Indian Christians, all of
whom celebrated the Saint's feast day on July 1. Although the church
was built in European fashion, in the early seventeenth century, its
caretaker was a Muslim.[7] When the Sultan of Golconda attacked the
region around Madras about 1646, there was a kind of Christian
reciprocity when the English were prudent enough to make peace
with him, and a Hindu temple was constructed.

Attracted by the security afforded by the fort, in addition to the
Portuguese, Indians, Armenians, and other assorted ethnicities soon
settled in the large, sprawling Black Town which quickly grew up
around the White Town, and became a desirable location for white
as well as non-white businesses.[8] Calicoes and chintzes were added
to the stores in the Company's warehouses, and 'madras' shortly
became not just the name of the settlement but also an adjective
describing the colourful plaid, striped, and checked patterns on the
fabrics that came from the brick and clay buildings of Black Town.

Madras prospered immediately. In 1639, the population of Madras
was numbered at 7,000; in 1674, the population, counting only adult
males, was 50,000. Only six years later, in 1681, it had ballooned
to 200,000, but now counting Portuguese, English, Indians, both
'Moors and Gentoos',[9] male and female. And in 1691, the population
was numbered at 400,000, including a surgeon and two chaplains.[10]
While one must allow for a certain amount of hyperbole in these figures, and even accounting for the fact that severe famines in 1646–47,
1658–59, and especially in 1686–87 drove people from outlying areas
into the settlement, by any measure, Madras' dramatic growth fully
justified Day's early optimism.

In 1654, Madras which until then had been subordinate to Surat,
was large enough and its trade significant enough to be declared a
presidency under Aaron Baker. It was he who had earlier persuaded
the Company to change its mind about allowing wives to accompany
their husbands to the Indies.

The Company's willingness to permit Elizabeth Baker to accompany her husband to India, albeit granted with some reluctance,
had opened the door for more women to also make the voyage
out. Underlining the Company's concern with the moral health of
its servants, a few years later, wives of chaplains were allowed to

accompany their husbands to India,[11] and specifically to Madras. The first reference to the Company providing allowances for the upkeep of houses for chaplains came in 1655,[12] and in 1661, Master Charles Walsh, 'an able orthodox divine who was well recommended…', was allowed to bring his wife with him to Fort St George.[13] Later, in July 1670, the Directors approved passage for the wife of Reverend John Hounsill, together with her maid, and the maid's child. Mrs Hounsill died shortly after reaching Fort St George and Reverend Hounsill himself died in July 1673.[14] What happened to the maid and her child is not recorded. Hounsill was succeeded as chaplain by Samuel Tutchin whose wife petitioned that she might join him. That petition was also granted and she, her young son, and her maid were granted passage but by the time she reached Fort St George, Tutchin had died and she returned home with her husband's estate 'in goods' and was allowed to land without paying the Company's dues.[15]

In providing for a family, however, chaplains faced the same problem everyone else did. Not only were their salaries low but private housing was hard to find. In Madras at least, all the houses in the inner fort were private property, and the Council did not have the power to allot a house to the chaplain without also paying the rent, which they could not do without the approval of the Directors, a process requiring well over a year to obtain. Reverend Penny gives the example of Thomas Consett who, in 1728, with the permission of the Directors, took his wife, three children, and a maid servant with him to Madras and got a special gratuity from the Company to provide for them on the voyage. On his arrival, Consett found his quarters in the inner fort too small for three adults and three children. The governor, James Macrae (1725–30) offered to enlarge their quarters but that could not be done without building on the top of them—a proposal that could not be carried out. Consett endured the inconvenience for over four months and then appealed for other less cramped and inconvenient quarters. He was given a choice to either hire a house for himself or to stay where he was. The records do not say which course he pursued, but in any case, he died in 1730.[16]

It was the presence of the Portuguese that altered the Company's policy from simply allowing English women to come to India to actually encouraging them to do so. Because the Portuguese in San Thomé knew the language and habits of the people among whom they had been raised, the Company's earliest agents at Madras, understanding their value as interpreters, tradesmen, office clerks, shop keepers, and soldiers, awarded them plots of land inside the fort, encouraged them to build houses both inside and outside the outer walls of the fort, and to bring their families with them.[17] They were also allowed the free exercise of their religion with the services of a priest under the bishop of San Thomé whose jurisdiction extended over the entire Coromandel Coast. By the end of the century, a Portuguese church would be on the north side of the fort opposite the first English church to be erected in India, St Mary's.[18] That would have been a remarkable gesture of religious toleration except that both militarily and financially, Saint George was very much dependent on Saint Thomas. It was Portuguese Catholics who formed the bulk of the military force and, as one report noted in 1680, '...our greatest income arises from the customs upon their commerce'.[19]

The commercial and military value of the Portuguese, however, had to be weighed against the equally powerful claims of religious orthodoxy, claims which were impossible to separate from political considerations. In 1659, the Reverend William Isaacson found himself at odds with the governor, Thomas Chamber, who opposed Isaacson's plan to expel two Portuguese 'mendicant' (presumably Franciscan or Capuchin) friars from Fort St George. The friars, Isaacson complained, visited women at night who were 'newly delivered' in order to baptize infants; they moved before corpses at burials with 'bell, book, candle, and cross', and tried to seduce the sick to their 'idolatrous custom' of setting the images of saints before them that they might pray to them. Then, touching what he no doubt knew would have been a sensitive nerve, he pointed out that 'all of this is to the great distress of those who knew not how to remedy it, living under the arbitrary government of one man, which will not advise with his Council in matters which concern the government of your Honours' town'.[20] Supported by the Council and also by many of the factors, Isaacson met with Chamber who explained that if he banished the Portuguese padres, the Portuguese soldiers in the Fort would desert. It was an obvious consideration. Painful though it might be, the friars would have to be permitted to stay.

Although the aim was for Protestant settlements, the Civil War had been nothing if not an argument that religious toleration was not only tidier but also much less expensive than bloodshed. As administrators in all the presidencies would quickly realize, granting religious toleration to the myriad populations under the Company's authority was one thing; marriage to a Catholic, however, especially if one intended to have heirs, was another matter entirely.

Thus, apart from the possibility of losing the services of valuable factors such as Aaron Baker, what was happening in Madras forced the Company to rethink its decision in the Keeling case. While it might indeed be a curse to keep a man and his wife asunder, the greater worry was that the factors were marrying Portuguese Catholic women. Indeed, when Day's companion, Andrew Cogan, left India to return to England to fight for the Royalist cause, one of his two sons dismayed his superiors by running off to San Thomé where he turned into a 'Papist rouge [*sic*]' and even went to Mass every day with his wife.[21] In the list of inhabitants for 1654, reference is made to the wife and daughter of Richard Potter, to the wife and daughter of Thomas Paine, to a Mrs Daardener, and a Mrs Newbegin, and to the wives of Richard Cogan, Thomas Bland, William Dawes, and Jacob Fuddle, 'a freeman of this Towne'.[22] There is a strong possibility, however, that few, if any, of these women were either English or Indian. A Catholic padre was present at Thomas Newbegin's death, suggesting the influence of a Catholic, possibly Portuguese or *mustee* wife.

What troubled the Company were not so much the marriages themselves as that the children of Englishmen who married *castees* or mustees were being brought up Catholic. Such marriages were not legal in England and succession to family property and honours depended upon legitimacy. Thus, property that could be claimed by the Company could also fall out of its hands. Several times, orders were sent out from Leadenhall Street that any man who was married by a Roman Catholic priest or did not have his children educated in the Protestant religion was to be sent home forthwith.[23] If one were not concerned about legitimacy, however, a rather obvious way to avoid compliance with the Company's orders was simply not to marry at all. In January 1676, the Reverend Patrick Warner, who was not in Holy Orders, but was described as 'a very good preacher, and of a sober peaceable disposition',[24] complained to the Directors from Fort St George:

Some [factors], after they have lived a long time in uncleanness, their whores persuade them to marry them, and several such have been married, who within a little time have found them treacherous and adulterous and thereupon have run away from them, or carried them along with them and sold them to the Infidels and Moores. Some unmarried persons keep whores in their houses, and some married whose wives are in England do the same. Most of those whores are popish Christians; and if those that marry them do not fall into the former inconveniences, they hardly escape being seduced by their wives and wives' families into popery.[25]

Interestingly, Warner did not think it necessary to prohibit such marriages, but he did want more careful inspection taken about the persons sent over to 'these places',

… for there come hither some thousand murderers, some men stealers, some popish, some come over under the notion of single persons and unmarried, who yet have their wives in England, and here have been married to others, with whom they have lived in adultery; and some on the other hand have come over as married persons, of whom there are strange suspicions they were never married.[26]

On the other hand, the worst threat to stable English settlements not only in India but throughout the Indies came not from European competitors or Indian foes, but from disease. Three years would remain the average duration of a European's life in India until the early nineteenth century, or, as it was rather quaintly put, 'two monsoons is the age of a man'. Dr John Fryer who traveled in India in the 1670s wondered,

Is this the Elysium after a tedious Wastage? For this, will any thirst, will any contend, will any forsake the Pleasures of his Native Soil, in his Vigorous Age, to bury himself alive here? For in Five hundred, One hundred survive not; of that One hundred, one Quarter get not Estates, of those that do, it has not been recorded above One in Ten Years has seen his Country.[27]

While women and children represented an unwelcome expense, and Dr Fryer's disquiet notwithstanding, the perpetually dwindling Protestant population of the factories was an even more formidable consideration. Thus, at the end of 1678, the Directors decided to send three or four 'plain, honest' women out to Fort St George on 'matrimonial speculation'. The three single women who arrived were Mary Gainsford, Ann Davys and Rebecca Randell.[28] The social and economic condition of the three women must have been quite desperate. Given the dangers and discomforts of the voyage out and the uncertainties they would face once they arrived, India could only have been a last resort. According to the Fort St. George *Consultation* from that year, the three women had

> neither relations nor recommendations to any person in this place, but say they knew noe otherwayes but that they were sent out by the Hon'ble Company, and therefore have made their request for subsistence upon their Accompt. They being in a low condition, and not able to maintaine themselves, it was therefore resolv'd to allow them 40 fanams per Mensum for their maintenance ... soe long as they remaine unmarryed.[29]

Ann Davys and Rebecca Randell had changed their condition by the end of the year but it took Mary Gainsford nearly three years before she married Robert Bowyer of the civil service in 1681. That same year saw another wedding when Triphena Ord, the sister of the schoolmaster, Ralph Ord, who had come to Madras in July 1678, married James Wheeler of the civil service. Another woman, Mary Milton, who had accompanied Triphena Ord, was married two years later to Captain Henry Burton, a master mariner.[30]

Still, ten years later, in 1688, there would be eleven christenings and thirteen marriages but over a hundred burials.[31] The high mortality combined with the scarcity of unmarried English women meant that if legal marriages were going to occur, they would still most often be to Catholics—or not occur at all. Ultimately, the government was willing to allow marriages for their own civil and military servants with Portuguese women but only on the condition that they be sacramentalized according to Anglican rites—and thereby contrary to Catholic canon law. The critical case seems to have come in 1680, two years after the arrival of Misses Randell, Davys, Gainsford, and Ord, when Phineas Brewster, who was a free merchant and thus not under the Company's direct supervision, married a Portuguese woman who was Catholic. She was the widow of an Englishman named Barrick and the marriage to Brewster was solemnized on March 22 by a Portuguese priest who then fled the jurisdiction of the Council to avoid punishment. Initially, the Madras Council decided to allow the marriage on three grounds: (*a*) although it was it was against the 1673 Test Act forbidding Catholics to hold office under the Crown, it was not against the law of God as found in Scripture; (*b*) because the Catholics in Madras were the offspring of foreigners, namely, Portuguese, they were not subject to the laws of England against Catholics; and (*c*) there were not enough English women for the men, and the small salaries of the common soldiers allowed them to maintain Portuguese women more easily than they could English women and children. Moreover, their women were 'not less modest than our ordinary or country people', and such marriages, hopefully, might gain many children to be brought up in the Protestant religion. After three days of consultation with other free merchants and the two chaplains in the settlement, however, it was resolved that the children of such mixed unions were to be brought up Protestants.[32]

That settled the matter for Englishmen with Catholic wives inside Fort St George, but not for those who married outside the fort and then came to live there. So in October 1683, the Council resolved that the children of seamen who married 'native women' and came to settle in Madras also should be raised Protestant, and recommended that soldiers within the fort be actually encouraged to marry native women in the hope that the children of such marriages might be brought up as Protestants. To that end, in early April 1687, just months before James II would be forced from the throne when his Catholic wife delivered a son, the Directors offered something of a bribe. Soldiers would be allowed to marry 'native women' but the day the child of such a union was christened in the Anglican faith, the mother would be paid a pagoda. However, they added, 'If you think it will not have any considerable effect that way, we had better keep our money.'[33]

The offer indeed had little effect. Although there are records of the pagoda being paid even as late as the surrender of Fort St George in 1746, the new Rules of 1680 and 1683 made it difficult for men to obtain wives among the daughters of the Portuguese Catholics. Rather than make the required promise, the Portuguese women would live with the men of their choice without marriage and so retain control over their children's religion.[34]

By making marriage to Portuguese Catholic women a bit more cumbersome, the 1680 and 1683 regulations should have worked in favour of Protestant English women coming to Madras for the purpose of getting married. Indeed, by the end of the seventeenth century, although wives of any race were still rare, the majority were English. In 1699, a listing at Fort St George 'and other places' on the Coromandel Coast, including Fort St David and Vizagapatam, showed 119 Englishmen, including Company servants and seafaring men who were not constant inhabitants, and 'freemen'. Of these, only forty-seven were married, the rest were bachelors. However, almost half of those who were married—twenty-six—were married to English women. Fourteen were married to castees, four to mustees, two to French women, and one to a Georgian.

On the other hand, the regulations may have made little difference. Even more interesting than the number of English women who were married is that the number of those who were not nearly equals those who were. Fourteen English women were widows and ten were 'young unmarried ladies'.[35] In giving those figures, J. Talboys Wheeler adds, 'It seems a great pity that ten young ladies should have been unable to find husbands amongst so large a community of unmarried gentlemen.'[36] In a company where there were seventy-two English bachelors, in addition to any number of unattached males of other races, the figures might suggest an extraordinary fastidiousness on someone's part. However, Indian concubines were still available, salaries had not been increased enough to enable a man to establish an English family, and, most constraining of all, the General Table was still in effect.

In 1678, pending the arrival of Ann Davys, Rebecca Randell, and Mary Gainsford, the Madras Council had appealed to the Directors to raise wages for married persons because 'the allowances they receive for Dyett and House rent are so small that they are not able to subsist thereupon, being at great expence unavoydable out of their own purses …'[37] The appeal did little good; the Directors did not significantly increase the salaries of their servants until the early nineteenth century.

The issue of the General Table had been raised earlier. In August 1674, the Council at Fort St George, then under the governor Sir William Langhorne (1672–78) appealed to the Directors:

And as for the young men without the Councill [*sic*], your Honours need not be informed how discreditable as well as unpleasing a thing it would

British Women in India

be for your Agent to be tyed to sitt like a pedant amongst his Boyes, especially heere being such a concourse of Dutch and French, either on business or civility, whom we cannot avoid entertaining at your table...[38]

The Directors were unsympathetic. Not only was it 'most honourable and convenient' to maintain the General Table but, they argued, the sitting of youths at the table, in no way abridged their freedom. Besides, it would set a good example and prevent them from keeping 'ill' company.[39]

Whatever good example the Table provided was apparently minimal. As late as 1710, the Directors were sorry to hear that, despite files of musketeers being sent to keep the peace at dinner time, 'there has not been a Sufficient Decorum kept up among our People, and particularly among the Young Writers and Factors'.[40]Although the General Table was abolished in 1722,[41] a decade later, the Directors still believed that the extravagance of their servants could have been avoided by maintaining the Table. While that was continued, they argued, 'our Servants were kept in decorum, and behaved suitably to their Superiours'. Then, ignoring the competition provided by the private or country trade, other European contenders, Indian princes, and pirates, the Directors remarked that because of the disuse of the Table 'our profits in Trade are every year so considerably diminished'.[42]

Although there continued to be complaints about Portuguese padres noisily parading with 'bell, book, and candle' at funerals and other processions, interfaith marriages became less problematic, albeit still mildly irritating. By the end of the century, the Portuguese threat had diminished both in Europe and in India, and the Enlightenment made religious toleration not only fashionable but sound economic policy as well. Henry Dobyns was privately married to Rachel Baker by a 'Romish priest' on 27 June 1698, but then the priest went to Bengal and the witnesses could not at first be found; so, because Dobyns could not prove he was legally married, he was ordered to remain inside Fort St George. Two witnesses to the marriage eventually did come forth and Dobyns was then released pending further consideration about what punishment should be inflicted. However, the matter apparently then was dropped.[43]

In 1719, again contrary to the Company's regulations, Portuguese priests presided over two marriages of people belonging to Fort St

George. The first case was the chief officer of a Company ship who married a French woman. When the bride refused to be married at St Mary's because of the 1680 regulation that the children of all marriages had to be raised Protestant, the chief officer renounced his religion for 'Romanism'. As in the Dobyns case, the matter was dropped. The second case involved a soldier named Dutton, described in the Consultations as 'an ordinary fellow' who married Ann Ridley, the orphaned daughter of a former governor who had been a ward of the ministers and churchwardens. The reason for refusing their consent, however, was not religious but that the man of her choice was not her social equal.[44]

Two years later, the Governor and Council agreed that the 1680 regulation ought to be repealed for three reasons: (*a*) the obligation of itself was unjust and a violation of the right of all parents to have their children raised in that religion they think most acceptable to God; (*b*) since the obligation was unlawful in itself, it could not bind anyone's conscience; and (*c*) Such a promise might have ill consequences, 'as in the instance now before us', that is, the case of Ann Ridley and Dutton.[45]

By the beginning of the eighteenth century, the Directors had to admit that 'we hear that almost all the Black people about Madras are either Gentues or Papists'. Instead of prohibiting Catholic baptisms, however, or insisting that the children be raised Protestant, and concerned too that 'we can never reckon upon the true strength of the place being at our disposal', the Directors shifted to the tactic of educating 'the natives' in the Protestant Religion.[46] Thus, church trustees, instead of simply railing against mixed marriages, wisely took on the care of orphans. The result was that less than two generations after Ann Davys, Mary Gainsford, Rebecca Randell, and Triphena Ord had arrived to counter marriages to Portuguese castees, a key hallmark of that 'most English' of the settlements in India, like that of its ancestor, San Thomé, was Madras' religious and racial diversity.

notes

1 John Ovington, *A Voyage to Surat in the Year 1689*, ed., H.G. Rawlinson (London: Humphrey Milford, Oxford University Press, 1929), 88.

2 Masulipatnam, famous for its chintz and calicoes, was the earliest English factory on the Coromandel Coast, having been established in 1611.

3 Henry Davison Love, *Vestiges of Old Madras, 1640–1800.* 3 vols, Indian Records Series (London: John Murray, 1913), I, 84. The grant from the *naik* is dated August 1639. Within a few years of the founding of Fort St George, the new town which had grown up around the Fort was commonly known to the natives as Chennaipatam, either in deference to the naik's wishes whose father had been named Channa or Channanapak Nayak or because the site had originally borne that name.

4 In 1630, following the rout of the Portuguese at Swally by a small force of English sailors, the Portuguese agreed to the Treaty of Madrid declaring that the English and Portuguese would abstain from hostilities against each other in the East. This was then followed by a convention in 1635 between William Methwold, then president at Surat, and the Viceroy of Goa establishing a truce for an indefinite period of time. It was not until 1654, however, that Cromwell was able to extract from the Portuguese a full recognition of England's right to trade in the East Indies. See H.H. Dodwell, ed., *The Cambridge History of the British Empire: British India*, Vol. IV (New York: Macmillan, 1929), 84–5.

5 John Keay, *The Honourable Company: A History of the English East India Company* (New York: Macmillan, 1991), 69. Andrew Cogan was later promoted to Bantam while Day left for England in 1641 amid charges of private trade.

6 Built in a square about a mile and a half in circumference, the fort extended only four hundred yards in length from north to south parallel with the sea and one hundred yards, east to west. See J. Talboys Wheeler, *Annals of the Madras Presidency.* 3 vols (Delhi: B.R. Publishing Corporation, 1985), I, 187.

7 'Mr. Samuel Purchas's Description of India 250 Years Ago' in J. Talboys Wheeler, ed., *Early Travels in India in the 16th & 17th Centuries* (Delhi: Deep Publications, 1974), 155.

8 The earliest mention of a 'Christian' town separate from the native Black Town is in 1661.

9 The terms 'Moors' and 'Gentoos' were both used with a good bit of imprecision. In general, 'Moors' referred to Muslim Indians and 'Gentoos' were usually but not always Hindus. By the late eighteenth century, however, the term 'Gentoo' was often being used to refer to any non-European.

10 Love, *Vestiges*, I, 547. See also *Vestiges*, II, 77. Love's figures are taken from a Thomas Salmon or Sammon writing of Madras in 1699 or 1700.

11 Several authors seem to sense that chaplains were generally bachelors but Penny discounts that. While Penny is perhaps correct, the truth also is that it was as difficult for chaplains as for anyone else to support a family.

See Reverend Frank Penny, *The Church in Madras Being the History of the Ecclesiastical and Missionary Action of the East India Company in the Presidency of Madras in the Seventeenth and Eighteenth Centuries.* 2 vols (London: Smith, Elder, & Co., 1904), I, 157.

12 Ibid., I, 5.

13 *Court Minutes*, 17 and 18 February 1661–62, cited in ibid., 39.

14 Ibid., 54–5.

15 Court of Committees, *Court Book*, vol. xxix, 27 October 1675, in Ethel Sainsbury, *A Calendar of the Court Minutes, etc. of the East India Company, 1674–1676* (Oxford: Clarendon Press, 1935), 231–3.

16 Penny, *Church in Madras*, I, 157.

17 Ibid., 26.

18 The foundation of St Mary's Church was laid on Easter Monday, 1 April 1678 by the governor, Streynsham Master, and was completed in 1680.

19 Cited in ibid., 78–9.

20 Cited in ibid., 27.

21 Indian Records Series, Vol. I, cited in Dennis Kincaid, *British Social Life in India, 1608–1937* (London: George Routledge & Sons, Ltd., 1938, reprinted 1939), 49.

22 Love argues that these were doubtless not the only female European or Eurasian residents of the place. See *Vestiges*, I, 117–18.

23 See for eaxmple, Penny, *Church in Madras*, 60–1. The letter is dated 24 December 1675.

24 Penny, 57, citing *Factory Records*, Miscellaneous, III, 141.

25 From Rev. Patrick Warner's letter to the Court of Directors, 31 January 1676, in Wheeler, *Annals*, I, 47.

26 Ibid.

27 John Fryer, *A New Account of East India and Persia Being Nine Years' Travels, 1672–1681*, ed. William Crooke, 3 vols (London: Printed for the Hakluyt Society, 1909), I, 180.

28 Love, *Vestiges*, I, 449.

29 Cited from the Consultations, P.C., vol. II, 25 July 1678 in ibid., 450. At Fort St George, c. 1685, a fanum was worth about four pence; forty fanums or one pagoda was worth about ten shillings, the pice was one half-penny. The rupee was valued at three shillings. See John Bruce, *Annals of the Honorable East India Company from Their Establishment by the Charter of Queen Elizabeth, 1600, to the Union of the London and English East India Companies, 1707–8.* 3 vols (London: Black, Parry, and Kingsbury, 1810 [Republished at Farnborough: Gregg Press Limited, 1968]), II, 561.

30 Footnote in Love, *Vestiges*, I, 450.

31 Wheeler, *Annals*, I, 193. Love has only fifty-seven burials and eight marriages. See *Vestiges*, I, 485. While the discrepancy is striking, both sets of figures indicate an appalling ratio of deaths to marriages and births.

32 Penny, *Church in Madras*, I, 78 citing Consultations, 22 and 25 March 1680.

33 Cited in ibid., 107 from Consultations, 8 April 1696.

34 Ibid.

35 Wheeler, *Annals*, I, 268–9.

36 Ibid.

37 Love, *Vestiges*, I, 397.

38 O.C., No. 3992, 20 August 1674, cited in Love, *Vestiges*, I, 396.

39 Cited in Love, *Vestiges*, I, 397.

40 Cited in ibid., II,170.

41 Wheeler, *Annals*, III, 105.

42 Love, *Vestiges*, II, 268.

43 Ibid., 252–3.

44 Penny, *Church in Madras*, I, 234.

45 Cited from Consultations, 10 April and 26 October 1721, in ibid., I, 236.

46 Cited from Despatch, 7 April 1708, para. 112 in ibid., I, 133.

5

the 'debauched' ladies of bombay

IN 1661, CHARLES II MARRIED THE PORTUGUESE INFANTA, Catherine of Braganza. Part of her dowry was Bombay, now known as Mumbai, the capital of the modern Indian state of Maharashtra. Although the marriage was designed to bring peace in Europe, trade rivalries, exacerbated by religious differences, continued to plague the Company's servants in the East. The Portuguese at Goa, who had churches and extensive lands in the northern part of the island, bitterly opposed the transfer. On the grounds of a 'misunderstanding', they argued that the treaty stipulated Bombay alone; the British insisted that it included the islands of Salsette and Tannah without which Bombay would have been worthless in that it could not be accessed. It was not until February of 1665 that the difficulties were settled and the island was actually handed over to English authorities. Two years later, in 1667, in return for a loan of £50,000 or £10 per annum,[1] Charles was glad to place Bombay into the hands of the East India Company. As tricky as the initial cession had been, Bombay, like Madras, very quickly became a centre of cultural and religious diversity—and for the same reason, trade. Within a decade, the population rose from 10 to 60,000.[2]

Bombay—modern Mumbai—the centre of Bollywood or India's Hindi film industry. That 'tag' and another mark of modernity, industrial pollution, point to a westward orientation that goes very deep into the city's history. There is evidence of visits to the Malabar Coast by ancient Greeks and Romans who came to trade. These Westerners did not, however, settle in India. That was left for the descendants of Zoroastrian refugees who, in the seventh century, had fled persecution from recently Islamized Persia. Eventually, these 'Parsis' as they came to be known, made their way to India and came to settle in Mumbai where they quickly established an exceptionally active merchant community. Even the derivation of the old name 'Bombay' is Western. It is usually thought to come from the Portuguese, 'bombaim' or good bay.

And good indeed it is. Flanked by parallel rows of hills, the island of Bombay itself, which is the largest of seven islands, is 11 miles long and 3 miles wide. The majestic harbour on its southwest end is about 5 by 7 miles and capable of holding scores of English vessels. Beyond the city lie coconut, mango, and palm groves, rice and paddy fields, and the Mahim wood for which Bombay is famous. Directly south of Bombay is Colaba or Old Woman's Island which became a pleasure-resort when the Company laid out a park, gardens, and a small zoo. In the seventeenth century, at the end of the town were a bazaar where cows and buffaloes roamed and several churches and convents in the hands of the Portuguese Jesuits and Franciscans who owned them.[3] The most conspicuous edifice on Bombay, however, was the Portuguese castle-fort with its cannons and guns on the southeastern side of the island.

Initially, Bombay was subordinate to Surat whose governor, George Oxinden, sent several deputies whose loose management resulted in what Dr Fryer described as 'anarchy'.[4] That ended with the appointment of Gerald Aungier (1669–77), who would prove to be one of the most competent administrators the Company had in the seventeenth century, indeed in its entire history. He was also one of the many extraordinary men whose efforts to stabilize a settlement in order to attract trade were vastly underappreciated by the Directors.

Under the new charter, Aungier established a mint in 1672 and started to issue copper and tin coins under the Company's authority.

Silver was not minted, however, until 1675, and in 1676, Charles II authorized the mintage at Bombay of rupees and other coins bearing the royal arms. The coinage helped trade on as well as off the island. The economic value of the Parsi population was obvious but Aungier also wished to see the old native trade guilds at Bombay receive official recognition as well and have native magistrates appointed for petty legal cases.

Bombay flourished at first. Along the waterfront rose the Company's warehouses, tiled or plastered with *chuman*, a material made from oyster shells which, when dried, gave a lovely marble-like translucence to the exterior of buildings. By the time Dr John Fryer arrived in Surat in the 1670s, the factory had obtained a sturdy house built of stone and timber from the Emperor Aurangzeb. Each floor was at least half a yard thick of plastered cement and, as would be the case with much of Anglo-Indian architecture, 'contrived after the Moor's buildings', the building had upper and lower galleries, or terrace-walks, a neat oratory, and a convenient open place for meals.[5] The president had spacious lodgings in the castle-fort, noble rooms for counsel and entertainment, pleasant tanks, yards, and a hummum, that is, an Eastern bath.[6] Outside the Fort, the castle gardens were said to be the most pleasant in India, 'intended rather for wanton Dalliance, Love's Artillery, than to make resistance against an invading foe'.[7]

Bombay had another advantage that Surat had lacked, but one shared with Fort St George. A man could build his own house on British soil, and the Company encouraged outsiders as well as its own servants, after their term of service, to settle there and engage in trade as long as their businesses did not compete with the Company's. Thus, while much of the collegial atmosphere remained within the Fort, family life might have become a bit more feasible.

It may have been with that in mind that the Directors, apparently concerned about the effects of the more relaxed virtue of the Restoration upon their servants in India, sent out a set of rules 'for the Christian and sober Comportment of all our Factors and Servants' almost as soon as they acquired Bombay from the Crown. Because there were ten of them, they became popularly known as the Ten Commandments.[8] Essentially the Commandments were a reiteration of the regulations the Company had been issuing since

British Women in India

its founding, and while nothing was said about transgressions of a sexual nature, fines which were to be kept in a box for the poor were levied for the usual cursing, swearing, blaspheming, drunkenness, for absence from prayers on Sundays and Wednesdays, and for leaving the fort without permission. In addition to the Ten Commandments and, as in Madras, in reaction to the horrific mortality and also to assure that what progeny survived would be Protestant, in 1668, the Directors ordered that a number of soldiers, with their wives and families, were to be sent annually to Bombay.[9] About the same time, several 'gentlewomen' also were sent out as potential wives to merchants.

The experiment was extremely disappointing for everyone. The presence of English women did little to uplift morals, and the breaking of the Ten Commandments, whether from Moses or the Company, continued unabated. In 1671, Philip Gyfford, a member of the president's council and Aungier's deputy governor, reported that 'the ladys that are unmarried begin to despaire and desire leave to goe home' if they could not find husbands within the next two months. Moreover, 'several persons of the ordinarie sorte come out of both sexes, whose lives and carriages not being enquired into, prove when they arrive heare soe strangely debauch[ed] and factious that they are not onely [sic] dangerous and troublesome, but are a disgrace both to their country and religion'.[10]

While terms like 'wicked' and 'debauched' may have some justification, they may also describe not the women themselves so much as the proclivities of the correspondents using them. Aungier, for all his administrative skill, did, after all, tend to be a bit puritanical.

Complaints of debauched or disgraceful behaviour should also perhaps be viewed in the unusual context of Bombay itself for, despite its great physical endowments, Bombay also had severe disadvantages that made the establishment of family life even more difficult than was usual at a factory. At almost the precise moment that the Company acquired Bombay, the great Maratha chief Shivaji (1627–1680) had begun to create a power in central India that would shortly rival the Moghuls themselves. By 1654, he had gained control of the Western Ghats and in three battles in the last months of 1660, he defeated superior forces, alarming Aurangzeb who, after assassinating his father, Shah Jehan, had seized the throne in 1658 and who had once scorned Shivaji as a 'mountain rat'. In January 1664, the English factors at Surat witnessed Shivaji's attack on that city. The factors saved their own property, valued at £80,000, but Shivaji plundered the town for six days and finally carried off immense booty.[11] Surat was plundered again in 1670, but again the English factory was spared. In the next decade, having consolidated power in Maharashtra, Shivaji turned his attention to Golconda, the Carnatic, and the Tamil country. What perhaps saved all the English factories from grave harm was that they were too insignificant to interest Shivaji very much. The turmoil, however, did the Company's trade little good. What had become increasingly clear since Hawkins' day and what the Maratha danger bore out so forcibly was that the old policy of propitiations, flattery, and begging for *firmans* had to be substituted for forts and careful alliances which, in India's tumultuous political climate, were constantly in flux. Nor did Shivaji's death in 1680 end the danger. The Marathas would continue to worry the Company until their final defeat in 1818.

More than princes, Marathas and Moghuls, however, Bombay's greatest enemy was disease. For all its advantages, Bombay was unhealthier even than Madras due partly to the habit of manuring the coconut groves around the island with a putrid fish called buckshaw 'that breeds Consumptions, Fevers, and Fluxes'.[12] Matthew Gray, Deputy Governor at Bombay from January to September 1670, wrote in July, 'Tis now a sickly time for fluxes and feavours, yet praised be God, wee have buryed but one man these three months past.'[13] The following month, however, three lives were claimed.

The combination of the threats from the Marathas and disease should have argued for a greater investment of both men and resources but the Company was unwilling to provide either. The high mortality required that native soldiers, 'sepoys', were employed and new recruits were sent out almost annually from England, but soldiers' salaries remained miserable. So low were they, in fact, that there was a small rebellion in 1674 when recruits complained that, among other things, they were owed a month's pay, could not afford to buy their own coats, and that inflation had pushed some foodstuffs beyond their means.[14] It goes without saying that, although they did not mention it in their list of grievances, supporting a wife, let alone children, would have been out of the question.

Nonetheless, the notion that English wives might have a calming influence brought a repetition of the experiment. In 1675, shortly before Reverend Patrick Warner asked for women to be sent to Madras, revolted by the drunkenness, gambling, dueling, and prostitution that flourished on the island, Aungier again asked that women be sent out to propagate Bombay and for the same reason—to prevent liaisons with 'foul women', that is, *castees* or *mustees*. 'Through their fathers' neglect', he complained, the children were being brought up in Roman Catholic principles, 'to the great dishonour and weakening of the Protestant religion and interest'.[15] He wanted gentlewomen for the factors and officers and 'other women'—'country girls' or even 'hospital girls'—for the troops. One 'suit of raiment' was to be allowed for each girl and they were to be given lodging for a year and a day at the Company's expense.[16]

By the standards of another age, both Aungier's petition and the earlier order in 1668 seem a bit callous perhaps, or at least ill-conceived. There is something of a cattle market flavour in expecting that the mere presence of an English woman would entice a man to prefer her to a Portuguese wife or an Indian concubine, or that a woman's role was simply to provide for Protestant progeny and raise the standards of civility. There is also a kind of 'throw away' quality about 'country girls' destined for soldiers whose lot was often brutal—and brutalizing—as opposed to the 'gentle women' targeted for the factors and officers whose kindnesses may have been only a little less unsympathetic. Aungier's petition, however, must be placed in the context of an age when marriage was less about romance than about economics, when sailors could be keelhauled and soldiers forced to run the gauntlet, and when human cargo was a staple of the trans-Atlantic trade. Moreover, as with Ann Davys, Mary Gainsford, and Rebecca Randell who appeared three years later in Madras, India may have been a last resort for young girls who must have been terribly poor, likely orphaned, and completely without other economic or social resources. One might expect, too, that something of a social revolution occurred on board and that by the time they reached India, all the young ladies had become 'gentle'.

In any case, Aungier's plan, like the earlier one, was frustrated from the outset. By 1677, the Company had found twelve young women to send out as prospective wives for the soldiers saying they had taken care to choose only 'civil' ones and they had not been able to get any 'country girls' of the kind asked for.[17] Many of the girls proved as troublesome as those who had arrived earlier, however, and soon there were complaints that their behaviour had 'grown scandalous to our nation, religion and government', and they had to be warned that if they did not 'apply themselves to a more sober and Christian conversation' they would be confined and fed on bread and water until they could be shipped back to England.[18]

What they were doing that so distressed Aungier is not recorded. Unlike peccadilloes involving drinking, gambling, quarreling, illicit private trade, and the like that merit terms such as 'wicked', 'vicious' or 'scandalous', the word 'debauchery' used by Gyfford in 1671 suggests transgressions that were peculiarly sexual.[19] That, coupled with the Council's complaint that their behaviour had offended 'our nation, religion and government' raises the intriguing possibility that their behaviour resembled that of the men with whom they lived—that is, instead of marrying English factors, the ladies found partners who were not English—possibly Portuguese and, thus, Catholic. Another possibility is that, like many English men, they may have simply dwelt in domestic harmony without benefit of the sacrament. Some may also have turned to prostitution in order to survive, but while that behaviour would have been 'debauched' it would not necessarily have threatened 'our nation, religion and government' to the degree that marriage to a Catholic would have.

The phrase also suggests another even more intriguing possibility—that these ladies may have been inclined to enter into some kind of sexual relationship with Indian men. It is somewhat difficult to imagine that they could have been induced to leave England—to endure the dangers and difficulties of the voyage to they knew not what—unless there was very little reason to remain at home. Whatever few constraints English society might have afforded them had probably dissolved before they had even boarded the East Indiaman that would take them far from English soil. Most importantly, the racial barriers that invaded even the private lives of Victorians simply were not there for their grandparents and great grandparents. Because India had not yet been conquered, Indians had not yet become 'inferior', or 'effeminate' or any of the pejorative terms that would later be attached to them. The Indians these women would have encountered—*banians*, *khitmutgars*, *khansamans*, and so on—would, like themselves, have belonged to the servant classes, and the comforts that a Protestant Englishman, especially an English soldier, might supply promised to be no better, and perhaps a good bit worse, than the comforts a man of any other nation might afford.

In any case, the presence of English women did as little to alleviate the 'contagion of the Air' as it did to alleviate the other causes of the 'dissolution of manners'. According to Dr Fryer,

> The Company have sent out English women, but they beget a sickly Generation; and as the Dutch well observe, those thrive better that come of an European Father and Indian Mother: Which (not to reflect on what Creatures are sent abroad) may be attributed to their living at large, not debarring themselves Wine and Strong Drink, which immoderately used, inflames the Blood, and spoils the Milk in these Hot Countries, as Aristotle long ago declared. The Natives abhor all heady Liquors, for which reason they prove better Nurses.[20]

While the object of sending English women to India had been marriage and the procreation of Protestant progeny in the face of the high mortality, Aungier's pleas for funds to drain the fetid tidal swamps in and around Bombay, which would have been far more sensible, were turned down on the grounds of expense. In 1671, shortly after his arrival in Bombay and about the same time the first English women had arrived there, he also ordered that a hospital be built but a number of obstacles including a scarcity of labourers and material, namely chuman, prevented its completion until 1676.[21] After a particularly long monsoon in 1675, a total of fifty men were buried between 1 October and 24 November.[22] Gray complained, 'We have diverse of our people sick and tis a harde sayinge when the surgeons tell them they have no medicines to give them, occasioned by the improvidence of those {to whom} our Masters intrust it at home, that neglected sendinge any out by the last three ships, which falls out unhappily to the loss of the Company's servants ...'[23]

Not only was London culpable for the lack of medicines but the Directors were more inclined to agree with the navy chaplain, John Ovington, who was rather certain that the appalling mortality rate could be attributed not so much to 'an impure Contagion of the Air, or the gross Infection of the Elements' as to 'the vicious Enormities' which had grown in the place.

> Luxury, Immodesty, and a prostitute Dissolution of Manners, found still new Matter to work upon. Wickedness was still upon the Improvement, and grew to such a Perfection, that no Vice was so detestable as not to be extremely vicious; whereby Satan obtain'd a more Despotick Author- ity in the Hearts of the Christians, than he did among the Gentiles in the Pageantry of Heathen Worship. And when the Seeds of Avarice and Prophaneness, of Envy and Injustice, and a thousand other black Infer- nal Vices grew up and flourish'd, and were made the Ambition of every Individual; we need not then admire, if the pure Luminaries of Heaven should set themselves against their Impieties, and dart their mortal Poy- sons on the Earth; if the Planets should wisely shed their venomous As- pects upon profligate Men, and thereby in Vengeance produce the mortal Fruits of Death.[24]

The Directors also baulked when Aungier pressed them for a grant of small allowances to care for destitute children of English parentage. If the allowances were not forthcoming, he pointed out, the children would either have been left to starve or be allowed to be adopted by the Portuguese padres and brought up Catholic.

Aungier died at Surat on 30 June 1677. Five years later, in 1684, Bombay became the site of a rebellion which, in the annals of British India, was so minor that it often becomes a footnote, if it is even mentioned, in the histories. Called the Keigwin Rebellion after its leader, Captain Richard Keigwin, it was essentially a military pro- test against what was perceived as civilian arbitrariness. In another sense, however, it was not entirely unrelated to the Company's ambivalent policy not only about wives, but also about the nature of its role in India. While it wanted settled families, the Company was chronically unwilling to part with the collegial ideal of a group of merchants quietly plying their trade, harmoniously eating together, sleeping together, minding the Company's business together, and needing little or no financial remuneration in order to raise families. Aungier himself who had left his wife in England had complained to the Directors in 1674 that he had drawn no salary for four years and was forced to pay for the expense of entertaining French and Portuguese dignitaries out of his own pocket.[25] Similarly, with Marathas and Moghuls both hovering around Bombay and with an appalling mortality among their troops, the Company was reluctant to allocate funds for the defence of the settlement.

The tiny revolt in 1674 had been over in a few weeks but Aungier had been fair and reasonable. Ten years later, the governor of Surat with responsibility for Bombay was Sir John Child who had been in India for about twenty years. Child was no Aungier. He was unscrupulous—not necessarily an unhappy malady—but worse, he was associated, wrongly, with Sir Josiah Child, the Company's unpopular chairman, whom he probably never met. Besides their name, the two men also shared an unrealistic view of the Company's strength in India. In 1683, only three years after Shivaji's death and with the Marathas now a very formidable power, John Child, obeying a directive from London to reduce expenses, cut military pay and reduced the Bombay garrison then under the command of Captain Keigwin. A former governor of St Helena, Keigwin had come to India in 1676 as a freelance planter, then had entered the Company's service, was appointed to the garrison, and in 1681, had taken a seat on the governing Council. When the cuts were announced, the garrison rebelled. Keigwin seized a ship in the harbour holding £50,000 in gold and for almost a year governed Bombay in which post he did rather well. Like Aungier, he was at some pains to pursue friendly relations with his Indian neighbours and keep Bombay a free port open to all traders, including interlopers. In 1684, news of the rebellion reached Charles II who, having endured the Exclusion Crisis and Monmouth Rebellion only a few years previously, understandably had no love for rebels of any kind, even those who, like Keigwin, professed loyalty to the Crown. The king ordered that Bombay be restored to the Company forthwith and Keigwin complied, surrendering the fort and the ship he had seized with the £50,000 in gold untouched. The participants were ultimately all pardoned but the reason given for the pardoning of one of them was that he was illiterate and under the influence of his wife, 'a wicked woman'.[26]

Whether the 'wicked woman' was English, Portuguese, or neither is perhaps irrelevant. The cutting of her husband's pay which had been low to begin with, and the trimming of the garrison in the face of the Maratha threat, would have caused stress to any wife. If there were children, the stress would have been insupportable.

In 1687, the seat of the presidency was transferred to Bombay, and Surat which had been the headquarters of the English from 1608 to 1687, languishing from its exposure to Maratha attacks, but also from the silting up of the Tapti River, and the intrigues of Moghul officials, gradually declined in importance. Bombay, however, fared ill, too. Poised between the Moghuls, Marathas, and Malabari pirates, Bombay also suffered from a line of governors who were often as incompetent as they were unlucky. Child would be drawn into a war with the Moghuls in 1688–91 when he challenged Aurangzeb's right to levy the *jizya*, or tax, on all infidels. The affair ended shamefully when two English envoys, with hands bound behind their backs, were forced to prostrate themselves before the emperor and allowed to resume trade on payment of 150,000 rupees and to 'behave them-selves for the future...'[27] Bartholomew Harris who succeeded Child as president of Surat and governor of Bombay upon the latter's death in 1690 was in a Moghul prison in retaliation for Child's seizure of Moghul ships. He and his companions were released in April but imprisoned again in August 1691.

There is a kind of irony in that the issue of interfaith marriage which so occupied the English authorities in Madras laid a far lighter claim on the attention of those in Bombay. Portugal's interest in India was not only roughly a century older than England's but it had also been heaviest along the Malabar Coast. Certainly the danger of English factors marrying castees or mustees and allowing their off-spring to be raised Catholic would seem to have been as prominent a concern there as in Madras. Unlike the pages of the Madras records which are quite liberally sprinkled with rather anguished questions of how to balance the need to use the commercial and military skills of the Portuguese against the onus of their Catholicism, the Bombay records are relatively quiet.

Bombay, however, faced problems that Madras also faced but on a far greater scale. It was unhealthy. When John Ovington visited the 'good bay' in 1689, he observed that of the children born, 'not one in twenty of them live to any Maturity, or even beyond their Infant days'.[28] By the end of the seventeenth century, Aungier's hope that Bombay could be a settled, safe home for English families had been sorely frustrated and Bombay had become something of a backwater, a status from which it would not recover until the nineteenth century.

After the few experiments of the 1670s, although the Company continued to allow women to go to India, usually in the company of a male relative, there is no evidence that it subsidized further 'fishing fleets' either to Bombay or to any other factory in its possession. What had become very clear was that English women in India, while they may no longer have been viewed as outright 'incumberances', had also displayed as little regard for the Company's Ten Commandments as the factors themselves. In 1728, the Directors included the behaviour of women in complaining,

> We are greatly concerned to hear that the mischievous Vice of Gaming continues and even encreases [*sic*]amongst our Covenant Servants, Free Merchants and others residing at Our Settlements in India for great Sums of Money, and that the Women are also infected therewith, by which Means many Persons have been ruin'd as well on board Ship as on shore....We do hereby peremptorily [*sic*] forbid all Manner of Gaming whatsoever in any of Our Settlements or elsewhere in India to the amount of Ten Pounds or upwards.[29]

The women who had landed at Bombay would have given Sir Thomas Roe ample confirmation of his judgement that women were indeed 'incumberances', for the presence of wives, rather than having a calming effect, had added yet another ingredient to what had always been a volatile social milieu. And the reason was not hard to find. Like the Company's servants, many women were learning how to use the Company's investment in India to their own benefit. That was primarily through marriage, or at least some kind of union but, one might fairly assume, not necessarily to Englishmen.

notes

1 Marguerite Wilbur, *The East India Company and the British Empire in the Far East* (New York: Richard R. Smith, 1945), 161.

2 Ibid., 163.

3 John Fryer, *A New Account of East India and Persia Being Nine Years' Travels, 1672–1681*, ed., William Crooke, 3 vols (London: Printed for the Hakluyt Society, 1909), I, 172, 174.

4 Ibid., 169

5 Ibid., 214.

6 For the very loose and somewhat inaccurate translation of the term, the author apologizes to any reader who has ever experienced an Eastern hummum.

7 Ibid., 165. John Ovington, who visited the place about fifteen years later, gives a similar description. See John Ovington, *A Voyage to Surat in the Year 1689*, ed., H.G. Rawlinson (London: Humphrey Milford, Oxford University Press, 1929), 227.

8 Reverend Frank Penny, *The Church in Madras Being the History of the Ecclesiastical and Missionary Action of the East India Company in the Presidency of Madras in the Seventeenth and Eighteenth Centuries.* 2 vols (London: Smith, Elder, & Co., 1904), I, 93.

9 John Bruce, *Annals of the Honourable East India Company, from Their Establishment by the Charter of Queen Elizabeth, 1600 to the Union of the London and English East India Companies, 1707–8.* 3 vols (London: Black, Parry, and Kingsbury, 1810 [Republished at Farnborough: Gregg Press Limited, 1968]), II, 226.

10 Sir Charles Fawcett, ed., *The English Factories in India: The Western Presidency, 1670–1677* (new series) (Oxford: Clarendon Press, 1936), I, 19.

11 J. Talboys Wheeler, ed., *Annals of the Madras Presidency.* 3 vols (Delhi: B.R. Publishing Corporation, 1985), I, 73.

12 Alexander Hamilton, *A New Account of the East Indies*, ed. Sir William Foster (London: The Argonaut Press, 1930), I, 106.

13 Fawcett, *English Factories: Western Presidency*, I, 16.

14 John Keay, *The Honourable Company: A History of the English East India Company* (New York: Macmillan, 1991), 137.

15 Cited in Philip Anderson, *The English in Western India, Being the Early History of the Factory at Surat, of Bombay, and the Subordinate Factories on the Western Coast* (London: Smith, Elder, & Co., 1856, 2nd ed.), 215.

16 Surat to Court, 17 January 1676, cited in Stephen Edwardes, ed., *The Gazetteer of Bombay City and Island.* 3 vols (Bombay: The Times Press, 1909), II, 62.

17 Fawcett, *English Factories: Western Presidency*, I, 177.

18 The Surat Council to Bombay, 18 December 1675 in Edwardes, *Bombay Gazetteer*, II, 62 (footnote).

19 Although it is a century later, that impression is reinforced by William Hickey who refers to a 'little baggage' named Nancy Harris who was dismissed by the Duchess of Manchester for 'debauching' her thirteen-year-old son. See William Hickey, *Memoirs*, ed., Alfred Spencer, 8th ed., 4 vols (New York: Alfred A. Knopf, 1921), I, 12.

20 Fryer, *New Account*, I, 179.

21 Fawcett, *English Factories: Western Presidency*, I, 141.

22 Fawcett, *English Factories: Western Presidency*, I, 143.

23 Ibid., 16.

24 Ovington, *Voyage*, 87.

25 See footnote in Edwardes, *Bombay Gazetteer*, II, 64.

26 Sir Charles Fawcett, ed., *English Factories in India: Bombay, Surat, and the Western Coast, 1678–1684* (new series) (Oxford: Clarendon Press, 1954), III, 193.

27 Ibid.

28 Ovington, *Voyage*, 88.

29 Cited in Warner letter in Wheeler, *Annals*, I, 249.

6

feathering their nests

BY THE MIDDLE OF THE SEVENTEENTH CENTURY, while the East India Company's trade gave ample opportunities for a man to, as William Hawkins had put it, 'feather my owne neste while doing you ser-vice',[1] it had become clear that, both at home and in India itself, women could also feather their nests. The records are filled with women who borrowed and lent monies to invest in goods being sent to India, and their petitions to the Court of Directors indicate that they expected to receive a return on those investments. Granted that these women were connected with male stock holders, their persis-tence in claiming dividends nonetheless strongly suggests that many of them kept a careful and knowledgeable eye on the market. Unlike other political institutions, joint-stock companies had constitutions that admitted women as voters on the same terms as men. They could acquire shares in the Company, attend stockholder meetings, and vote on questions put to shareholders. As early as 1691, fifty-six women were shareholders in the East India Company, twice as many as in 1675.[2]

Normally, however, their claims happened within the context of marriage, and gave the Company further reason to consider them 'incumberances'. The records frequently show widows, children, and other family members petitioning the Company for some kind of remuneration.[3] Because a woman was normally dependent on the income of a husband, father, brother, or other male relative, and in the absence of life insurance policies or government or company pensions, when the monies sent home to support a family were ended by the death of a man in their employ, the Company was the only recourse a woman had for financial support and, as with the tolerance of private trade, partially explains the low salaries it paid servants. Their requests usually sound reasonable and the Company's response is normally forthcoming, albeit not overwhelmingly generous. Like the women themselves, however, the Company obviously would have preferred women to remain married to living husbands who could support them rather than becoming widows, dependent on the Company's dole.

Moreover, there could be difficulties for the Company if a woman's creativity matched her persistence. When her brother died in 1637, Mary Haines offered the Court of Directors to take only half of his estate which she said was worth about £5,600. It was also encumbered with debt, both owed and owing. The Court, remembering her brother's gaming, private trade, and unsavoury partnership with a Mr Burt from whom he seems to have acquired the bulk of that estate, was unenthusiastic about helping her, at least not to the extent she was asking. Moreover, the investment he had taken out to sell in India was small and he could not, they pointed out, have 'honestly' gained so much in the short time he had been there. They asked her to reconsider her demand. That she did but by the time she returned two weeks later, they also had reconsidered and were willing to grant her £700 or £800. Miss Haines, however, was not to be so easily dismissed. She replied that she would accept £1,200 if the Court would also give her the right to recover the debts owed her brother. Again, the Court asked her to reconsider. When they met a month later, a compromise was reached whereby she was granted a little over £1,000.[4] The lady's importunate bargaining would not have been amiss in an Indian bazaar where, had the Company been able or willing to hire her, she might have been a valuable asset.

Despite the obstacles the Company itself was responsible for erecting, namely the low salaries and the deliberately monastic character of the factories themselves, there was a persistent belief that the mere presence of English women would induce the factors in India to marry them. The Directors were not alone in that expectation. John Ovington who visited India in the late 1680s thought that

> a Modish Garb and Mien is all that is expected from any Women that pass thither, who are many times match'd to the chief Merchants upon the place, and advance thereby their Conditions to a very pitch. And considering what trouble attends the Passage, especially of Women, considering the Hazard, as well as length of the Voyage, with some other Casualties that sometimes happen on Board, a modest Woman may very well expect, without any great Stock of Honour or Wealth, a Husband of Repute and Riches there, after she has run all this Danger and Trouble for him. And indeed the fond Indulgence of the Husbands, as well as their Wealth, is another valuable Recompense to Women for the Toil and Trouble of the Voyage.[5]

Obstacles notwithstanding, Ovington's view of marital possibilities in India continued to carry some weight, and not without good reason. Marriage was the most promising investment that a woman could make and one that the Company really wanted her to make. The one marketable asset that an English woman—and no other woman, concubine, *castee*, or *mustee*—enjoyed was that under English law, only an English Protestant wife could provide a man's progeny with legitimacy and, thus, title to that man's property. There was, therefore, a congruence of interests in that no consciences needed to be unsettled nor burdens placed upon the Company's coffers if the wives and children of its servants could be provided for by the gains they made in private trade. At the same time, especially if she made an advantageous marriage, India represented a chance for a woman that might not have been available at home to move up the economic ladder. And as the Mary Haines case indicates, both the Company and the women themselves were willing to negotiate the claims that could be made upon a man's property.

Marriage was such a serious economic enterprise that a woman could be capable of profound mendacity to see either herself or her daughter profitably married. Anne Brown was such a woman. Wily enough to use the law to her daughter's advantage, she almost succeeded in suing a man for breach of contract. Unfortunately, the target of her ambitions was far less wealthy than she had hoped and almost, but not quite, as unprincipled.

Anne was the widow of Dr Samuel Brown, by whom she had had a daughter, Elizabeth. In 1700, Mrs Brown married John Foquet who had entered the Company's service in 1687.[6] In 1707, apparently at her mother's instigation, Elizabeth Brown brought a suit for breach of a marriage contract against Captain Henry Cornwall who had left the navy in 1700 after twelve years' service and entered the Company's service where, through the influence of friends, he hoped to be speedily promoted. From 1704 to 1706, he is listed among the seafaring inhabitants of Madras where he encountered the Brown women. Expecting to get preferment in England through Anne Foquet, he entered into a formal written contract with Elizabeth Brown early in 1707. Rings were exchanged in the presence of witnesses, and Cornwall even gave Miss Brown a thousand-pound bond as well as his estate in India, and left a will in her hands naming her as the executrix as bond for the performance of the marriage. Before leaving for England, Cornwall also apparently repeatedly told Anne Foquet that if he could not better himself, he would 'by no means think of complying with that obligation'.[7] Things got murky, however, even before he left. Apparently, Mrs Foquet had never seriously intended for the marriage to take place. According to Cornwall's testimony, which she did not contradict, she had told the mayor, Robert Raworth, that she had refused Cornwall marriage to her daughter before he left for home because she was sure he would marry in England which would then give her the opportunity of prosecuting the obligation.

In England, as Mrs Fouquet may have anticipated, her friends proved of no use, and Cornwall's own relatives, being 'strangers to trade' also refused help. Possibly in the interests of furthering his fortunes, he married another woman, ran up a considerable debt, and was lucky to finally get command of a small ship to return to India to try to restore his finances. He had barely landed when on 12 February 1711, Elizabeth (prodded no doubt by her mother) petitioned William Fraser, governor of Fort St George, and his Council for a thousand pounds from Cornwall, 'a poor reparation for all the injustice he hath done us'.[8] Although a Padre Lewis had asked both mother and daughter 'to accommodate matters amicably with Captain Cornwall...and not drive things to extremity', the Brown women had no intention of complying. Instead, they contended that

Cornwall had sent a letter to Miss Brown 'made up of all the ill nature and ill language he is master of; and … to think at last to run us down, and to carry his point by calumny and slander…'

The dispute ended when the governor and Council decided that since Cornwall had indeed married a wife in England, he was liable to a penalty amounting to £1,000, but 'considering the present circumstances of Captain Cornwall which are but moderate, having met with great losses, and he generously offering a moiety of what he has in the world, and having cleared the reputation of said Mrs. Brown both parties were called in, reconciled and made friends…'[9]

In early 1718, Elizabeth Brown married the Reverend Charles Long who was not in good health. Within a year, he was ordered to return to Europe because he did not perform his ministerial duties and was thought to be mixed up with some commercial transaction in Europe which, by Company regulation, was strictly forbidden.[10] Upon his return to England, he took several academic degrees and was installed at a vicarage in Chieveley in Berkshire, hopefully to the satisfaction of his mother-in-law.

If it could be had, marriage could offer not only emotional comfort and financial security to a woman, but occasionally even a partnership of sorts with her husband. One of the more extraordinary examples of that is the case of Catherine Gyfford whose connubial career began at the tender age of thirteen or fourteen in 1709 when her father literally sold her to John Harvey, chief of the Karwar factory, who was 'a deformed man and in years'.[11] Despite his physical limitations, before he died a little over a year later, he had taught Catherine enough so that she was apparently able to help him straighten out his accounts which had become hopelessly entangled with those of the Company. Before she was twenty, she had been widowed two more times, leaving her not only with a claim to Harvey's estate which the Bombay Council, in a fit of sympathy, awarded her, but also with a claim to reimbursement for gifts that her third husband, William Gyfford, had been killed in his attempt to deliver to the rani of Ashure. Catherine then engaged the Company in a series of litigations, and her case was still in the courts when she died at Madras in 1745.[12] Like Mary Haines and perhaps many other women, she had the wit and the business acumen to challenge what, by then, had become the largest corporation in England. And not lose her case.

Catherine Gyfford was not alone in becoming her husband's business partner. Alexander Hamilton, who travelled in India in the early eighteenth century, encountered Anthony Weltden, then governor of Fort William. Weltden, who had earlier made a fortune—and an unsavoury reputation—in private trade, arrived in Bengal in July 1710 with his wife, Mary, and his daughter, also named Mary, a son, two maidservants, a manservant, and an enormous pile of luggage that included 'tons of books, another of linen, a barrel of pewter, a bundle of bedding, six cases or small tubs of provisions, four hampers of cider, ten chests of beer and ale, about the same quantity of wine, an escritoire, a harpsichord in a case, and 4,000 pounds of bullion'.[13] According to Hamilton, Weltden was 'shy in taking bribes, referring those honest folks who trafficked that way to the discretion of his wife and daughter and to pay the money into their hands'.[14] The Directors recalled Weltden, albeit for other reasons, and he left Bengal before the charge of bribery on the part of the Marys could be proven, but not before they had given fair testimony to the fact that many women did not mean to leave the feathering of nests to men, nor were they any more averse than men to using any means available to do so.

As Catherine Gyfford's story suggests, a woman could make the most of widowhood. There are a large number of multiple marriages made by women in India but many women lived out the rest of their lives in India as widows. A good part of the explanation is that the journey home remained fraught with dangers, difficulties, and discomforts, and India, especially in the presidencies, provided a very good life. Under Elihu Yale, Madras' second governor (1687–92), authority was granted to levy an assessment to pave a street in Madras' White Town in proportion to the area of pavement in front of each house. The levy fell heaviest upon Yale himself but three widows, all of whom owned the most valuable properties on Middle Street which then was one of the 'best' streets', were levied almost as heavily.[15] They were Ursula O'Neale, Margery Fleetwood, and Elizabeth Monke who could also lay claim to two houses, the one in Middle Street and another in Chowltry Street.

Ursula O'Neale had been granted passage to Bengal on the death of her husband, Captain Philip O'Neale, but returned to Madras where she appears on the list of residents for many years as a widow. Her house was worth a yearly rent of one pagoda, Margery Heathfield's was valued at two pagodas, and Yale's own house in that street was worth three pagodas.

Margery Heathfield had been widowed twice. When her first husband, Robert Fleetwood, who had been chief at Madapollam, a small factory on the Coromandel Coast, died, he left Margery with two houses but considerable debt as well. So when she married the surgeon John Heathfield in May 1678, she did so in her shift; that is, she divested herself of everything connected with her first marriage so that her second husband would not be liable for any of Fleetwood's debts. Four days later, Fleetwood's two houses were sold and the proceeds were brought into the Company to credit Fleetwood's account. Dr Heathfield, however, was not poor. In addition to a good quantity of the furniture, he was wealthy enough to bring to the marriage 'two slave wenches and a slave boy'.[16] Shortly after the marriage, he petitioned to enter the civil service, but then reverted to his original profession[17] in which he apparently flourished. He died in 1688 but the now twice-widowed Margery, besides owning the 'substantial' residence in Middle Street, also possessed a garden house in the suburb of Peddanaikpetta which she sold in 1707 to several weavers who intended to build their houses and 'conveniencys' thereon in order to carry on their trade. Margery herself survived until 1723.[18]

While marriage was perhaps the safest path to economic security for a woman, it was not the only one. The kinds of businesses they entered into were confined to the compound itself and separate from the Company's trade. Normally, this involved running a deceased husband's affairs—if he had left her any to run. By the last two decades of the seventeenth century, however, when some regularity had emerged in the three major factories, it was possible for a woman to manage a business on her own. The most common was running a tavern or a punch house. A tavern was not merely a pub or a bar. It was also an inn. The larger ones were also places of formal entertainments. A close modern parallel might be an upscale hotel. A punch house resembled a tavern in that food and alcoholic beverages were provided, but not lodging. Both businesses were fairly lucrative, since the amount of alcohol consumed by the Company's servants was gargantuan. Sobriety had not become a fashionable virtue in England either but in India it was so markedly rare that Thomas

Pitt who governed Madras from 1698 until 1709 noted in one of his reports that 'there is a general complaint that we drink a damnable deal of wine this year.'[19] Because of complaints that arrack punch was at least partly responsible for the high mortality rate and in an effort to control drinking, at least by 1678, taverns, entertainment houses, and hotels had to be licensed. The licence included fixing prices for the liquor, rules for proper conduct, and that two cots for strangers be kept in their houses with clean linen, good accommodations, and 'wholesome Diet and Liquor'.[20] Happily, as in England and in North America, women seemed to have encountered either little or no stigma in entering the tavern business. At least one woman, Mrs Deningo Ash, operated one so successfully that when she was over a month late renewing her licence in 1704, the authorities simply renewed it but with no fine.[21]

On the other hand, despite the 'damnable' amount of liquor that was consumed, operating a tavern did not guarantee prosperity. When the widow Elizabeth Monke applied for and received a licence for an arrack house in October 1695, she complained of no profit. Fortunately, she was not destitute. Her husband, Richard, had left her with the house in Middle Street.[22] Normally, what difficulties a woman did encounter had less to do with her sex than with her own conduct. In March 1688, the wife of a Lieutenant Francis who had been killed in Bengal arrived in Madras quite poor. However, her petition to keep a punch house was denied because, having 'lived very scandalously' before in Madras and being 'a notorious bad woman', she was not permitted to keep a public house, 'lest it be the occasion of many debaucheries and disorders; she having lived very scandalously formerly here'. She was ordered to the West Coast, and allowed 'something out of the proceeds of the prizes, to provide her necessaries, in consideration of the loss of her husband in the late unhappy Bengal expedition'. Afterwards, she was sent home to prevent 'further scandals in our city'.[23]

Katherine Nicks was either the most enterprising of all the English business women in seventeenth-century India or one who could easily be manipulated by the men who surrounded her. Or perhaps both. Although she was married, it was not through marriage nor by owning a tavern that she made her way but through what might cannily be called 'private trade'. Katherine Barker had been one of only five unmarried women in White Town when she married John Nicks in 1680.[24] Nicks had come out to Fort St George in 1668 as an apprentice, made factor in 1678, became secretary and fourth in Council in 1685. In 1688, the Council appointed him to be chief of Conimere, a new factory on the Coromandel Coast between Madras and Pondicherry. It was here that his wife's very active business career began. In September 1689, the Court wrote approving the fortification of Conimere, confirming Nicks' chieftainship but on the condition that 'he do carefully prevent the Companys [sic] prejudice by his Wife's crafty trading, which we understand the method of, and cannot bear if we find. She makes her gains of our loss...'[25] What exactly her 'crafty trading' was is unclear but the following February, 'that expensive and unjust person Mr Nicks' was expelled from the Company's service for 'the wrong sorting of calicoes' and placed under house arrest.[26]

John Nicks' disgrace in no way deflated Katherine's career. 'To the scandal of Christianity among heathens'[27] as Wheeler puts it, she came to live with Elihu Yale at his garden house where Mrs Hieronima de Pavia, the widow of a Jewish diamond dealer, was also living with their children.

Yale's own private life had been colourful.[28] In 1672, he had come out to India as a writer. His superior, Joseph Hynmers, had helped Yale advance rapidly and in November 1680, six months after Hynmers died, Yale had married his wealthy widow, Catherine. Theirs was the first wedding in the newly constructed St Mary's Church which had been dedicated only a week earlier. One of the new Mrs Yale's bridesmaids had been Katherine Nicks.

Besides enough wealth to enable Yale to enter the diamond business, Joseph Hynmers had also left three children but one child was shipped home in 1680 shortly after the death of his father. By Catherine, Yale had a son, David, who died at Madras at the age of four in 1687, about the time Yale was appointed governor of Madras. Catherine Yale returned to England. Yale then found comfort with Mrs De Pavia and her three children. By her, he had another son, Charles.[29]

It was into this lively household that Mrs Nicks moved. On 20 December 1692, Judge Advocate John Dolben heard the case against Mrs Nicks. Compounding the 'several notorious frauds by her committed in Conimere', she was also accused of causing the Company's warehouses to be broken open, and had taken 'great quantities of cloth of the first sort', which she then applied to Yale's private use. Dolben wrote her a letter requiring her, 'being a woman notoriously known to be a separate Merchant from her husband', to answer personally for the damages the Company had sustained. She refused and Dolben issued a warrant for her arrest. When Mrs Nicks still refused to obey, Dolben ordered the Captain of the Guard to send a file of musketeers with a corporal to place her under house arrest, 'being under suspicion that she designs to fly from justice'. Unfortunately for Mrs Nicks, only a few days after she was arrested, Yale was replaced as governor by Nathaniel Higginson. For their 'malpractice' at Conimere, Higginson fined John Nicks 8000 pagodas, and Katherine 600.[30]

Yale continued at Madras till 1696, but Higginson disappeared from both Yale's and Mrs Nicks' life shortly after he came into them. In July 1693, leaving his wife, Elizabeth, in Madras, he embarked for Bengal and died there in November.

John Nicks and Yale both returned to England in 1699 but Katherine Nicks' business career continued, and it is this second part of her career that is most remarkable. She clearly engaged in private trade for herself and was still doing business either with or for Yale as late as 1701 when, in a letter to her sister—the first letter, incidentally, from an English woman in India[31]—she mentioned having sent ten ps.[?] of 'chints' to England which she hoped her sister had sold for her. How she appropriated the chintz is unclear, but it raises three most intriguing possibilities. First, as her earlier career suggests, she could have stolen them from the Company's own warehouses. Since she had been caught in the act a decade earlier, however, she may have learned either to avoid doing it again, or done it in such a way as not to get caught. Secondly, she may have legitimately purchased the cloth from an English factor. Thirdly, she may have purchased them directly from an Indian source. If that is the case, then she is one of a tiny handful of English women in the entire history of the British involvement in India to have engaged in direct commercial transactions with Indian merchants, either through a *dubash* or *banian*, or possibly even directly without an Indian intermediary. By then, she may have acquired enough knowledge of local dialects and the complexities of dealing with the bazaar to have negotiated the exchanges herself.

However she acquired the chintzes, she clearly understood the local market. She requested that her sister deliver the 'produce' of them to Mr Yale who then would 'pay you what you shall disbust for my Children' and complained that losses have been so great that she despaired of ever seeing her sister.[32] A year before that, on 19 February 1700, she had written a letter to John Pitt, Thomas Pitt's nephew, at Masulipatnam in which she appears to have been acting as Pitt's agent. She had received a 'parsell' of lace from Pitt the previous month but because the markets were so low, she doubted that he would ever recover the cost, let alone make a profit on the lace. She had carefully watched the local market where, at a public auction, a Mr Proby had not been able to sell two or three hundred pounds worth of lace at even half their cost. She offered to 'use my utmost Indeavours [sic] to dispose of it if possible' or deliver it to 'your Lady when she comes'. She had also taken on the task of refurbishing a palanquin which he had sent her without bed (cushions?) or tassels. She had silver and tassels added for which she was enclosing an account and now 'I think the Pallakeen is good and cheap.'[33]

Her differences with John Dolben, however, had also been resolved for, through him, she also sent her sister gifts, substantial enough to indicate that she had prospered quite well. Included in the package were a Japan dressing box containing a gown, twelve aprons, two pieces of chintz, six fans, six pairs of gloves, forty China 'pectars' (pictures?) and a dressing box.[34] By then, Mr Dolben had himself been dismissed from the Company's service for taking bribes. John Nicks returned to Madras and presumably Katherine again took up residence with him. She died in 1709; John, two years later.[35]

A secondary character in the Katherine Nicks' story, Elizabeth, the wife of Governor Higginson, also continued to flourish. Following her husband's death in Bengal, she accompanied her son Richard to Madras in 1722, and purchased Thomas Cooke's house. In 1731, when the 21-year lease granted Cooke was about to expire, Mrs Higginson asked for power to renew it. It was referred to the Directors who granted it 'in consideration of the good Services we have received from that Family'.[36]

Elihu Yale's fortune, acquired in part with the assistance of two widows and the crafty Mrs Nicks, was substantial enough to allow him to bestow goods worth over £500 upon the new Collegiate School of Connecticut to erect a new building. For his generosity, the building was named for its benefactor and soon the entire college became Yale College. Katherine Nicks' name was bestowed upon nothing other than her gravestone.

By the end of the seventeenth century, it had become clear that while the activities of some women might have bordered on the illegal as in the case of Katherine Nicks and the Weltden ladies, the Company could take some comfort in knowing that, at least financially, the women they were allowing to go to India had as little interest in becoming encumbrances as the Company itself had in bearing the burden of supporting them. Indeed, the casual morality and shrewd eye for a profit of many of these women, both at home and especially in India, allow one to almost feel a bit of pity for the Company's unwillingness to employ such people. Quite without the religious or moral motives that originally animated discussions about them, the resourcefulness of women in managing their own and often their deceased husbands' properties was a powerful argument in favour of allowing women to go to India either as wives or to find husbands, and by the end of the century, there was no longer even a discussion about the matter.

More importantly, as tiny as their numbers were, the presence of women had a singularly important effect in that it changed the very nature of the factories themselves. The monastic, collegial nature of the factory was fundamentally inconsistent with family life. Quite simply, Leadenhall Street could not have both, but before the Directors would abandon the ideal of the factory, they had to be convinced that families were more economical than trying to maintain it. By the end of the century, the presence of women and settled English families had made the factory an anachronism.

notes

1 Clements R. Markham, C.B., F.R.S., ed., 'The Journals of Captain William Hawkins', in *The Hawkins' Voyages During the Reigns of Henry VIII, Queen Elizabeth and James I* (London: Printed for the Hakluyt Society, 1878), 402.

2 Susan Stave, 'Investments, Votes, and "Bribes": Women as Shareholders in the Chartered National Companies', in Hilda Smith, ed. *Women Writers*

and the Early Modern British Political Tradition (Cambridge: Cambridge University Press, 1998), 259–60.

3 The desperation of many of these women was noticed by Samuel Pepys in his diary entry for 10 July 1666 when he was Clerk of the Acts to the Navy. The Navy yard, he says, was full of more than three hundred women who had come to get money for their husbands and friends who were prisoners in Holland. '…and they lay clamouring and swearing, and cursing us…their cries were so sad for money, and laying down the condition of their families and their husbands, and what they have done and suffered for the King, and how ill they are used by us…' See *Diary of Samuel Pepys*, ed., Robert Latham and William Matthews, 11 vols (Berkeley and Los Angeles: University of California Press, 1983), VII, 199–200.

4 Court of Committees, *Court Book*, Vol., xvi, 319 (10 May 1637), 328 (24 May 1637) and 339 (21 June 1637) in Ethel Sainsbury, *A Calendar of the Court Minutes etc. of the East India Company, 1635–1639* (Oxford: Clarendon Press, 1907), 264, 268, 281.

5 John Ovington, *A Voyage to Surat in the Year 1689*, ed. H.G. Rawlinson (London: Humphrey Milford, Oxford University Press, 1929), 88.

6 See footnote in Henry Davison Love, *Vestiges of Old Madras, 1640–1800*. 3 vols, Indian Records Series (London: John Murray, 1913), I, 569.

7 The entire story is told in J. Talboys Wheeler, ed., *Annals of the Madras Presidency*, 3 vols (Delhi: B.R. Publishing Corporation, 1985), II, 105–10.

8 Her petition against him is in the Fort William Council Minutes on 12 February 1711. See ibid.

9 Ibid.

10 Reverend Frank Penny, *The Church in Madras: Being the History of the Ecclesiastical and Missionary Action of the East India Company in the Presidency of Madras in the Seventeenth and Eighteenth Centuries*. 2 vols (London: Smith, Elder, & Co., 1904), I, 149, 151.

11 Cited in Colonel John Biddulph, *The Pirates of Malabar and an Englishwoman in India Two Hundred Years Ago* (London: Smith, Elder & Co., 1907), 258.

12 Love, *Vestiges*, II, 317.

13 Charles R. Wilson, *The Early Annals of the English in Bengal*, Vol. II, Part 1 (London: W. Thacker & Co., 1900), 318–19. See also the passenger list at 342.

14 Cited in ibid., vi, from Alexander Hamilton's *East Indies* (edition of 1727), II, 10.

15 See Love, *Vestiges*, I, 538, 560.

16 Cited in Penny, *The Church in Madras*, I, 68 from Factory Records, Masulipatnam, Vol. 2 in Oriental and India Office Collections (OIOC).

17 Footnote in Love, *Vestiges*, I, 483.

18 Footnote in ibid., II, 61, 174.

19 Colonel Henry Yule, *The Diary of William Hedges, Esq. during His Agency in Bengal; as well as on His Voyage Out and Return Overland (1681–1687)*. 3 vols (London: Printed for the Hakluyt Society, 1887–89), III, v.

20 From P.C. Vol. II, 28 August 1678 and in Love, *Vestiges*, I, 449.

21 William Bolts, *Considerations on Indian Affairs Particularly Respecting the Present State of Bengal and Its Dependencies* (London: Printed for J. Almon, 1772), 256.

22 Love, *Vestiges*, II, 62 (footnote).

23 Wheeler, *Annals*, I, 137.

24 Ibid.

25 Hedges, *Diary*, II, cclviii.

26 Ibid., cclix. See also Wheeler, *Annals of the Madras Presidency*, 1692–98, Vol. I, 260–1.

27 Wheeler, *Annals*, I, 218. Wheeler's editorial comment betrays a nineteenth-, not a seventeenth-century sensibility. Rarely are Indians referred to as 'heathens' in the seventeenth and throughout most of the eighteenth century. When they are not identified by race, for example, Pathan, Rajput, Jat, and so on, they are often called simply 'Moors', 'Gentoos', or 'Hindoos'. It is also unlikely that, in that rather Pepysianesque world, anyone would have been scandalized.

28 Elihu's father, David, had come to New Haven, Connecticut, in 1638 and Elihu had been born near Boston, Massachusetts, in 1649. Two years later, David Yale returned to England and the rest of the family followed in 1652.

29 Love, *Vestiges*, I, 454. Mrs Pavia is buried at the Cape of Good Hope beside her child Charles Yale, 'styled one of the former Governors of Madras'. From J.J. Cotton, 'List of Inscriptions', cited by Love, *Vestiges*, I, 486 (footnote).

30 Love, *Vestiges*, I, 553 and Wheeler, *Annals of the Madras Presidency*, I, 195–6. Reference is also made to her story in *Hedges Diary*, cclix.

31 It has long been mistakenly thought that the first letter from an Englishwoman in India was written by Jane Smart describing the visit to a zenana in 1741. See Chapter 7.

32 Wheeler, *Annals*, I, 216–7.

33 Yule, *Hedges Diary*, cclix.

34 Ibid., cclxi.

35 Love, *Vestiges*, II, 67.

36 Cited in Love, *Vestiges*, I, 236.

7

when east meets west

FOR ANYONE WHO IS NOT IRREPARABLY JADED, India simply astonishes.
Even before she set foot on Indian soil, the first thing an English
woman might have noticed would have been the smell that many later
generations of her countrymen would recall with nostalgia—at once
pungent, intoxicating, sensuous, a mixture of spices—ginger, tur-
meric, cloves—of jasmine, coconut, and mango, mingled with dust,
animal dung, and earth.[1] She would have noticed the heat, of course,
and then, especially if she arrived between June and September, she
would have noticed that the gentle rains of an English summer were
no preparation at all for the torrents of a monsoon that come suddenly and end just as suddenly.

The weather and the smells, indeed—but it is India's very life that
might have amazed her. There would have been birds with brighter
plumage than she ever could have seen in England—peacocks and
parrots, mynas, spotted cuckoos, purple-hooded pigeons, flamingoes,
red jungle fowl, shrikes, bustards, cranes, ospreys, and hornbills.
And in the immense foliage—jackfruit, plantain, palmyra, balsam,
and tamarind, great spreading banyan trees—there were chattering
monkeys, bawling elephants, shrieking hyenas, jackals, lemurs, wild

asses, mongooses, tigers, and the snakes that she would learn could kill her.

And what might have been her reaction when she approached the city—any city? She would have been accustomed to livestock wandering the streets in her home, so cows lumbering about the streets unmolested might not have surprised her, but would she have been prepared to discover that they were sacred? What would she have thought of the palanquins—some of which were quite ornate—being carried about the crowded streets by their bearers? Or the great bullock buffaloes pulling wagons heavily laden with goods that she may have only heard of but not seen? Would she have been prepared for the throngs of vendors crying out their strange wares—curries, warm chapattis and coffees from Arabia? What would she have thought of India's atonal music? Would it have struck her ears harshly?

What would she have thought of the people she saw, especially the women? Would she not have been slightly envious of them with their hair tied back in long braids, falling simply down their backs, while her own crimped hair was scrunched under a cap? Wrapped in her yards of petticoats and hoops, corsets, and bum rolls, would she not have felt just a touch of envy for their loose, colourful, and comfortable saris woven of fabrics softer and finer than her own rough fustian? Two centuries later, Fanny Parkes would articulate what must have been the sentiments of many of her earlier predecessors:

> In Europe, how rarely—how very rarely does a woman walk gracefully! Bound up in stays, the body is as stiff as a lobster in its shell; ... English dresses are very unbecoming, both to European and Asiatics. A Musulmani lady is a horror in an English dress; but an English woman is greatly improved by wearing a native one; the attire itself is so elegant, so feminine, and so graceful.[2]

Yet, of this world, an English woman would see very little. Like her compatriots who journeyed to North America and came to new Englands in Charleston or Boston or Williamsburg and saw little of the world of Pottawatomies or Narrangansetts, her home too would be a little England surrounded by a vast and, as Hawkins and others had discovered, an often dangerous Indian ocean.

India is and always has been Hindoostan, the land of Hinduism, and no conqueror has ever changed that essential identity. It is easy to forget that, before the British held India, another foreign power, the Moghuls, ruled the subcontinent, and they had changed India just as little as Britain would. Indeed, like a rough mother, India often intrigues, puzzles, astonishes, overwhelms, and finally moulds her conquerors rather than being shaped by them.

On the other hand, India is also a land of many separate, discreet communities, possessing distinctive dress, cuisine, language, festivals, architecture, and sometimes physiognomy. One might immediately think of caste and certainly geography as segregators, but even within fairly narrow geographical limits and caste notwithstanding, it is fairly easy to distinguish one community from another. Sikhs, Rajputs, Jains, Marathas, Jats, Parsis, Gurkhas, Gujaratis, Bengalis—while distinctively Indian are also sharply unique. While a member of the Parsi community, for instance, is decidedly Indian, only the most obtuse would mistake him for a Sikh or a Gujarati. And the minute a Bengali opened his mouth, he could not possibly be mistaken for a Rajput or a Punjabi.

For a relatively short period, Anglo-Indians joined this jumbled collectivity and, in the distinctiveness of their communities, they somewhat resembled it. Like many of their Indian neighbours, they lived in separate enclosed enclaves, with a unique language, dress, manners, and social regulations, belonging to India as much as the Parsis, for instance, do, and yet, like the Parsis, separate. The Parsi, however, would not have looked across half a globe for his 'home', or for the regulatory agencies that formed his social, commercial, and political organizations. The English man or woman, unlike the Parsi, was an alien in India.

Contact with the India in which the British lived was, at best, superficial for men as well as women, and the divide was never entirely the fault of the British. When Jehangir's sister-in-law invited Frances Steele to visit her, it was out of curiosity, not because she wanted to cultivate any deep friendship with her. She wanted to see what an English woman looked like, pure and simple. Cultural barriers were at least as formidable on the Indian side as they were on the British. In the mid-eighteenth century, John MacDonald, visiting Bombay with his master, Colonel Thomas Keating, observed that when the Colonel's wife had asked three Indian associates to bring their wives to her, she had been told, 'Madam, we are much obliged to you for your invitation, but we cannot do this: to let our wives visit any European, nor let them visit us; if we did we should lose our caste, and be despised by our relations and every one of our religion.'[3]

Despite the temptation to adopt some of the manners and customs of the Indian merchants with whom they traded as equals, what impressed visitors such as Hamilton was the very Englishness of the settlements. Later Victorians were chided for fostering an elaborate 'cult of home'—trying to cultivate English pansies and daffodils outside their bungalows within the confines of a walled compound, or insisting on having pianos despite the humidity. Nonetheless, while English, Anglo-India, like colonial North America, was not quite a transplanted England either, and the cultural barriers, formidable as they were, were enormously porous. Especially among men, apart from concubines, deep friendships and trusted confidences were frequent. Englishmen served in Indian armies, at Indian courts, and were at ease in the Indian bazaar.

The contacts with Indians available to English women, however, were bound to be fewer and not intimate. One woman's assessment of Indians as 'queer kittle-kattle'[4] in the nineteenth century seems to have been the assessment of Indians about Englishmen in the seventeenth. In 1678, Shah Reza, a minister of the king of Golconda, expressed curiosity about the manner of worship and on a Sunday in December, he came to Masulipatnam and stayed until the sermon was read, 'observing with much attention the performance thereof, wherewith he seemed to be pleased'. Not so well pleased, however, that he remained for the entire thing, for a quarter of an hour after the sermon was finished, he departed. Shah Reza then told the king about it and the king too desired to see the service. So the following Sunday, a seat was prepared for His Majesty and he and Shah Reza and some of his principal servants were conducted into the hall where he 'observed heedfully the manner thereof; and taking notice that the women made use of books, desired to be satisfied whether they could read; and calling for the Chief's Bible and Common Prayer Book gave them into the hands of Mistress Field and Madam Mainwaring, who according to his desire read before them'.[5] After this, he went to the Dutch factory at Masulipatnam where he was entertained in like manner, presumably with the Sunday service, and 'with music and dancing wenches belonging to their Chief's lady in the very place where just before they had performed their devotions'.

An English woman may have been invited to a Hindu wedding or religious festival but she would have understood and participated in the goings-on about as fully as Shah Reza and his king would at a Christmas Mass or a Church of England funeral. In this, women differed little from the Company's servants. Although the Directors consistently encouraged their merchants to learn Hindustani and Persian, there was not much success with either. At a time when delicate negotiations were going on at the court of Delhi (c. 1715), no one could translate even the titles of the Persian documents.[6] On the other hand, as with many of the Company's other directives, there was a disconnect with the realities in India itself where, rather often, neither of those two languages was of much use in the daily give-and-take of the Indian bazaar.

India in the late seventeenth and early eighteenth centuries was an even more dangerous place than it had been when William Hawkins had landed there. As centralized Moghul authority slackened following Aurangzeb's death in 1707, local rulers contested with each other for control. Having learned early and painfully the harsh lesson that a policy of neutrality endeared them to no one, the Company's servants in India were drawn into that vortex which, because of the presence of the French, was also played out in Europe and North America.

In the midst of this strife, Frances Benyon, the Madras governor's wife, had occasion to visit an Indian princess. Mrs Benyon had been Frances Davis, the daughter of Richard Horden and widow of Sandys Davis, chief of Vizagapatam who had died at that station in 1734. Richard Benyon had also been married before, to Mary Fleetwood, the granddaughter of Margery and John Heathfield.[7] The account of her visit was written by Jane Smart to her son in England. Jane, her husband, Jonathan, and their daughters, Jane and Elizabeth, had gone out to Madras in 1740.

In 1739, about a year before the Smarts reached India, Persia's Nadir Shah had sacked and brutally looted Delhi. Among the treasures he had seized was the Peacock Throne, symbol of Moghul sovereignty. The sack of Delhi had left the Carnatic open to incursions from the Marathas, among others, but the disintegration of Moghul authority also left the field open for any number of princes to claim power for themselves. In September 1741, one of the contenders for power in Carnatic, Safdar Ali, came with his wife, mother, son, and all their attendants, numbering in the 'many thousands' to Madras. Safdar Ali was in an extremely vulnerable position in that he had not been confirmed by anyone in a capacity to do so as Nizam of Hyderabad. He was coming to Madras essentially to provide for his family's safety but, following a sixty-one gun salute, he was received not as a refugee but as a guest. His intent to make the Haj to Mecca was given as the reason for the splendour of the entourage. He stayed only a fortnight as a guest of the Company, but his wife and the rest of the entourage remained in the Black Town.

It was after his departure that Frances Benyon decided to visit Safdar Ali's wife and invited a Mrs Beard and her eldest daughter, as well as Jane Smart, and several other women to accompany her. Given the magnificence of his arrival, Jane Smart makes the understandable mistake of calling Safdar Ali the prime minister to the Moghul emperor himself in her *Letter from a Lady at Madrass*.[8] According to Mrs Smart, the English ladies dressed 'in the very best of every thing we had' and went to the governor's house where they breakfasted. Then, with music playing and 'Thousands of People looking at us in our Way thither' they walked about a mile accompanied by their own attendants to the residence of Safdar Ali's wife.

When they arrived, they were led through two halls to a large garden and a large, spacious pavilion covered with fine carpets at the end of which was seated the nawab's lady on a richly embroidered crimson velvet settee overhung with another embroidered carpet. Mrs Benyon was received 'with the utmost Gentility and good Breeding'. The nawab's lady was a thin, genteel, middle-sized person with black eyes painted at the edges; her fingernails, toenails, and lips were painted red, and every other tooth was painted black to resemble ebony. She had thirty attendants all painted the same. What impressed the English ladies the most was the vast number of precious jewels worn by all the women. They were served tea flavoured with cinnamon and rose-water, as well as betel served in filigree boxes made of gold. The betel was a large green leaf which the Indians chewed but which the English often found disagreeable. Nonetheless, 'we were forced to comply with that out of Compliment'.

Afterwards, a large silver board was brought in, covered with a carpet on which there was a fine 'Moor's Coat, with a couple of rich Gold-Veils'. That was given to Mrs Benyon but then all the ladies got the same gift. This kind of gesture would be repeated scores and scores of times by scores and scores of women, Indian and British—a gift, regarded highly by the Indian and, until the late eighteenth century, given with grace, was received with grace by the British women.[9] The nawab's wife and her ladies all admired the English ladies but thought their dress 'very odd' and were astonished at the hoop pet-ticoats they wore. 'To end all, we were the first English Women they had ever seen, and I doubt not but we appeared as odd to them, as they did to us.' Their numerous riches were all the enjoyment they had, Mrs Smart noted, for the women would not be allowed to go out and when they were obliged to travel, their palanquins would be curtained so that no one could see them, for 'it would be Death to any Man to attempt to see a Moor's Lady'.

The story ended rather sadly. Safdar Ali made several trips back to Madras, the last in August 1742, and was assassinated that October. Two years later, Richard Benyon resigned the governorship and sailed to England where he married a third time; so apparently Frances her-self had died either in India or shortly after arriving in England.[10] One can rather hope that her death came before she knew that the family of her hostess would be supported by the French in the struggle with the English for the Carnatic in the late 1740s and 50s.

As with Frances Steele a century earlier, despite the fact that both women were in a position to be vitally interested in the political events that involved their husbands, the visit was not the kind of thing of which enduring friendships could be made. The nawab's lady, like Frances Steele's hostess, simply wanted to know what an English woman was like.

India could always be frightening for men as well as women, but the first part of the eighteenth century could be downright horrific, as the career of Catherine Gyfford illustrated. The rani encountered by Mrs Gyfford was a far cry from Frances Benyon's gracious, bejeweled hostess. Nor was Catherine Gyfford's India at all like the relatively safe environment of Mrs Benyon's Madras. Like many English women in India, she was married more than once but, even for that age, her connubial career was extraordinary. It began at the extremely tender age of thirteen or fourteen. The daughter of a gunner at Fort William, Gerrard Cooke,[11] and already renowned for her beauty, Catherine was sold by her father in 1709 to John Harvey, chief of the Karwar factory.[12] About a year later, Harvey decided to wind up his affairs in India and return home. After paying himself what he thought he was due from the Karwar treasury, he and Catherine went on to Bombay.

After the dullness of Karwar, Bombay must have been completely delightful. Part of its charm was no doubt due to two new acquaintances, a young, newly arrived factor named Thomas Chown and a twenty-three-year old writer named William Gyfford. Catherine's Bombay holiday was cut short, however, by the death of Harvey's replacement at Karwar and the need for Harvey to return there to adjust some more accounts.

Harvey himself, however, died about four months after their return to Karwar and Catherine then took over his affairs. She laid claim to his estate which, according to custom, had been taken over by the Company. Two months later, Chown arrived at Karwar as a factor and married the new widow. In November 1712, Catherine now 'heavy with child', presumably Chown's, left for Bombay to enforce her claim to the Harvey estate. They sailed in the ketch *Anne* with two other vessels. A day out from Karwar, the tiny fleet was attacked by square-rigged Maratha frigates called 'grabs'. Chown was hit in the shoulder by a cannon ball and bled to death in Catherine's arms. The *Anne* was boarded and the surviving crew, including Catherine, was taken captive and confined in the Maratha stronghold of Colaba, about fifty miles down the coast from Bombay. Her captor was the dreaded Maratha chief Kanhoji Angrey (also called Angria) who was just beginning to found a naval power that would last half a century and be the scourge of the Company on the Malabar Coast for twenty years. Kanhoji and the plight of his captives, including the delectable Mrs Chown, quickly became the talk of Bombay and were soon provoking the settlement to no end. There was even talk of an Anglo-Portuguese alliance against Kanhoji who, being not dim-witted, offered an olive branch. If 'an Englishman of credit' were to be sent to Colaba, wrote Kanhoji, he was ready to discuss terms. A Scotsman named Mackintosh gallantly offered to go. With 30,000 in rupees, he set off, met with Kanhoji, and found Mrs Chown in such a state of undress that he was obliged to cover her with his own clothes to conceal her nakedness. Following her rescue, she duly gave birth to Chown's child.

Catherine then married William Gyfford who shortly thereafter was appointed chief of the factory at Anjengo, a fairly recent but important factory on the Malabar Coast. Anjengo had belonged to the Rani Ashure of Attinga who had fallen in love with a 'beautiful' young English emissary who 'satisfied her well'. As a result, the rani had found it difficult to refuse his countrymen anything. Later, however, disgusted by the intrigues of both the Dutch and the English, the rani had withdrawn her support from both. She had died in 1700 and, according to Colonel Biddulph, under her successor, also a woman, the English did everything they could to wound native sensibilities. Gyfford was no more diplomatic than others had been, but in 1721, he proposed restoring an old custom of giving presents yearly to the rani in the name of the Company. He proposed taking a large supply of cowries, pepper, and cloth (purchased with the Company's funds) to the rani. As he was about to present the gift, a bad fracas ensued. Gyfford was taken, his tongue cut out and nailed to his chest. He then was nailed to a log and sent down the river. Catherine and the two other English women from the Anjengo factory were taken aboard a native longboat. Four weeks later, dishevelled and destitute, they appeared in Madras. Catherine, not yet twenty years old, was for the third time a widow. Before leaving Anjengo, however, she had had the presence of mind to take the factory records and a sum of money which she claimed belonged to her late husband.

It is her subsequent career, however, that proves that, like her contemporary, Katherine Nicks, this Catherine too was easily as clever and as grasping as any other businessman in India. When she returned to Madras in 1743 and applied for a pension, it was granted by Governor Benyon on the grounds that in 1721, 'when she was not in such indigent Circumstances', she had avoided putting the Company to the expense of twenty-five pagodas a month which had been offered to her. Unlike Mrs Steele or Mrs Hudson, she had not committed the unforgivable sin of being an economic 'incumberance'. Her petition mentions that her father had died in the Company's service and that she had been married three times to 'Gentlemen of Station in the Service' and that after the death of her last husband, she had been barely been able to support herself and 'is now reduced to want a Subsistance, and that at a time of Life when she is in most need of Help, and is, by unavoidable Accidents and Misfortunes, deprived of any Relief from such as could heretofore Assist her'. Nonetheless, her case was still in the courts when she died at Madras in 1745.[13]

The two Indias experienced by Catherine Gyfford on the one hand and Frances Benyon and Jane Smart on the other were extremes. Most Indian women obviously were neither heavily jew-elled, sheltered princesses like Safdar Ali's wife, nor ranis who would order a fairly horrible death for an Englishman. Nor were most Indians pirates. Unfortunately, the two archetypes, the dangerous, cruel, treacherous Indian, and its opposite, the gaudy, empty-headed, effeminate (if a man) Indian, would, in a future generation, become facile categorizations for encountering India.

Neither Jane Smart's letter, however, nor Colonel Biddulph's account of Catherine Gyfford had anything to do with contributing to those images. Jane Smart's letter is still largely unknown. Colonel Biddulph's tale of Catherine Gyfford was not published until 1907 when memories of the 1857 Mutiny were still fresh and, in the light of the beginnings of the Indian nationalist movement, the public was more than ready to believe tales of the atrocities committed upon innocent English women and men by Indians who, without the con-straints of British power, would become totally unhinged.

By the time Catherine Gyfford died, India was changing. The effects of the disintegration following Aurangzeb's death in 1707, followed by the catastrophic invasion of Nadir Shah twenty-two years later, allowed local officials, intent on creating and preserving their own independence, to disregard the immunities and privileges that had been extended to foreigners. Chief among these were the Sikhs in the Punjab, and the Jats in the area south of Delhi around Agra and, in the Deccan, the Marathas contended with Moghul offi-cials. For a time, Bengal remained relatively stable but in the west the Marathas, under Catherine Gyfford's captor, Kanhoji Angria, ruled the seas, and Bombay was required to build a naval force against him. In 1740, a Maratha attack on the Nizam of Hyderabad threatened garrison towns all the way to Calcutta.

The European companies, particularly the English and French East India Companies, had already learned that they could remain aloof from these quarrels only at their peril. They had little choice but to fortify their settlements, but defence brought with it a new measure of involvement in the intricacies of local politics. It was from Madras that the Company made the first in the series of actions, culminating in the Battle of Plassey in 1757, that would give it a pre-eminent political position in India. In the south, on the Coromandel Coast, between the British forts, St George (Madras) and St David, lay Pondicherry in the hands of the French East India Company (Compagnie des Indes). Nearly a hundred miles down the coast from Madras, Pondicherry had enjoyed a lively commerce since its founding in 1683, thus making it a serious trading rival of the English Company. Unlike Madras, it had also been heavily fortified, primarily against the Marathas who had captured the Carnatic capital of Arcot. In 1742, one of the most formidable enemies the Company was ever to face, Joseph Dupleix, arrived in Pondicherry.

Two years earlier, the hostilities that would ultimately become the War of the Austrian Succession had broken out in Europe, but war was not formally declared until 1744, and news of it did not reach India until the next year. The first to hear of it was the governor of Mauritius, Admiral Bertrand-François Mahe de la Bourdonnais, who immediately prepared to launch an attack on Madras. Despite orders from home to avoid hostilities with the English in India, Dupleix began to make strategic alliances with Indian potentates in an effort to oust the English from the Carnatic while at the same time proposing to the officials at Bombay, Madras, and Calcutta that hostilities be avoided. His proposal was rejected, thus allowing him to accept La Bourdonnais' offer of help and to persuade the nawab of the Carnatic to join the French cause.

After being bombarded for a few hours in September 1746 by La Bourdonnais, Madras surrendered unconditionally. Her fortifications were destroyed and the garrison imprisoned, but the town itself was largely spared. Dupleix then set about destroying Fort St David, about fifteen miles south of Pondicherry. In that garrison was a young officer named Robert Clive who, finding the life of a writer dull, had petitioned the Company to be moved to the military.

One of the Indian allies Dupleix had sought was Mohammed Ali Wallahjah, who claimed the throne of Arcot, but that prince allied himself with the Company against Dupleix and the French client, the Nizam of Hyderabad. Mohammed Ali seized Trichinopoly, a key fortress in the south, where he was besieged by the French and their Indian allies. Robert Clive, with Major Stringer Lawrence who had been hired by the Company to run military matters out of Madras, defeated the French at Arcot. The move to relieve the siege at Trichinopoly was successful. French ambitions in the Carnatic were ended and Madras would be returned to British control by the Treaty of Aix la Chapelle about two years later, but the centre of the Company's interests in India was shifting from graceful, elegant Madras to the youngest of the three presidencies, Calcutta.

Not only was India changing but so was the Company and in ways that would have dismayed Thomas Roe. Roe had argued strongly against military involvement, but even as he had done so, military involvement had been and was still unavoidable. But the Company in India was changing in another way too. Before Jane Smart encountered the nawab's lady or Catherine Gyfford had been captured, Thomas Pitt, under whom Madras had experienced something of a 'golden age', foresaw a growing Anglo-Indian rift when he wrote,

> When the Europeans first settled in India, they were mightily admired by the natives, believing they were as innocent as themselves; but since by their example they are grown very crafty and cautious and no people better understand their own interest so that it was easier to effect that in one year which you shan't do now in a century; and the more obliging your management, the more jealous they are of you.[14]

notes

1 Interestingly, India's particular smell is not noted by any travellers until the nineteenth century. The most obvious explanation for that omission might be that the noxious smells on the ship they had occupied for many months might have dulled any olfactory sense. However, if they had come from London or any other city of significant size where venomous smells were as much a part of daily life as the dirt, rats, and animal waste, one might expect them to remark on how relatively pleasant India's smell really is. The earliest English travellers who left written records, Ralph Fitch, John Mildenhall, and Thomas Coryat, had travelled in the Levant before reaching India and by the time they reached India, peculiar smells were simply part of their experience.

2 Fanny (Parlby) Parkes, *Wanderings of a Pilgrim in Search of the Picturesque, during Four and Twenty Years in the East,* 2 vols (London: P. Richardson, 1850), I, 383–6.

3 John Macdonald, *Memoirs of an Eighteenth Century Footman. 1774–1779,* with an introduction by John Beresford (London: George Routledge & Sons, Ltd., 1927), 138.

4 Dennis Kincaid, *British Social Life in India, 1608–1937* (London: George Routledge & Sons, Ltd., 1939), 208.

5 Reverend Frank Penny, *The Church in Madras: Being the History of the Ecclesiastical and Missionary Action of the East India Company in the Presidency of Madras in the Seventeenth and Eighteenth Centuries.* 2 vols (London: Smith, Elder, & Co., 1904), I, 70. In a footnote Penny here draws attention to the difference in the honorific. 'Madam' Mainwaring was the wife of a member of the Masulipatnam Council and 'Mistress' Field was the wife of a young merchant and the daughter of Robert and Margery Fleetwood.

6 Charles R. Wilson, *The Early Annals of the English in Bengal.* 3 vols (London: W. Thacker and Co., 1900), II, Part I, lxvii.

7 See Chapter 6. It is worth pointing out again how many families like the Fleetwoods were claiming India as their home as early as the seventeenth century.

8 *A Letter from a Lady at Madrass to Her Friends in London: Giving an Account of a Visit Made by the Governor of That Place, with His Lady and Others, to the Nabob (Prime Minister to the Great Mogul) and His Lady, &c., in Which Their Persons, and Amazing Richness of Dress, Are Particularly Described* (London: Printed for and sold by H. Piers, Bookseller, High Holborn, 1743).

9 The custom became a problem after the promulgation of Cornwallis' proscriptions against gift-taking, designed to protect Indians from the extortions and bribes which had occurred in the years following the Battle of Plassey. Lady Loudon, wife of the Marquis of Hastings, once found herself trapped between Indian custom and government regulations and the trap was one that many English women would find themselves helplessly enmeshed in for some time. To refuse a gift from an Indian hostess is an insult. Yet with the promulgation of Cornwallis' proscriptions against gift-taking, a woman had little choice but to turn down expensive articles offered by Indian princesses. When Lady Loudon accompanied Lord Hastings to a durbar in 1814, a wife of the prince offered her a very expensive necklace and Lady Loudon, of course, refused it. The *begum* then tried several times to throw the necklace over Lady Loudon's shoulders and the 'bustle' which resulted became so violent that Hastings himself had to intervene and explain why the necklace could not be accepted—an explanation, incidentally, which he was certain the begum did not understand. See Francis

Rawdon, Marquess of Hastings, *Private Journal of the Marquess of Hastings* (Allahabad: The Panini Office, 1907), 46.

10 Henry Davison Love, *Vestiges of Old Madras, 1640–1800.* 3 vols, Indian Records Series (London: John Murray, 1913), II, 272.

11 A passenger list for the Loyall Bliss, sailing 9 March 1708, includes 'Cook the gunner and his wife, two daughters and a son'. See Wilson, *Annals*, 345.

12 Her entire story is told in Colonel John Biddulph, *The Pirates of Malabar and an Englishwoman in India Two Hundred Years Ago* (London: Smith, Elder & Co., 15, Waterloo Place, 1907, 258.

13 Love, *Vestiges*, II, 317.

14 Beckles Willson, *Ledger and Sword or the Honourable Company of Merchants of England Trading to the East Indies, 1599–1874.* 2 vols (London, New York, and Bombay: Longmans, Green, 1903), II, 43.

part two

The age of the nabobs, 1757–1805

TWO CENTURIES AFTER WILLIAM HAWKINS had appeared at the court of Jehangir, the Company, in a period of just over four decades, beginning with the Battle of Plassey in 1757, was transformed from a group of quarrelling, avaricious merchants precariously clinging to straggling factories into administrators faced with the challenge of managing possessions of which, even though they had been there for a century and a half, they actually knew very little. Those decades were dramatic, not only in terms of military and political changes but in the ways in which India itself came to be viewed. In administrative terms, it might be argued that the most dramatic of the many dramatic events in those decades was not military triumphs at all, but Robert Clive's decision in 1765, following the defeat of the Moghul emperor, Shah Alam, and his ally, the nawab of Oudh, at Buxar to 'stand forth as diwan', that is, to assume the right to collect revenue on behalf of the emperor, for Bengal, Orissa, and Bihar.

For many Britons, the *diwani* was a happy surprise, promising untold opportunities to 'shake the pagoda tree' of India and amass great fortunes. Indeed, the period between 1757, but especially after 1765, and roughly 1784 when Warren Hastings left India is often referred to as the infamous 'age of the nabobs' a period of unbridled plunder and rapacity, of greed and moral squalor from which India would finally be redeemed by the Pitt Act of 1784 and the reforms of Charles Cornwallis (1786–93) and Richard Wellesley (1798–1805).

Greed and moral squalor indeed there were, enough to make the sturdiest of angels weep, as well as danger, uncertainty, and ambiguity, but, happily, it was men of the highest, not the lowest, calibre who emerged to give shape to an empire not merely *in* India but *of* India. The grant of the diwani had thrust upon the Company the responsibility for administering large tracts of land inhabited by some thirty million people, products of a long, rich, and complex history who spoke languages and dialects of languages which were not only structurally different from English or any European language but written in characters that had to be learned too if they were to be mastered. They had to assess and collect revenue with only the scantiest knowledge about the wealth of the districts and people from whom they were collecting it. Perhaps most trying of all, they had to cope with Directors who were at least six months distant and who were themselves frequently embroiled in quarrels with a Parliament which then, perhaps unfortunately, did not empty out when the subject of India was raised. Quite simply, how were these people to be administered?

Upon his arrival as Governor of Bengal in 1772, Hastings determined that since India had been thrust upon him, India would be ruled as much as possible according to her own traditions and laws. This meant that to deal with India's present, it was necessary to understand her past. To that end, he sponsored translations of Persian histories, founded a madrasah in Calcutta, and the first Bengali printing press. His most important contribution, however, was the founding of the Asiatic Society with the help of Sir William Jones who arrived in 1784. Jones would join Hastings himself, John Shore, Henry Thomas Colebroke, and Charles Wilkins in making the society a vehicle for organizing and dignifying the collection of information about India.

While Plassey changed the physical world in which Anglo-Indian women lived, two important features of the earlier factory remained. First, India had always represented a chance to 'feather one's nest' but, especially after 1765, that lure was almost irresistible. Two monsoons was still the proverbial life of a man and the race for wealth was a race against time, death, and the investigations of the Directors. And it was for money—and not for respect, or keeping up appearances or doing good or for imperial power—that women, no less than men, were willing to forfeit honour, health, and even their lives. They simply intended to enjoy with unabashed vigour and zest life, money, and the things money could buy.

Second, despite the victory at Plassey, the Company was still engaged in war with Indian powers. Indians had, therefore, not yet been decisively shown to be weak, docile, depraved, or effeminate. Nor could any Anglo-Indian boast of his moral purity as against the moral helplessness of the Indians, for if he did, there were enough critics at home to admonish him.

Third, and closely related to their fragile position in India, Anglo-Indians exhibited an openness to the Indian communities that stood outside its boundaries. Even mildly educated women were children of the Enlightenment and while they could not belong to the Oriental Society and most probably knew little or none of its work, they shared with those scholars a lively and open curiosity about India, and more importantly, a sense of the essential oneness of humankind.

Most of these people were avaricious. They drank, ate, danced, and lived at a frenetic pace, but they were not particularly vicious, nor, like the earlier factors, were they very good racists. Racism would come later.

8

fishing fleets

FOR WOMEN, INDIA HAD ALWAYS REPRESENTED AN opportunity, albeit a last and often desperate one, to improve their economic and social lot. The scramble for wealth following the grant of the *diwani* made India a tremendously attractive pond in which to 'fish' for a rich husband, and it is in the period from 1765 to about 1784 that the great fishing fleets arrived bearing young—and not so young—ladies openly pursuing rich husbands.

The majority of the women who had come out to India in the seventeenth century had been married to or were sisters or daughters of factors, seamen, and soldiers. After its first dismal experiments of sending out hospital girls as wives for their servants in Bombay and Madras, the Company freely allowed but never again deliberately sent out women with the specific intention of marriage, or, for that matter, any other purpose. Until its dissolution in 1858, the Company's policy about women in India seems to have been centred firmly where it had been in 1615, that is, ambivalent. While women, primarily as wives, could provide some kind of spiritual or moral or civilizing influence, they could also be, as the Company had long since learned, at least mildly troublesome, and the Directors were, according to William Carey, 'chary' of increasing the number of European ladies in their possessions.[1]

Until well into the nineteenth century, any illusion that marriage was simply an emotional matter was dispelled by the quite substantial financial investment required to go to India. For passage and outfitting, the cost was about £500, plus a £12 licence fee which might be waived.[2] Presumably, one would not make that kind of an investment unless India was something of a last resort. Francis Fowke, writing to his nephew, made that clear. 'Your sister [Margaret] goes out now, I suppose,' he wrote, 'to get her a husband, which she has not beauty or fortune enough to get here.'[3]

While the Directors may have been 'chary', the newly founded *Calcutta Gazette* enthusiastically boasted that the presence of 'our numerous beauties, who charm the eye and enthrall the ear' would contribute to 'the rapid progress we are daily making in all those polite and refined entertainments, which have so strong a tendency to humanize the mind, and render life pleasing and agreeable'.[4]

Polite and refined though the entertainments might have been, the 'beauties' who charmed eyes and enthralled ears, entered a world that, like the earlier factories, was competitive, aggressive, more than a little crude, and still essentially commercial. The fact that it was so openly a fortune that many women pursued, far from being frowned upon or ridiculed, was taken very lightly, even paraded. There was, therefore, a zest about the game, an unabashed vigour, and something of frenzy about it because the object of securing a husband had never been guaranteed by simply setting foot on Indian soil.

As always, however, India represented an opportunity to occasionally move a notch or two upwards on the social scale, not a chance to leap all the way from the bottom to the top. Nonetheless, tales of the vast fortunes being made, even though they were fantastic, were compelling. It often took only a few letters from a friend in India telling of the luxury of Calcutta, the beauty of the garden houses, the elegance of the 'budgerows' and snake boats on the Hooghly River, and especially the initial reception there to turn the eyes of any unmarried girl to the East instead of towards the rebellious colonies along the Atlantic coast. As one woman put it, 'The attention and court paid to me was astonishing; my smile was meaning and my articulation melody; in a word, mirrors are useless things in

Calcutta, and self-adoration idle; for your looks are reflected in the pleasure of your beholder, and your claims to first rate distinction are confessed by all who approach you.'[5]

Exactly how many single ladies came out in each fishing fleet angling for husbands varied, but a lady writing to her cousin in 1779 reported that she had come in the company of twenty-nine other women seeking husbands, and they were, she tells us, of all ages, complexions, and sizes with little or nothing in common but that they were single and wished to get married. 'Some were absolutely old maids of the shriveled and dry description, most of them above the age of fifty; while others were mere girls just freed from the tyranny of the dancing, music and drawing masters at boarding school, ignorant of almost everything that was useful, and educated merely to cover the surface of their mental deformity.'[6]

This woman landed at Calcutta and what she went through next is probably typical of what happened also at Madras and Bombay. The first thing done

is for the captains to give an entertainment, to which they issue general invitations; and everybody, with the look and attendance of a gentleman, is at liberty to make his appearance. The speculative ladies, who have come out in the different ships, dress themselves with all the splendour they can assume, exhausting upon finery all the little stock of money they have brought out with them from Europe. This is in truth their last, or nearly their last stake, and they are all determined to look and dance as divinely as possible.[7]

Most of the ladies were disposed of at this Captain's Ball, but the ball may also have led to crowning disappointments. This lady, at any rate, was not terribly impressed with the crop of prospective mates for whom she had primped and powdered herself. 'They are', she said,

of all ranks, but generally of pale and squalid complexion, and suffering under the grievous inflictions of liver complaints. A pretty prospect this for matrimonial happiness! Not a few are old and infirm, leaning upon sticks and crutches, even supported about the apartments by their gorgeously dressed servants, for a display of all kinds of splendour on their part is no less attempted and accomplished.[8]

These 'old decrepit gentlemen' addressed themselves with supreme confidence in their purses, if not in their limbs, to the youngest and the prettiest, and the youngest and the prettiest were often inclined to respond in like manner to the purse, generously overlooking the sticks, crutches, and livers of their owners. The ball proved less successful to others, however, and it was 'really curious, but most melancholy, to see them ranged round the room, waiting with the utmost anxiety for offers, and looking with envy upon all who are more fortunate than themselves'.[9]

If the Captain's Ball did not bring a woman to the successful completion of her marital enterprise, however, there was certainly no need to despair. For the first three or four nights after the landing, she was exhibited to the settlement in the house where she was residing. This was what William Hickey called the 'disagreeable and foolish ceremony' of setting up,[10] a new and peculiarly Anglo-Indian custom, neither imported from England nor practised in the earlier factories. It was a means of introducing or rather exhibiting newcomers to the settlements. Single women frequently obtained a number of offers from the wealthier merchants of the community and many matches were concluded even before the third evening's 'setting'. The purposes of the custom aside, however, it was fatiguing and the calls required afterwards could exhaust a woman for several weeks. When it finally did cease in the early years of the next century, it was most probably the women themselves who ended it. Even if it resulted in a 'catch', the ignominy of being exhibited like cattle plus the burden of the obligatory calls seems not to have been worth it. It had also become redundant. Everyone knew when a new arrival was expected and where she would be staying and other methods had been found for meeting potential mates.[11]

If setting-up failed to accomplish a woman's objective, there was always the church. The arrival of a ship from Europe loaded with marriageable females brought more men to church on the following Sunday than any holy day or admonition from the Court of Directors ever did. The ladies would be carried in a slow progress in palanquins to the Customs Office in the Old Fort, which was used for services until the erection of St John's Church in 1787. At the entrance, they were presented with what must have been the truly edifying sight of the bachelors of the settlement, however old, infirm, or suffering from the food, drink, and conviviality of the night before, jostling each other for the right to escort the ladies to their seats.

Here, as at the Captain's Ball, the candidates for her hand may not have impressed a woman very much. They may have had foul livers and worse tempers but their wealth and/or the prospects of wealth and their loneliness may have made them not only easy 'catches' but lucrative ones as well.

If neither church nor setting-up accomplished the marital objective there were countless balls, dinners, breakfasts, concerts, fetes-champêtres, and theatre parties where a woman might hope to win the prize she sought. Those women who were still unmarried after a lapse of about three months would all unite in giving an entertainment at their own expense to which all of the gentlemen of the settlement would be invited. Three months was about the most that India's climate and the savage cosmetics[12] she had brought with her would grant a woman's beauty, so it was a matter of pressing urgency for a woman to marry before the bloom had entirely left her cheeks. Those who failed to do so found themselves 'old stock' who had little choice but to marry a military officer and live up-country on half pay, or the ignominy of failure and retreat to England. Or worse.

William Hickey tells of a Scottish girl, a Miss Dundas, who was seduced by a cavalry officer when she was only fourteen years old. She left home (or was forced to leave?) for him and came to India where he was later killed. Left destitute and friendless, she turned to prostitution.[13] For obvious reasons, it is not possible to discover how many women, like the unfortunate Miss Dundas, did turn to prostitution or what their motives for doing so might have been. The death or desertion of her male guardian, however, would have left any woman in an extremely precarious social and financial position. In 1761, there had been only three unmarried European ladies in Calcutta but twenty years later they were not uncommon.[14]

As in the generations before Plassey, the Indian El Dorado proved an illusion to many men and so did the hopes of scores of women who hoped to marry rich nabobs and live in luxurious happy-ever-afters. Philip Francis' brother-in-law, Alexander Mackrabie, suggested to a friend that he advise any ladies who wished to be married to go to America instead where 'the good people are marrying one another as if they had not a day to live' and avoid India as a marrying ground.[15]

The major impediment to marriage remained the low salaries paid to the factors. A senior merchant was paid £40 per annum, a junior merchant, £30; factors received £15; and writers, £5.[16] After 1758, the Court of Directors increased the salary of governors from £300 pounds a year to £2,700, that of a member of a Council in Madras, Bombay, or Calcutta from £100 pounds to £132.17s and that of a writer from £5 to £27.[17] There were further increases ten years later but a writer's salary went up to only £50 per annum and a senior merchant's to only £81.[18] There was the expectation that salaries would be supplemented with other sources of income but suitable housing for an English family remained a very heavy burden, and only a very few senior merchants in the Company's service could afford to marry an English wife and maintain her and a family. Anglo-Indian society had always been terribly extravagant and ostentatious but it was even more so in the eighteenth century, and the result of competition among both men and women in dress and ornament, housing, carriages, and servants could have brought ruin to many houses.

Servants remained a major and a necessary expense. The Directors were very legitimately concerned that young civilians would ruin themselves on the acquisition of more servants than they could afford on their wages and, beginning in 1759, the Directors tried several times to fix the wages for servants. Still, by 1801, they were almost three times as high as they had been in 1759.[19] The regulation of salaries was about the only recourse the Company could take to cut down the expenses of its servants, but the more servants a man had the greater his social prestige. And the servants themselves encouraged large expenditures. It was obviously more prestigious and profitable for Indian servants to go out in a very rich livery and to be associated with a very wealthy master rather than a poor one who could barely clothe them.

Aside from the expense of servants and housing, there were expenses for dress, and male dress in the eighteenth century was as elaborate as that of women. William Hickey tells us that when he arrived in Bengal, 'everybody was dressed splendidly, being covered with lace, spangles and foil'. So the genial Hickey, 'who always had a tendency to be a beau, gave in to the fashion with much good will, no person appearing in richer suits of velvet and lace than myself'.[20]

Men's dress required lace and ruffles, ribbons and powder, buckles and breeches, black and white hats, thunder and lightning coats, stockings of various colors, and waistcoats, plus a substantial stock of linen, shirts, and underclothes to be changed several times a day, owing to the climate. Hairdressers also were as indispensable to men as they were to women. Men usually got their hair done twice a day. It would be furiously powdered and pomatummed and the lowest pay a native hairdresser received was two rupees monthly, but their fees often went much higher and gentlemen needed their services as well as those of a barber. If ladies could be critical of fashions, men were no less so. Mackrabie attended a public function at Government House in 1784 and, in addition to his annoyance over the heat, the confusion, the lack of 'Regularity', and the absence of guards or anyone to receive or show the way about, Mr Hastings had not even put on a ruffled shirt![21]

In addition to dress, there were charges for table accessories, carriages and/or palanquins, and entertainments. To add to these expenses the additional expense of a wife and further expenditure on children was far beyond the capacities of all but the most senior merchants, and explains why ladies so often found only 'old decrepit gentlemen' as suitors. An English wife was costly, but precisely because of the expense, she was also a status symbol, a mark of wealth in an age that loved to show off its wealth.

On the other hand, any argument that the simple presence of European women would encourage connubial regularity had long since been disproven. There were still too few of them to have much of an impact. By 1810, Captain Thomas Williamson gave a figure of 250 European women for all of Bengal while male inhabitants 'of respectability', including military officers, were 4,000.[22] That accords with Holden Furber's estimate that the total number of European women (British and others) did not exceed a few hundred at a time before the end of the eighteenth century.[23] Concubinage remained an easy and less expensive alternative to an English wife and had become too well established to be much affected by new arrivals, male or female. The cost of supporting an Indian 'companion' and her attendants depended upon the circumstances and disposition of the man but it normally could be done for about Rs. 25–40 a month or roughly £50 a year. An English wife, on the other hand, meant an expenditure of £600 a year. Between 1757 and 1800, only one in four covenanted servants, one in eight civilians and one in ten army officers actually married in India. Between 1767 and 1782, over half (54 per cent) of the children baptized in St John's Church in Calcutta were of mixed parentage and illegitimate.[24]

As in the earlier factories, society accepted a man and a favourite concubine as husband and wife and accorded the title 'Mrs' to the woman out of courtesy whether they were married or not. That happened when William Hickey set up housekeeping with his lovely servant Jemadanee, following the death of his English 'wife' Charlotte whom he had never bothered to formerly wed either.

Even when a woman was lucky enough to 'catch' a husband in India, she was likely to discover that she was simply trading economic insecurity for disappointment as did one woman who wrote to a friend,

> True it is I am married: I have attained that for which I came out to India—a husband; ...What a state of things is that, where the happiness of a wife depends upon the death of that man who should be the chief not the only source of her felicity. However such is the fact in India: the wives are looking out with gratitude for the next mortality that may carry off their husbands, in order that they may return to England to live upon their jointures; they live a married life, an absolute misery, that they may enjoy a widowhood of affluence and independence.[25]

At home, the view of marriage as a mercenary and therefore artificial arrangement had come under attack even before 1757. William Hogarth's biting tableau, *Marriage a la Mode*, completed in 1745, was, at its heart, an argument that marriage be taken as a loving arrangement between equal partners. While wealth and social position would continue to set the criteria in seeking a potential spouse, the consumer revolution of the eighteenth century had expanded women's roles in investment, spending, and consumption. That allowed them to challenge the purely mercenary objectives in marriage and demand, if not full equality in a marriage, then conduct approximating, if not love, then at least respect.[26]

Nonetheless, as difficult as a marriage might become, eighteenth-century English law did not favour a woman's suit for a divorce. On marriage, a woman became subject to her husband's domicile, even if she did later become separated or divorced from him. Divorce in England was normally granted only at the husband's suit and on the grounds of adultery. A wife's suit for divorce on the grounds of adultery, however, had to be accompanied by proof of cruelty or desertion, and what constituted cruelty was only physical, endangering life, limb, and health. Moreover, it required an Act of Parliament.

In 1785, Mrs Harriet Ann Mackenzie brought a divorce suit against her husband, Major Robert Mackenzie, charging him with adultery and maltreatment. The major admitted committing adultery in Bombay before his wife had arrived there. And with her knowledge. But when the couple came to Bengal, the major embarked on another round of adulterous liaisons of which Harriet was, for a time, kept ignorant. She tolerated not only the adultery but also the maltreatment which had begun in Scotland before either she or the major had even come out to India. In November of 1784, the major struck her so hard that a surgeon was called in. Even then, however, she did not leave him—and one suspects that by now she was perhaps afraid to for fear of even further abuse. At the divorce proceedings, she acknowledged that when she had accompanied him to Cawnpore, it had been against her will, and then she had finally been able to desert him there. The Court mercifully granted her the divorce.[27]

Nevertheless, the distance from home and the censure of friends and relatives and the very fluidity of Anglo-Indian society could work to a woman's advantage. The Act of Parliament granting a divorce was impractical, and divorces were therefore more easily obtained in India than they perhaps would have been in England. Harriet Mackenzie's suit on a mere charge of adultery would probably have gone nowhere in India, but the charge of maltreatment might have won her the divorce in England as well as in India.

The dissolution of the marriage between Anthony and Eliza Fay, however, involved no such clear-cut case of physical abuse. Eliza had simply married a muddling fool who was petty, stupid, and ill-bred. Those unlovely traits, however, did not become apparent to her until they came to India where Fay, a barrister, intended to practise law. On their landing at Madras in November 1779, they had become prisoners of Haider Ali. After about a month and a half, they were told that they would be freed but the promise was then revoked and Fay, losing all self-control, rushed in a rage toward the throne of Haider Ali's lieutenant-governor, seized him bodily, and insisted on fulfilment of the promise. That act could have cost them their lives except that the Indians thought Fay had gone mad and, according to Eliza, 'regard the sufferers under these complaints with a superstitious awe'.[28] On their arrival at Calcutta, following their release, they were received by the cream of Calcutta society, but Anthony Fay was drawn into one of the numerous schemes against Warren Hastings. Once he was admitted to the bar there, he ordered Eliza not to call on any of the judges' wives while he worked secretly for the impeachment of chief justice, Elijah Impey. Finally, after two years, Eliza left him by which time he had run into debt and fathered an illegitimate child. Eliza did obtain a divorce from Fay and in a remarkably short period of time.

Divorces, however, although relatively easy to obtain from the legal standpoint, were prohibitively expensive. One woman observed,

> No wonder lawyers return from this country rolling in wealth. Their fees are enormous; if you ask a single question in any affair you pay down your gold mohur, and if he writes a letter of only three lines, twenty-eight rupees! I tremble at the idea of coming into their hands; for what must be the recoveries, to answer such immense charges![29]

Still, despite the legal and financial difficulties facing a woman who was divorced, Georgian society at home was less apt to ostracize her than the Victorians would be. And this was the case also in India. Eliza Fay did indeed drop into a lower social rank, but her outspokenness may have made her a rather tiresome guest in any case.

Many divorcees could take some comfort in the fact that at the very pinnacle of Anglo-Indian society there was a divorcee. Maria, the second wife of Warren Hastings, had been the wife of a German portrait painter named Imhoff who had applied for and received a cadetship in the Company's service.[30] Hastings had met the pair on his second voyage out to India in 1769, following his appointment by the Directors as second member of the Council at Madras and with a title to succeed to the governorship of that presidency. Hastings was fifteen years her senior, had been a widower for almost twelve years, was almost entirely bald, and needed spectacles for reading. Maria was intelligent, witty, and vivacious. During an illness Hastings suffered en route, Maria nursed him back to health and by the time the ship docked at Madras, a strong affection had developed between the two. Imhoff went to Calcutta shortly before Hastings' own transfer there as Governor-General in 1772, but the Directors ordered Imhoff to resign the service and to leave India immediately—by force, if necessary. At that point, Maria made clear her desire for a divorce in order to marry Hastings, and Imhoff was disposed to grant it.

In March 1773, Imhoff sailed for Europe and, with funds provided by Hastings, secured a divorce in Germany in 1776.[31] In the interval between 1773 and the date of the divorce in 1776, Maria was maintained by Hastings, and Calcutta was allowed to believe that Imhoff would return as soon as he could get reinstated in the service. Almost as soon as the divorce was sealed, Hastings and Mrs Imhoff were married. The divorce and remarriage did some social damage but Calcutta society was not nearly as worried about respectability as it became in the next century. Hastings' own character was above reproach but he certainly had enough enemies, notably Philip Francis, who could have used the relationship to harm Hastings politically. But Francis himself was charmed by Maria and admitted that she was really an accomplished woman who behaved with perfect propriety in her new station and deserved every mark of respect.[32] Her wit and vivacity together with Calcutta's own rather looser morality apparently put the entire affair quite beyond the reach of scandal.

Madame Grand who was seduced by Francis did not have the advantage of a high social position in Calcutta society. She was not European and her husband who, although respectable enough, was not quite so far beyond moral reproach and scandal as Hastings, and Francis himself certainly was not. Yet, after the seduction and all the attendant political repercussions, Mrs Grand was not only established in a house by Francis where he was careful to see that she was visited by the very cream of society, including members of the Council and, of course, Maria Hastings. Francis' career never did fully recover from the scandal. Madame Grand, however, survived rather well. She eventually became the wife of France's capable Foreign Minister, Charles Maurice de Talleyrand in 1802.[33]

While the number of English women who were in India did slightly increase, the fishing fleets, in themselves, did not change the essential nature of Anglo-Indian society in the late eighteenth century any more than they had in the seventeenth. In most respects, the behaviour of most of these women—and men—resembled their grandparents and great grandparents more than it would their children and grandchildren; that is, they remained acquisitive, cantankerous, and somewhat gaudy. Despite a growing sense that marriage might or ought to involve emotional fulfilment as well as financial security, the idea of marriage as essentially an economic arrangement never did lose its currency, and, although many women found that the voyage was not worth the effort, fishing fleets continued to arrive in India until the 1857 Mutiny.

notes

1 William Carey, *The Good Old Days of Honorable John Company, Being Curious Reminiscences during the Rule of the East India Company from 1600 to 1858*. 2 vols (Calcutta: R. Cambray, 1906), I, 84.

2 Suresh Chandra Ghosh, *The Social Condition of the British Community in Bengal, 1757–1800* (Leiden: E.J. Brill, 1970), 63.

3 Cited in ibid., 62.

4 *Calcutta Gazette*, 21 October 1784.

5 Phebe Gibbes [Sophia Goldborne], *Hartly House, Calcutta* (Calcutta: Thacker, Spink and Co., 1908 [Reprinted from the 1789 edition]), 36.

6 Cited in Carey, *Good Old Days*, I, 93.

7 Ibid., 94.

8 Ibid.

9 Ibid., 95.

10 William Hickey, *Memoirs of William Hickey*, ed., Alfred Spencer, 4 vols, 8th ed. (New York: Alfred A. Knopf, 1921), III, 159.

11 Eliza Fay had to endure the thing as late as 1807 in Bombay. See Eliza Fay, *Original Letters from India*, ed. E.M. Forster (London: Hogarth Press, 1986), 233.

12 See Chapter Ten for a discussion of the cosmetics.

13 Hickey, *Memoirs*, III, 231.

14 Mark Naidis, 'Evolution of the Sahib', in *The Historian*, XIX (August 1957), 430.

15 Philip Francis, *The Francis Letters*, ed. Beata Francis and Eliza Keary, 2 vols (London: Hutchinson and Co., 1901), I, 90.

16 Carey, *Good Old Days*, I, 33.

17 Ghosh, *The Social Condition of the British Community*, 66.

18 Ibid.

19 See Carey, *Good Old Days*, II, 61–2, and Henry Busteed, *Echoes of Old Calcutta*, 4th ed. (London: W. Thacker & Co, 1908), 128.

20 Hickey, *Memoirs*, II, 138.

21 Francis, *Letters*, I, 210.

22 Captain Thomas Williamson, *The East India Vade-Mecum or Complete Guide to Gentlemen Intended for the Civil, Military, or Naval Service of the Hon. East India Company*, 2 vols (London: Printed for Black, Parry, and Kingsbury, 1810), I, 453.

23 Holden Furber, *John Company at Work* (Cambridge: Harvard University Press, 1948), 25.

24 Christopher J. Hawes, *Poor Relations: The Making of a Eurasian Community in British India, 1773–1833* (Richmond, Surrey: Curzon Press, 1996), 6.

25 Carey, *Good Old Days* I, 93.

26 Ingrid Tague discusses 'conduct writers' who became 'unfashionably fashionable' by challenging the mercenary character of marriage in 'Love, Honor, and Obedience: Fashionable Women and the Discourse of Marriage in the Early Eighteenth Century', *Journal of British Studies*, 40, no. 4 (October 2001), 76.

27 *Calcutta Gazette*, 30 June 1785.

28 Fay, *Letters*, 141.

29 Gibbes [Goldborne], *Hartly House*, 122.

30 A. Mervyn Davies, *Strange Destiny. A Biography of Warren Hastings* (New York: G.P. Putnam's Sons, 1935), 53–4.

31 Ibid., 191.

32 Francis, *Letters*, I, 285.

33 They were separated after Waterloo. She returned to England, then Paris where she died in 1835. See Carey, *Good Old Days*, II, 235.

9

a city of palaces

WHEN JEMIMA KINDERSLEY ARRIVED IN 1764, she thought Calcutta looked 'as if all the houses had been thrown up in the air, and fallen down again by accident as they now stand...so that all the English part of the town, which is the largest, is a confusion of very superb and very shabby houses, dead walls, straw huts, warehouses, and I know not what'.[1] Eliza Fay, arriving about fifteen years later, however, discovered the slopes, banks, and ramparts along the Hooghly River, covered with the 'richest verdure', the beautiful Esplanade fronting the Fort, the variety of vessels continually passing on the surface of the river, and the elegant mansions and garden houses lining its banks—all of this was 'a magnificent and beautiful moving picture; at once exhilarating the heart, and charming the senses'.[2]

The dramatic change in only a decade and a half suggests the almost frenetic haste of a frontier town, a city on the move. Just as the earlier walled, fortified factory had revealed a cautious community on the defensive against India, so did the elegant mansions of Eliza Fay's Calcutta reveal a richer, more confident, and decidedly European identity, but an identity still willing to borrow from and blend with India. The neo-classical columns and ornamented pediments proclaimed Europe's Baroque grandeur, but the lovely *chuman* of India was still used to cover the thick, brick exterior walls. Other architectural features, resulting from accommodations to the climate and borrowed from Indian styles, were new. The interior walls which had either been left unpainted or whitewashed in the earlier period, had begun to give way to plastering in colored panels, usually in two shades, to soften the starkness of the high walls. Indian mats or Persian carpets covered the floors. Since glass had to be imported from Europe and was therefore expensive, the windows were either lattice-work grilles or covered with bamboo blinds. The blinds were not only elegant but more practical in that they could be closed and barred against the weather while at the same time permitting the free passage of air throughout the house. Until the hanging punkah came into use near the end of the century, fans or chowries waved to and fro by 'kettesol boys' made the hot weather more tolerable.[3]

Unlike European households, furnishings, because they could harbour vermin, continued to be sparse and light. The *Calcutta Gazette* regularly advertised large stores of furniture being sold either at the Europe shops or by individuals who were leaving for home and trying to get rid of as many household furnishings as possible. However, as Jemima Kindersley observed,

> Furniture is so extraordinarily dear, and so difficult to procure, that one seldom sees a room where all the chairs are of one sort; people of first consequence are forced to pick them up as they can...so that those people who have great good luck, generally get their houses tolerably well equipped by the time they are quitting them to return to England.[4]

The trouble with such elegant houses is that they were prohibitively expensive on even a senior merchant's salary unless, of course, he could supplement his income from other sources, licit or not. The cost of renting was also extremely high. Philip Francis paid £500 a year to rent a house without a single glass window which he described as a barn.[5] One way of getting around the high rents was for men to rent quarters in the Writers' Buildings or to live together in a house, but either arrangement, like the earlier collegial factory, would hardly have been attractive if one of them were married.

In addition to the desire to parade wealth, the Anglo-Indian community retained another characteristic of the earlier factory, that is, there remained a remarkable degree of social fluidity. Anglo-India remained an insular, albeit a cosmopolitan, society that knew and respected official and military rankings but was far freer of class prejudice than its model at home and thus much less likely to place any particular group or people—Indians or women—in a position of irrevocable inferiority. And while there was a distinction between the officials and the military, there were also professional people—doctors, lawyers, engineers, European shopkeepers, tavern owners, tradesmen, and chaplains—who remained relatively free of the influence of either and who, in their turn, had a great deal of social status. Hastings himself would have been the last to grant that the Governor-General's authority was firm even in Bengal, let alone in Madras and Bombay. Any deference paid him or his wife by Calcutta society had to be earned, even demanded. Yet Hastings' personal accessibility and his wife's own charm and warmth determined that whatever pomp and formality might attach to their positions (and consequently, to those of anyone else, at least in the civilian services) accrued only to the position and not to the person and thus militated against the formation of rigid social hierarchy.

Other remnants of the factory also remained. The Directors would continue to prohibit gambling, drinking, and dueling, and, as usual, their directives would be largely unheeded. A Sunday congregation was somewhat assured by regular directives from the Directors, but, in the generation before Evangelicalism swept Britain and then India, church would by no means render one's conscience uneasy for the morals of the clergy in India still resembled those of their flocks. As servants of the Company, their salaries remained extremely low and they often supplemented them with shares in certain monopolies such as salt, betel nut, and tobacco when they were honest, or they speculated, extorted, and extracted 'presents' when they were not. Mackrabie noticed that although clergymen in India were not numerous, they were 'thoroughly orthodox'.

> One rivals Nimrod in hunting—a second supplies Bullocks to the Army—another is a perfect Connoiseur in Chinese Gardening. I endeavour to obtain some Light from them all, but the Fear of God is not the kind of Wisdom most in Request in Bengal.[6]

The English in India continued to eat and drink very well. Someone had told Eliza Fay before she left England that the heat of Bengal destroyed the appetite. Perhaps for the sake of their constitutions it should have but Eliza's informant could not have been more wrong. The bill of fare for the Fays alone for a single dinner consisted of a soup, a roast fowl, curry and rice, a mutton pie, a forequarter of lamb, a rice pudding, tarts, 'very good cheese, fresh churned butter, fine bread', and some excellent Madeira which she noted was very expensive, although the eatables were cheap.[7] Practically every variety of food or drink that even the most discriminating palate could require was available so that Englishmen did not really have to acquire a taste for Indian food, although many, like the Fays, did. The Europe shops carried English and Dutch cheeses, pickles, vinegar, oil, mustard, fish sauces, pickled tongues, beef, pork, preserved fruits, mandarin oranges from China, and garden seeds of every variety also made fresh vegetables available.[8] A universal favourite was a burdwan stew made of everything at the table—fish, fowl and flesh—and supposed by many to be no good unless prepared in a silver saucepan.

Thomas Pitt's observation about the 'damnable amount of alcohol' his countrymen drank in the early part of the century remained valid. The amount of alcohol that could be consumed at any one sitting can quite stagger the imaginations of a more abstemious generation. Heavy drinking was typical of the age, however, rather than a peculiar addiction of Anglo-Indians. Alcohol, beers, ales, and wines were as abundant and varied as the food, although some of the wines were rather expensive since they were imported. Eliza Fay, for instance, did not expect to produce much English claret for her tables because of the high prices, but wines, often mixed with water, were generally drunk at dinner as well as at supper. After dessert, a few loyal toasts would be drunk, and the men would then sit down to the more serious business of disposing of three bottles of claret apiece. The ladies also drank, although with a bit more restraint, but as one woman observed, at a single sitting, 'every lady, even to your humble servant drinks at least one bottle per diem, and the gentlemen four times that quantity'.[9] The deadly arrack punch that had taken so many lives continued to be consumed but apparently not in the lethal quantities of the earlier factories since it is listed as a cause of death far less frequently.

A nap after dinner was followed by evening airings on the racecourse where 'everyone goes though sure of being half suffocated with dust'.[10] Despite the dust, the evening airing was an 'event' that no one dispensed with unless sick nearly to the point of death. Since the entire point of seeing and being seen was to show off one's wealth and to compare that with everyone else's, the carriages and palanquins were as extravagantly designed and furnished as their owners could possibly afford. Carriages, phaetons, and tack in the latest European styles could be obtained from the Europe shops and were as elegant as perhaps anything of the like in Europe.

The airing on the course was followed by tea. After tea, either cards or music filled the interval until about 10 p.m. when supper would be announced. Formal visits might also be paid in that interval. These were normally very short since each lady had perhaps a dozen calls to make at a time and a party waiting for her at home besides. Here, as with the carriage rides, little sets of formal 'rules' developed. Women shortly learned at least one Indian phrase, *darwan-e bund* or 'the door is closed' indicating that a woman was not dressed properly; she was ill or otherwise not disposed to receive the person making the call.[11] She learned too that if she asked a gentleman to put down his hat, it was considered an invitation to stay for supper and many hats were left dangling in the hands of their owners for up to half an hour before they were finally compelled to leave.[12]

Supper was as opulent as dinner. Mackrabie, who attended a supper with the Elijah Impeys at the Claverings,[13] was one of the many perhaps who went to supper joylessly. 'Entre nous,' he wrote, '...the evening was stupid enough, and the supper detestable; great joints of roasted goat; with endless dishes of cold fish. With respect to conversation, we have had three or four songs screeched to unknown tunes; the ladies regaled with cherry-brandy; and we pelted one another with bread pills a la mode de Bengal'.[14]

Pelting each other with little pellets of bread was actually an improvement over a previous custom of gentlemen throwing chickens at one another's heads, while the ladies pelted each other with sweetmeats and pastries.[15] Both sexes enthusiastically engaged in bread pelleting and Hickey tells us that some people could discharge the pellets with enough force to cause considerable pain when struck in the face. Richard Barwell got so proficient that he could snuff out a candle at the distance of three or four yards several times in succession. Pelleting finally came to an end about 1780, however, when a Captain Morrison who had frequently discussed his abhorrence of the practice warned that if anyone struck him with one, he would consider it an insult and 'resent it accordingly'. When a pellet thrown by a recent acquaintance did strike him, Morrison, without the slightest hesitation, picked up a dish containing a leg of mutton and hurled it at the offender with such force that it knocked him from his chair and gave him a severe cut on the temple. A duel ensued in which the pelleter was shot through his body, lay upon his bed many months, and never perfectly recovered.[16]

There was a possibility, albeit a small one, that one could retire for the night following supper. But on those rare evenings when there was no ball or concert accompanying supper, men and women would go to the card tables. The stakes were outrageously high. Literally, fortunes could be lost at the gaming tables. As with the eating and drinking, gambling had never been absent from Anglo-Indian life nor was it unique to India nor was it an exclusively male activity. Women at home also gambled heavily and apparently could lose more than mere money, for a little poem of the period ends with the lines,

And when the Fair One can't the Debt defray,
In Sterling Coin, does Sterling Beauty pay.[17]

There is, however, no indication that Anglo-Indian ladies ever lost anything more than money at the gaming tables. Besides loo, tredille and whist were also favourite games. Ladies seldom played whist, however, because while the stakes were relatively moderate, bets frequently ran so high among the men that those who sat down for mere amusement were often rendered anxious 'lest others should lose by their blunders'.[18] While some women may have been 'rendered anxious' at whist, others were either skillful or lucky enough to clean a man's pockets without either playing whist or marrying him. A Mrs Rumbold of Madras relieved Hickey of nearly three hundred pounds before she reluctantly allowed him to withdraw from a game of loo.[19]

Another extremely popular and more recent entertainment was the theatre. The first theatre built in Calcutta was destroyed in the siege of 1756.[20] The Calcutta Theatre erected after the destruction of the old one was financed by subscription and completed in 1775.[21]

As in Britain, the stage itself was largely a male preserve, and it was usually men who took all the roles, produced, and directed the plays. Since they were all amateurs, the quality of the performances could be fairly uneven. It was reported, in fact, that some people went to see a tragedy for the purpose of enjoying a laugh.[22] Nevertheless, what was attempted was impressive. The theatre in England had been fairly mediocre in the early half of the century but by the 1760s, David Garrick, Richard Brinsley Sheridan, and Oliver Goldsmith in particular had lent it an air of respectability, and this was reflected in Calcutta and Madras. *She Stoops to Conquer* and *School for Scandal* were performed in Madras and a good many farces, along with Shakespearean presentations and even Handel's *Messiah* in its entirety, were done in Calcutta. If the presentations did not meet very high dramatic criteria, they were attended and praised enthusiastically. Even the relatively respectable and contained *Calcutta Gazette* rarely gave a performance a bad review.

There were also private theatres and these gave women an opportunity to develop dramatic talents more fully in India perhaps than would have been possible in England. The most favoured was Emma Wrangham Bristow's in her own house in Chowringhee. It was she who, following the lead of Mrs Siddons in England, set the fashion of ladies appearing on the stage and even took the leading parts in plays she herself produced.[23] Her own strong points were reported to be in comedy and 'humorous singing'.[24] Dramatic criticism was not refined and Emma Bristow would probably have won the most fulsome praise from the Calcutta papers if she had walked through the part of Lady Macbeth. One paper noted, 'She went through the whole of the humorous part of "The English Slave in the Ottoman Seraglio" with a justness of conception and success of execution most admirable. Magnificently decorated by Art, and more beautifully adorned by Nature, the extravagance of the amorous Sultan seemed justified by her charms.'[25] It may be fair to assume that Emma Bristow well deserved the praise her performances won. On the other hand, it might also be fair to wonder if India did not provide an opportunity to develop her dramatic skills that she would not have had if she had remained in England.

There were also a number of less esoteric entertainments available to Anglo-Indians. The members of a Tent Club used to go weekly into the jungles within fifty miles of Calcutta to catch hogs.[26] Carey says nothing about the membership, but one gets the distinct impression that whatever women were physically capable of doing, their male associates were perfectly willing to allow them to do. The reigning belle of Calcutta in the early 1780s was Emma Wrangham Bristow whose 'natural flow of spirits', according to William Hickey, frequently led her 'into follies of rather too masculine a nature'.[27] She rode horseback astride, and could leap over hedges and ditches that even the 'most zealous sportsmen' would not attempt. She was an excellent shot, rarely missing her bird, and 'understood the present fashionable science of pugilism and would without hesitation knock a man down if he presumed to offer her the slightest insult'.[28] What other women in the settlement thought of her is unknown, but the men were absolutely captivated by her. A.J. Hicky, publisher of the *Bengal Gazette*, had no qualms about dragging the most innocent reputations through the slime, yet she was affectionately alluded to in his paper as 'turban Conquest' and 'Chinsura Belle'.[29]

Concerts were also another decidedly European entertainment. The Europe shops provided harps, horns, bassoons, hautboys, organs, piano-fortes, harpsichords, guitars, violins, cellos, flutes, and also music[30] but many people would bring their instruments and music with them from home. There was a concert in Calcutta every Tuesday night and as with the balls, supper was often a part of the evening's entertainment. As in Madras, the performers, both vocal and instrumental, were women as well as men but they may have been international affairs as well. The author of a poem, 'Lady to a Friend in England', leads one to believe just that, for she writes,

Come, let's away, 'tis Tuesday night,
The CONCERT'S various charms invite;
Where Blacks with Britons swell the notes
And ladies strain their tuneful throats;
Th' auxiliary Dane with these unites,
To raise the soul in rapt'rous flights.[31]

This is the only mention of the inclusion of Indians in musical performances and even if she is correct, there is no indication that any orchestra or band ever attempted to play Indian music. While the Europe shops did not stock Indian instruments, these, of course, could have been obtained from Indians themselves. Nonetheless, what music and how it should be played, and melodic and harmonic tastes were widely divergent. There is no evidence of an individual or group subscription to a concert offering a programme of Indian music, and most Europeans would have found it dissonant, and arhythmical. Nonetheless, why 'Blacks with Britons' would want to 'swell the notes' is not clear either. European music could have been no more pleasing to Indian ears than Indian music to British ones. Yet the advertisement attests again to a society where cultural barriers were bridged fairly often and easily.

The most popular entertainments by far were the balls. These were exclusively British entertainments, but like the occasional concert, they reveal an openness to India that would be lost two or three generations later. Masquerades were as popular in India as they were at home. When given privately they were a means of not only having a good time or disposing of eligible marriage partners but also an occasion on which to display wealth. Men would show up in women's costumes and vice versa, but both sexes would sometimes appear in Indian costumes as well. At a ball given by Mr Creighton, the owner of the Harmonic Tavern in March 1785, there were a lady dressed as Night, a fruit girl, Tancred, a Harlequin, a Darby and Joan, a chimney sweep, a landlady, a witch, a Spaniard, two Hussars, a shepherdess, the Devil, sailors, and various other European costumes. But there were also several ladies in Hindustani dress and also the costumes of a subahdar, and some Persian and Muslim costumes,[32] evidence, albeit small, that worries about 'going native', if they existed, were shallow.

Indians, with or without masks, even if they had been invited, would not have come to a ball to participate in the dancing. Notions about what a dance is and who was to do the dancing were part of that cultural barrier between the two communities. Unlike Indian dancing which is a public performance done by professional dancers and *watched* by an audience, English dances, of course, required partners of both sexes, themselves *doing* the dancing. As James Forbes remarked, 'An Indian of respectability could never consent to his wife or daughter dancing in public, nor can they reconcile the English country-dances to their ideas of female delicacy.'[33]

The Indian dance to which most Europeans were exposed was something called a nautch. Often performed by women who were well-educated, sophisticated, physically beautiful, young, and charming, the nautch was partly a religious activity that included sexual seduction.

> Being always women of considerable personal attractions, which are heightened by all the seductions of dress, jewels, accomplishments and art, they frequently receive large sums in return for the favours they grant.... Nor is this very much to be wondered at, as they comprise among their number, perhaps, some of the loveliest women in the world.[34]

Mrs Kindersley tells us that an Indian would compliment a European by treating him with a nautch to which English wives would also often be invited. But she also notes that the favourite women of the Indian host would never appear themselves on these occasions, 'for they are equally jealous of their concubines as of their wives'.[35] Nor would an Indian man's sense of female propriety permit him to engage in much meaningful conversation with his women guests. In the 1790s and early years of the next century, in Calcutta, British men and women had open invitations to nautches hosted by a wealthy businessman named Sooknay Roy. The reaction was mixed. Of one of his nautches, given in 1792, it was reported that the nautch was pleasant enough because two large punkahs cooled and circulated the air but the only novelty was an attempt to introduce some English tunes in the midst of the Indian music. 'This was not', the account ran, 'attended, as might be supposed, with much success, owing to the indifferent skill of the musicians.'[36]

Closed though much of the Indian world was to them, many British women were also capable of unabashedly enjoying another Indian amusement—the hookah. They could often become as addicted to the former as men as a French traveller observed.

> The rage of smoking extends even to the ladies; and the highest compliment they can pay a man is to give him preference by smoking his hookah. In this case, it is a point of politeness to take off the mouthpiece he is using, and substitute a fresh one, which he presents to the lady with his hookah who soon returns it. The compliment is not always of a trivial importance; it sometimes signifies a great deal to a friend, and often still more to a husband.[37]

In a letter that accompanied some betel, Eliza Draper's sister, Mary, confessed that she had not 'smoaked' since she last saw Eliza.[38] Hookahs were very expensive and often very ornate. They also required the hiring of a *hookahburdar* who, if one wanted to make a decent impression at all, had to be attired in a rich and colorful livery. They were therefore fashionable, indeed almost indispensable in elegant, respectable houses. In 1779, the Governor-General and Mrs Hastings sent cards of invitation to a concert and supper requesting each guest to bring his own hookah and hookahburdar.[39] The hookah was brought to the theatre, to card rooms, and supper parties and ladies even made hookah rugs to present to their friends or relatives as gifts.[40] The hookahburdars would prepare the rich, soft tobacco mingled with fragrant spices, fresh treacle and rose-water in an adjoining apartment and then would enter the room all together after the dessert and present them to their masters and mistresses. Then for about half an hour the group would puff away in perfect silence except for the gurgling of the pipes. The fashionability of the hookah was, however, relatively tenuous. William Hickey, for whom a splendid hookah had been prepared at the home of Daniel Barwell, found it quite disagreeable and wanted to know if he really had to become a smoker. He was told that he would be quite out of fashion if he did not smoke. Nevertheless, he dismissed the hookah and never tasted another one.[41] Its taste which some men and women did find disagreeable, and its expense, more than the presence of English women or anything like an increasing insularity in the Anglo-Indian community seem to have hastened its decline.

As with the nautch, there was a studied curiosity about other Indian amusements—the exhibitions of jugglers, street musicians, yogis, fakirs, snake charmers, and the like. Some women—and men—enjoyed such spectacles while others did not, but in general, their reactions underline the openness of all British society, in home as well as in India, to the novel, the curious, the bizarre, the exotic. India was 'Other', as it always had been, but many British women simply found India and its people and its cultures deeply interesting. Scores of miniatures and paintings show them in Indian dress, lounging about on carpets or couches, smoking hookahs, or watching a nautch, often with an exotic animal in the background. One woman may not have been exaggerating when she claimed that everyone took the trouble to 'learn to ask for what they want in Gentoo phrases'.[42]

Generally, the entertainments engaged in by Anglo-Indians of both sexes were those they would have enjoyed in Europe, and although they did not inaugurate any of them, English women entered into the social, cultural, and artistic activities with all the exuberance, flamboyance, the lack of religious enthusiasm, and the extravagance of the Georgian age. Like the men, their activities were conditioned by the frontier that had newly opened in India. Such 'indianizing' influences as there were upon the Anglo-Indian community were at best largely superficial. Most of these people rarely understood Indian musical forms or dances. They did not, with the notable exception of the Orientalists, make India a subject for their serious scholarly pursuit. They modified European styles in architecture, furnishings, and their own dress, not because of any admiration for Moghul or Hindu styles, but because of the materials available and because of the need to make concessions to the climate. What is significant is the unabashed, unembarrassed curiosity of the women about India, found in the very trite selection of an Indian costume for a masked ball, or the use of the turban as a fashionable headdress.

There is no evidence that any women were worried at all about whether Indians should be educated in English or Hindustani or whether they should be educated at all. They were horrified by sati, child marriage, and infanticide but they had no intention of obliterating them. In short, the burden of empire borne by the Victorians troubled many of their Georgian ancestors not at all. In fact, most of them were not even aware that they had an empire to worry about yet. They knew little of how to prevent the diseases they suffered and died from, and they ate, dressed, and danced to perilous extremes, and were completely baffled by the longevity of the Indians. But they often had more understanding and empathy with the peoples among whom they lived than their grandchildren would. The result was that Calcutta, Madras, and Bombay in the last half of the eighteenth century were gayer, freer, and more ostentatious than they ever had been or would ever be again.

notes

1 Mrs Jemima Kindersley, *Letters from the Island of Teneriffe, Brazil, the Cape of Good Hope and the East Indies* (London: Printed for J. Nourse, 1777), 273–4.

2 Eliza Fay, *Original Letters from India, 1779–1815*, ed., E.M. Forster (London: Hogarth Press, 1986), 172.

3 For a more complete description of these mansions, see R. Pearson, *Eastern Interlude* (Calcutta: Thacker, Spink, & Co., Ltd., 1954), 81 ff.

4 Kindersley, *Letters*, 270.

5 Philip Francis, *The Francis Letters*, ed., Beata Francis and Eliza Keary, 2 vols (London: Hutchinson and Co., 1901), I, 221.

6 Francis, *Letters*, I, 233.

7 Fay, *Letters*, 181.

8 See, for example, *Calcutta Gazette*, 6 May 1784, or almost any advertisement page in that paper.

9 Phebe Gibbes [Sophia Goldborne], *Hartly House* (Calcutta: Thacker, Spink and Co., 1908 [Reprinted from the 1789 edition]), 135.

10 Fay, *Letters*, 189.

11 William Carey, *The Good Old Days of Honorable John Company, Being Curious Reminiscences during the Rule of the East India Company from 1600 to 1858*. 2 vols (Calcutta: R. Cambray & Co., 1906), I, 110.

12 Fay, *Letters*, 189–90.

13 Sir Elijah Impey was Chief Justice and General Sir John Clavering, a member of Council.

14 Francis, *Letters*, I, 256.

15 Ibid., 220.

16 William Hickey, *Memoirs*, ed. Alfred Spencer, 8th ed., 4 vols (New York: Alfred A. Knopf, 1921), II, 137.

17 Jay Barrett Botsford, *English Society in the Eighteenth Century* (New York: The Macmillan Company, 1924), 246.

18 Fay, *Letters*, 189.

19 Hickey, *Memoirs*, II, 196.

20 Carey, *Good Old Days*, I, 42.

21 Henry Busteed, *Echoes of Old Calcutta*, 4th ed. (London: W. Thacker & Co., 1908), 143.

22 Fay, *Letters*, 194.

23 Sydney Grier, ed., *The Letters of Warren Hastings to His Wife* (Edinburgh and London: William Blackwood and Sons, 1905), 227.

24 Busteed, *Echoes*, 213.

25 Cited in ibid., 214.

26 Carey, *Good Old Days*, I, 114.

27 Hickey, *Memoirs*, III, 377.

28 Ibid.

29 See, for example, *Bengal Gazette*, 24–31 March 1781.

30 See, for example, *Calcutta Gazette*, 16 September 1784.

31 *Calcutta Gazette*, 12 August 1784.

32 Ibid., 14 April 1785.

33 James Forbes, *Oriental Memoirs*, 4 vols (London: White, Cochrane and Co., 1813), III, 81.

34 Edward Sellon, *Annotations on the Sacred Writings of the Hindues*, New edition (London: Printed for Private Circulation, 1902), 56.

35 Kindersley, *Letters*, 230.

36 Ibid. Sooknay Roy was not the only Indian to try to ingratiate himself with Calcutta's new rulers. Another wealthy and respected merchant, Sheikh Ghoolan Hossein, also attempted to accommodate English tastes. In 1814, the *Calcutta Gazette* reported that he gave 'a splendid entertainment' that included 'an excellent dinner dressed in the English manner', Indian dishes, and a fireworks display in addition to a nautch. See *Calcutta Gazette*, 29 September 1814.

37 Cited in Carey, *Good Old Days*, I, 100

38 Arnold Wright and William L. Sclater, *Sterne's Eliza* (London: William Heinemann, 1922), 23.

39 Busteed, *Echoes*, 142.

40 Carey, *Good Old Days*, I, 100.

41 Hickey, *Memoirs*, II, 136.

42 Gibbes, *Hartly House*, 57.

10

passages to india

IT IS PERHAPS UNNECESSARY TO POINT OUT that the manner in which one reacts to a new, or even a familiar environment, depends less upon that physical environment than upon one's own individual emotional and intellectual circumstances. The happily married wife of a judge is likely to react quite differently to the Taj Mahal, or to a crowded bazaar in Bengal, for instance, than a newly divorced woman who has just survived captivity upon her arrival in India. The women discussed in this chapter were shaped by very different circumstances but, in addition to their gender and nationality, they shared another characteristic; often unwittingly, they approached India with the same kind of curiosity with which the men of the Asiatic Society did.

In his discussion of the eighteenth-century Orientalists, Amal Chatterjee identifies two schools of thought regarding India's Sanskritic past, the 'primitive' and the 'degenerate'. The 'primitive' school which would find its most aggressive proponents in Charles Grant, John Shore, and, later, James Mill, argued that Hinduism was and always had been immoral, absurd, pernicious, and barbaric, and they blamed India's stagnation on the oppressive heat which bred disease, induced lethargy, and retarded progress.

The 'degenerate' school to which William Jones and most of the early Orientalists subscribed argued that at some time in its ancient past, Hinduism had been more moral, even 'glorious' but that there had been degeneration caused largely by an excess of Brahminical influence.[1] In that view, there was an ancient body of Hindu learning for which they had sympathy and even admiration, and a less ancient body of Muslim learning for which they had less sympathy.

There were people in India, however, both Indian and European, who did not necessarily view India through the prism of a Sanskritic past, or really much of any past and who, unlike the Orientalists, seemed unaware that anything had degenerated or needed to be reformed. Besides the 'primitive' and 'degenerate' elements in eighteenth-century Orientalism, there was a third, far more personal dimension that, for want of a better term, might be called 'indifferentism' and it is into this category that the perspective of someone like William Hickey, for instance, falls. It is also the category into which the women discussed below fall.

The education of women in the eighteenth and nineteenth centuries often included learning to sketch and draw. Women were not considered 'artists' in the sense of a J.M.W. Turner perhaps or a Joshua Reynolds, but the quality, charm, precision, sensitivity, and real skill of their work have been vastly underappreciated. Two women, Elizabeth Gwillam and Mary Impey, inaugurated a body of visual representations of India by women that would continue to grow until 1947. While both women left substantial bodies of work detailing Indian animals, birds, flowers, and landscapes, neither did portraits of Indian people. That would wait until the next generation.

While her husband served as a justice on Madras' Supreme Court, Lady Elizabeth, the daughter of an architect, did scores of paintings of Indian birds as well as plants and other animals.[2] One of the more impressive artists of either sex to ever portray India, however, was Lady Mary Impey, the wife of Calcutta's first Chief Justice, Sir Elijah Impey. After the damp cold of her native Yorkshire, India apparently thrilled Mary. Upon his arrival in Calcutta, Sir Elijah immediately set out to learn Persian and Bengali in order to understand the people that he was about to help govern. But Mary was not to be left out of India. While her husband became involved in the legal and political turmoil surrounding his friend, Warren Hastings, Mary picked up her brushes and paints and explored the forests, rivers, mountains, and villages of Bengal. Brightly coloured parakeets, cuckoos, spotted pigeons, animals of all sorts, flowers, trees, bright moths and butterflies, and lavish landscapes splashed onto her canvases in exquisite detail. Her vast collection, now housed with the Linnean Society, became the cornerstone of British knowledge of Indian natural history.

Had that been all, Mary Impey's legacy would be impressive, but she did not stop there. She developed an affection for Indian miniaturism and employed three major Indian artists, the Hindus Ram Das and Bhawani Das and the Muslim Sheikh Zain al-Din, to draw India's flora and fauna. While the genre had been fairly common in the Middle Ages and Elizabethan period, miniaturism was not then at all fashionable either at home or in Calcutta where the rage was for larger scale works. Lady Impey's appreciation for the extraordinary skill, delicacy, and refinement of Indian miniatures must have made her cringe at the clunky stuff that was being churned out to be hung on the walls of newly rich nabobs clamouring for portraits of themselves and their 'ancestors'.

For Indian miniaturism, Lady Impey could have found parallels in European art, but for Indian music there was no such comparable tradition. Of all the arts, music might have been the one Europeans would have had the most difficulty appreciating. The Indian instruments, modes, and genres all were vastly different from anything in the Western legacy. Nonetheless, for Elizabeth Plowden, India was music. And Lucknow. Sophisticated, debauched, and glittering, Lucknow, the capital of the large, rich, and strategically vital province of Oudh, was a very different world from Calcutta. It was a city of squalor and perfumed orange groves, of hucksters and fortune-seekers, and people so poor they must have envied the rich diets the nawab, Asaf ad-Daula, ordered for his horses.

Elizabeth was the middle-class wife of Richard Chichely Plowden, assigned to Asaf ad-Daula's bodyguard. In Lucknow, she moved in a world she could only have imagined had she remained in England. She nibbled on pistachoes, pomegranates, and dates while watching elephant fights. She attended a cock fight hosted by Colonel Mordaunt that became immortalized in a canvas painted by one of the most prominent European painters in India, Johann Zoffany.[3] Evenings would be spent at lush banquets with friends or with the nawab, or perhaps at home with a nautch after dinner.[4] Her close friends were the crème de la crème of Lucknow society.[5] One of the closest was the nawab who had ascended the vacated throne following the defeat of his father, Shuja ad-Daula, by the Company's forces at Buxar in 1764.[6] Fat, dissolute, and incompetent, Asaf not only lacked the political and military qualities of his father, he did not want them. Having been forced to cede a good bit of territory and about half his revenue to the Company, he was content to leave political matters to a favourite, Murtaza Khan, while he incurred heavy debts, including the £3,000 that he owed Elizabeth's husband. He adored the arts, however, and turned Lucknow into an artistic centre that surpassed Calcutta. He liked Elizabeth Plowden, and not only bestowed toys on her seven children but also granted her a *sanad* making her a *begum*, that is, a noble woman.[7]

How much musical training Elizabeth had had before coming to India is uncertain. Handel and Bach had died but their music as well as that of Mozart and Haydn, her contemporaries, had been in the air around her in England. Sir William Jones was doing major analyses of Indian musical forms but whether Mrs Plowden was either aware of that work or even interested in it is almost irrelevant. She apparently simply liked Indian music for its own sake. Happily, her dissipated friend, Asaf ad-Daula, shared her passion. By the time she left India in 1789, she had acquired a substantial collection of copies of music.[8]

Before Plassey, only two women—Katherine Nicks and Jane Smart—had left anything in writing. The letters of both women deal exclusively with personal experiences; Mrs Nicks' details her business transactions and Mrs Smart's, her visit to a *zenana*. Neither letter was meant for an audience beyond their own families. Beginning with the publication in 1777 of Jemima Kindersley's *Letters*, however, many women would clearly be writing for a public audience rather than an exclusively private one and, although the writing is in the form of letters and the style is deeply personal, even, in some cases, intimate, the scope of interest in India is much wider than that of either Mrs Nicks or Mrs Smart.

Jemima Kindersley, nee Wicksted, known to her friends as 'Pulcherima', was the wife of a Bengal Artillery officer, Lieutenant Nathaniel Kindersley. She sailed to India with their two children to join her husband via Brazil and the Cape of Good Hope arriving in 1765, about the time the Company stood forth as *diwan* but before any administrative reforms had altered the government of India. She was there for four years, largely in Calcutta and Allahabad, departing before Warren Hastings and William Jones had begun the work of resurrecting India's past. Articulate and well-educated, she used her *Letters* to give an account of India's history, its current situation, and the structure of the Company's government. Echoing Montesquieu whose *Spirit of the Laws* had been published about a generation earlier,[9] she traced many of India's 'ills' to the climate.

> ... even immediate self-preservation scarcely rouses them from it ... their aversion to action is so extreme, that when themselves or children are in danger of being crushed by horses or carriages, they will neither move themselves, or put out a hand to draw their infants nearer to them till the moment they are forced to it; and then do not withdraw an inch farther than they are obliged.... Ease with them is the greatest good; and nothing surprizes [*sic*] the Indians so much as to see Europeans take pleasure in exercise; they are astonished to see people walking who might sit still.[10]

Like many of her own and later generations, she found the Indians 'indolent', an attribute noticed by few, if any, travelers before the eighteenth century, and one that said less about India than about the onset of the Industrial Revolution in Britain with its emphasis on industry, hard work, and productivity. The length of time it took for tailors, embroiderers and other craftsmen to finish a job thoroughly annoyed her. 'This extreme slowness', she thought, 'is the cause of all the works being excessively expensive; ... the length of time they are about every piece of work, makes it costly at the end.'[11]

Although she was in Calcutta almost two decades before the founding of the Asiatic Society, she anticipated those later scholars in decrying the decadence of learning among both Hindus and Muslims, criticizing the Brahmins for keeping the masses of people in a state of ignorance. Nonetheless, 'the great virtue of the Hindoos is their extensive charity: the Brahmins inculcate, with the utmost zeal, the necessity of building and endowing pagodas (where themselves are maintained in ease and plenty), feeding the hungry, relieving the poor, and providing against the distresses of their fellow-creatures, whether of their own religion or strangers'.[12]

Again, in the spirit of the Enlightenment, she was ready to go beyond cultural differences to the motivations common to all human beings. Of Hindu polytheism, she wrote,

> It is no wonder that being taught to revere and preserve a cow on account of its utility, or to admire an elephant for its sagacity and strength; and the river Ganges, as causing the fertility, and facilitating the commerce of their country; and these opinions delivered to them in the lofty and figurative style of the East; it is no wonder, I say, that they should rank the two first in the number of their demy gods, and believe that the other is able to cure diseases, and wash away sin.[13]

She reminded her readers that certain medieval church customs, notably celibacy, long outlived the ends for which they had originally been established. And, echoing the 'degenerate' school of Orientalists, she found it not at all surprising 'that the ancient customs of the Hindoos should yet be observed, although the use of them is either lost, or not understood'.[14]

Eliza Fay's entrance into India, fifteen years after Mrs Kindersley's, was far more turbulent and, with four separate voyages, the first in 1779 and the last in 1816, more prolonged. Like Mrs Kindersley, Mrs Fay is alert, sensitive, witty, and reasonably pious but not religious. There, however, the similarities end. Although both women use the device of letters, Mrs Fay's writing is fundamentally autobiographical and more intensely personal. She writes not of India but of herself *in* India. Not surprisingly, given the greater tumult in her personal life, her style lacks the calm, detached polish of the earlier visitor. Mrs Kindersely was consciously writing for a wider public; it did not occur to Mrs Fay to think of publication until May 1816 when she was heavily in debt and needed funds to pay her creditors.

Possibly the daughter of a sailor, she was nonetheless fairly well read. She knew French and Italian, learned Portuguese and some Hindustani in India, and was able to cite, among others, Petrarch, Pope, Richardson and Samuel Butler. She was passionate, and now and then, she could be delightfully sarcastic, albeit never mean. One evening after a harpsichord recital in which Lady Chambers had played a sonata by Nicolai on the harpsichord, someone asked Mrs Fay if she did not think the 'jig' played by Lady Chambers was not the prettiest thing she had ever heard. 'He meant the rondo,' she wryly observed, 'but I dare say "Over the water to Charley" would have pleased him equally well.'[15] Far more than Mrs Kindersley, it is easy to read Eliza Fay's moods, to not only see her world but almost to feel it as she does.

There is another major difference between the two women. While Mrs Kindersley says very much about India's past but very little of the really dramatic political and military events around her, Mrs Fay does exactly the opposite. She says absolutely nothing of India's past history, very little of Hinduism, nothing of India's music or architecture, art or literature, and is seemingly unaware of even the existence of the Asiatic Society, let alone any of its activities. Anticipating a number of later women, she is very aware of what is going on immediately around her. She comments on the Hastings–Francis duel[16] but political affairs interest her because she not only knows the people involved, their fortunes are often intimately linked with her own. Similarly, she is very interested in affairs in the Carnatic because of her hatred of Haider Ali. She mentions the defeat of Colonel William Baillie at the hands of Haider Ali at Polilur near Madras in September 1780, and understandably, she hopes that 'that fine old veteran Sir Eyre Coote ... will strike those undisciplined hordes with terror'.[17]

She was also the first woman to use India as a mirror through which to look critically at the behaviour of her countrymen. Like Mrs Kindersley, she never witnessed a sati but whereas Mrs Kindersley hoped that the British would 'prevent those Nabobs we are in alliance with' from permitting sati,[18] Mrs Fay's view of the custom, coloured very much by her own sufferings in the separation and divorce from Anthony Fay, allowed her not only to find an analogy in European cultures, but to articulate a critique on the condition of women in her own country.

> I cannot avoid smiling when I hear gentlemen bring forward the con-
> duct of the Hindoo women, as a test of superior character, since I am
> well aware that so much are we the slaves of habit *every where* that were
> it necessary for a woman's reputation to burn herself in England, many
> a one who has accepted a husband merely for the sake of an establish-
> ment, who has lived with him without affection, perhaps thwarted his
> views, dissipated his fortune and rendered his life uncomfortable to its
> close, would yet mount the funeral pile with all imaginable decency and
> die with heroic fortitude. The most spacious sacrifices are not always

the greatest, she who wages war with a naturally petulant temper, who practices a rigid self-denial, endures without complaining the unkindness, infidelity, extravagance, meanness or scorn of the man to whom she has given a tender and confiding heart, and for whose happiness and well-being in life all the powers of her mind are engaged;—is ten times more of a heroine than the slave of bigotry and superstition; who affects to scorn the life demanded of her by the laws of her country or at least the country's customs and many such we have in England.[19]

Except for their servants, the contacts with Indians available to English women remained few and not intimate. Whatever business associations they had touched neither the Company's interests nor those of Indians, and contact with Indian men was likely to be disappointing. Contact with Indian women was likely to be no different from what Jane Smart, Frances Benyon, and Frances Steele had experienced earlier. The zenana was puzzling. Jemima Kindersley entered one and her reaction, unlike that of Jane Smart, was pity.

As the Mahommedan principles do not allow women any share in religion, so of course they have no public state in government, or any other, except the influence of a beautiful face over an ignorant and voluptuous prince.

These poor women, not only are never seen, but, if possible, they are never named out of the Zanannah; a Mahommedan never speaks of his wives and it is thought a very great affront and indelicacy to enquire after them.

The Indian women have often children at twelve years of age; and by the time they are turned of twenty are thought old women and are really so in point of beauty; for after fifteen their complexions grow every year darker; the climate, as it hastens their maturity, likewise hastens their decline.[20]

And Mrs Fay, who did not enter a zenana, came close to expressing the same sentiments when she wrote of Indian women,

Their whole time is taken up in decorating their persons: the hair—eye-lids—eye-brows—teeth—hands and nails: all undergo certain processes to render them more completely fascinating; nor can one seriously blame their having recourse to these, or like artifices—the motive being to secure the affections of a husband, or to counteract the plans of a rival.[21]

Oddly, Mrs Fay who owned a millinery shop saw no similarity between wearing wigs and chewing betel to enhance one's person in the pursuit of a husband, nor did Jemima Kindersley see the similarity in the Indian woman's bar to a 'public state in government' and her own. Both women here indicated a tendency that had been foreshadowed from the moment Frances Steele entered the zenana of Jehangir's sister-in-law—that is, English women and Indian women rarely came even close to intimacy, and the zenana was as much to blame for that as the mentality of the British women themselves.

As in the earlier factories, their servants were the most sustained contact many British women had ever been able to have with Indians and practically no one of either sex was exempt from utter frustration with them, nor from downright hatred of the *banians*. British impatience with either or both groups was rarely, however, transferred to Indians as an entire race. If other Indians were disliked or found contemptible, it was because of an actual experience. There were, after all, things in India that were considered distasteful, barbaric, and really painful to put up with and Eliza Fay illustrates that. She hated Haider Ali most cordially for the very sound reason that she had been his captive, but she hardly held him or all other Indians in contempt or found them all 'tigers'. Nor did she seem to pity or hate anything in Indian cultures that produced the likes of Haider Ali or view all Indians as physically, intellectually, or morally inferior because of her captivity. In other words, her hatred was just that—healthy, normal, cold hatred. At one point, utterly exasperated by banians, she blurted out, 'You may likewise perceive that human nature has its faults and follies everywhere, and that black rogues are to the full as common as white ones, but in my opinion more impudent.'[22] Yet she spoke gently of her own banian, Dattaram Chuckerbutty,[23] and wished 'these people would not vex one by their tricks; for there is something in the mild countenance and gentle manners of the Hindoos that interests me exceedingly'.[24]

The intellectual openness of women like Eliza Fay and Jemima Kindersley to Hinduism and Mary Impey's delight in Indian art or Elizabeth Plowden's affection for Indian music may not have been unusual. What was unusual was a novel that came from the hand of a woman who never went to India at all but who was able to capture the spirit of toleration and sympathy that characterized many of her contemporaries who did go there. The only son of Phebe Gibbes died in Calcutta and it is most probably upon his letters that she relied for her novel, *Hartly House, Calcutta*. Like Fay and Kindersley, she used the device of letters as her medium. Unlike Kindersley and Fay, however, Gibbes was the first woman to consciously, deliberately, and purposefully write not only for a public audience but for the specific objective of influencing that audience. In her 1804 petition to the Royal Literary Fund, she claimed that the novel was written as a celebration of the subcontinent and she intended to use a work of literature to counter prejudice against India and to discuss the position of women in colonial society.[25] Most importantly, she showed that women were able and willing to take a hand in shaping opinion about England's role in India.

Written as a series of letters to her friend, Arabella, in England, the author, 'Sophia Goldborne' leads the reader into a world seen through eyes that are completely charmed by India. When she is perhaps in her early twenties, Sophia enters India with her newly widowed father, an East India Company official who had returned to England following the death of his wife and decided to bring his daughter with him back to India. She and her father then reside in the luxurious mansion of a Mr and Mrs Hartly whence she enters the whirl of Calcutta society. She is soon courted by a Mr Edward Doyly whose person is 'so pastoral, and his sensibility so oriental'[26] but whose poverty renders him ineligible as a husband. It is India itself, however, that immediately and completely charms Sophia. 'The grave of thousands!' she exclaims, 'Doubtless, my good girl, in the successive years of European visitation, the eastern world is, as you pronounce it, the grave of thousands; but is it not also a mine of exhaustless wealth! the centre of unimaginable magnificence! an ever-blooming, an ever-brilliant scene?'[27]

Although well aware of a number of the darker aspects of Hinduism, she nonetheless finds Hindus to be 'the most tranquil and temperate people on earth' and concludes that it is the 'doctrine of the metampsychosis' which has 'so effectually restrained the sons and daughters of this Eastern world from committing the wantonest acts of cruelty towards the brute creation'. Compared with 'the arrogance and ferocity daily manifested by the several nations around them, their hearts are softened into a tender concern for the kind treatment of every creature living'. Even sati, 'if properly directed', she finds, is an 'honour to the female world'. 'We laugh at the Gentoos', she says, 'and their plurality of gods—but truly ridiculous our wisdom must appear, which, instead of being exerted in the cause of happiness, its whole end and aim is to teach us to be miserable with a good grace, and undo the benevolent work of Providence with our own prophane [*sic*] hands.'[28]

In that her roseate view is rather one-dimensional, it could lead to just as many misunderstandings as the equally one-dimensional view of all Hindus as 'depraved'. What keeps Sophia's enthusiasm for Hinduism from being offensive, however, is that it springs from her affection for a young man she refers to as 'my Brahmin' whom she meets at Hartly House and it is this man who, apart from Sophia herself, is the real hero of her story. Following Doyly's departure for England 'with some important dispatches', the Brahmin's onslaught upon Sophia proceeds apace and is not rejected, although always on a high spiritual and moral plane, since both have committed themselves to celibacy. One day, in the presence of Mrs Hartly, he says of himself that, although born a Brahmin, 'he submits to, as the will of Heaven—and that you are the loveliest of women, he acknowledges with pious resignation'. Sophia is astonished 'and the Bramin retired, with more emotion than quite accorded with his corrected temper, as if he felt he had said too much'.[29] His death leaves Sophia telling Arabella 'that I doubt not but I shall meet him, where parting is an evil no longer to be apprehended; and sin and sorrow have no place'.[30] His death is followed shortly thereafter by the reappearance in Calcutta of Doyly whose fortunes, conveniently improved by the timely death of a disreputable uncle, allow him to ask for Sophia's hand in marriage. And she accepts.

As A.L. Basham points out, for a respectable English girl to even think of rousing sexual feelings in a 'native' would be considered so immoral in the days of Kipling and even E.M. Forster that she would not have dared confess it to herself let alone put it on paper.[31] When the first edition of *Hartly House* appeared in 1789, however, the possibility of deep affection, with or without sexual activity, was neither inconceivable nor derided. Significantly, what *Hartly House* indirectly intimates is that the ladies who had landed at Bombay in the previous century very possibly had entered into liaisons with

Indian men not entirely unlike Sophia's with her Brahmin. Given the differences in both social class and education between Sophia and the earlier women, however, those liaisons may not have been simply platonic friendships.

Hartly House as well as Eliza Fay's *Letters* and Elizabeth Plowden's collection of Indian music also suggest that, for some women, India was more than a matter of simple intellectual curiosity. It was specific, personal, and could become intensely emotional. At least two British women were recruited to join an Oudhi harem. In the early 1830s, Fanny Parkes saw a mosque in honour of one of them, a Miss Walters, at Lucknow where she also encountered one of the 'Angrezi begums'.[32] The fabulous Begum Johnson who had been born in India of English parents in 1725 at Fort St David near Pondicherry had four English husbands in India and died at Calcutta in 1812. But she enjoyed the intimate friendship of the widow of Ali Verdi Khan, Siraj ud-Daula's grandmother, and spent only about nine years in England in her whole life and showed very little desire to return there in her declining years.[33]

Women like these, vigorous in body and in mind, were far from worrying about the effect of their behaviour upon 'the natives' or doing good, or improving them or anyone else. And had they been able to affect the policy-makers, they would hardly have been inclined to close Indians or Indian cultures from their areas of interest. Ketaki Kushari Dyson speaks of the practical, pioneering outlook of these women and, in a single phrase, distinguishes them from their descendants. They accepted the difficulties of living in a foreign country, she says, 'with a greater measure of common sense than many of the women writing at a later period'.[34]

notes

1 Amal Chatterjee, *Representations of India, 1740–1840: The Creation of India in the Colonial Imagination* (New York: St. Martin's Press, Inc., 1998), 88.

2 Sir Henry Gwillam's service was from 1801 until 1809 when he was recalled as a result of disputes with the Madras government. By then, Elizabeth herself had died in 1807. Her collection is now at the Blacker-Wood Library, McGill University, Montreal.

3 The canvas, entitled *Colonel Mordaunt's Cock Match*, was commissioned by Warren Hastings.

4 Maya Jasanoff, *Edge of Empire: Lives, Culture, and Conquest in the East, 1750–1850* (New York: Alfred A. Knopf, 2005), 61.

5 Among them was Claude Martin, who, by 1800, would have acquired a fortune worth £400,000, making him possibly the richest European in India and richer than many princes in India or anywhere else for that matter.

6 It was the presumed spoliation of the wealth of his mother and grandmother, the 'begums of Oudh', that would be one of the chief charges against Warren Hastings.

7 Jasanoff, *Edge*, 61. A *sanad* is an official government diploma or deed granting a privilege, an office, or a right.

8 Ibid., 61.

9 In 1748.

10 Mrs Jemima Kindersley, *Letters from the Island of Teneriffe, Brazil, the Cape of Good Hope and the East Indies* (London: Printed for J. Nourse, 1777), 180–2.

11 Ibid., 240.

12 Ibid., 119.

13 Ibid., 136–7.

14 Ibid.

15 Eliza Fay, *Original Letters from India, 1779–1815*, ed., E.M. Forster (London: Hogarth Press, 1986), 192.

16 Ibid., 185.

17 Ibid., 186. Baillie's defeat at Polilur was catastrophic. Sixty of the eighty-six officers were killed along with about 2,000 European and Indian troops. About a thousand more were taken prisoner. To add humiliation to the defeat was that a magnificent mural commemorating the battle decorated the walls of the palace at Hyderabad. Mrs Fay's hope, however, that Coote would reverse the loss was fulfilled but the gains made against Mysore would remain modest until the fall of Tipu Sultan at Seringapatam in 1799.

18 Kindersley, *Letters*, 180.

19 Fay, *Letters*, 203.

20 Ibid., 226–7.

21 Ibid., 207.

22 Ibid., 162.

23 Ibid., 207.

24 Ibid., 163.

25 Michael J. Franklin, 'Radically Feminizing India. Phebe Gibbes's *Hartly House, Calcutta* (1789) and Sydney Owenson's "The Missionary: An Indian Tale (1811)"', in Michael Franklin, ed., *Romantic Representations of British India* (London and New York: Routledge, 2006), 154.

26 Gibbes, *Hartly House*, 159.

27 Gibbes, *Hartly House*, 1.

28 Ibid., 240.

29 Ibid., 185.

30 Ibid., 237.

31 A.L. Basham, 'Sophia and the "Bramin"' in *East India Company Studies. Papers Presented to Professor Sir Cyril Philips*, eds, Kenneth Ballhatchet and John Harrison (Hong Kong: Asian Research Service, 1986), 16.

32 Fanny (Parlby) Parkes, *Wanderings of a Pilgrim in Search of the Picturesque, during Four and Twenty Years in the East*, 2 vols (London: P. Richardson, 1850), I, 417–18.

33 William H. Carey, *The Good Old Days of Honorable John Company: Being Curious Reminiscences during the Rule of the East India Company from 1600 to 1858*, 2 vols (Calcutta: R. Cambray & Co., 1906), II, 220.

34 Ketaki Kushari Dyson, *A Various Universe: A Study of the Journals and Memoirs of British Men and Women in the Indian Subcontinent, 1765–1856* (Delhi: Oxford University Press, 1978), 132–3.

11

the merchant princes in retreat

FROM THE TIME IT HAD ENCOUNTERED the enterprising Mrs Hudson, there had not been a time when women were not actively invested in the Company's fortunes. Most often, they had managed the income or the pension of a male relative, but they had also been shareholders in their own right. In 1783, 16.2 per cent of the shareholder accounts in East India Company stock belonged to women and that amounted to 12.5 per cent of all India stock, with an average holding of £911 per woman. Moreover, some women were buying shares for themselves, either directly on Exchange Alley or by using brokers as intermediaries.[1]

They were also capable agents for male investors. Mary Barwell, born in 1733, was the oldest of the ten children of William Barwell. Her brother, Richard, born in 1741, was appointed to the four-man Calcutta Council created by the Regulating Act in 1774. While gaining fame with his bread pelleting prowess, he found that he also needed an agent in London to represent his interests, and named Mary. To advance their fortunes, he sent Mary money, bills of exchange, and jewels, but also supplied her with information on which she could trade India stock.[2] By the time he returned to

England in 1780, Mary had garnered a fortune large enough to enable Richard to buy a seat in Parliament.

Acquiring an independent fortune of her own in India, however, was another matter. While a woman would not normally have come to India for specifically commercial reasons[3] and if marriage proved to be a disappointment, there were a number of opportunities by which a woman could support herself. Taverns and punch houses continued to provide women with opportunities for employment either as partners with their husbands or as proprietors in their own right, but in the eighteenth century, two other enterprises also opened, the millinery business and operating boarding schools either alone or with a male companion—normally, a husband.

Women had been operating taverns since the late seventeenth century and often with some success. In 1796, twenty-three people were granted licenses for taverns and punch houses in Madras. Of these, two were women.[4] In Calcutta, the most important tavern was the Harmonic, operated by a Mr Creighton, but there were smaller ones managed by women. Hannah Hall, the wife of a man who had 'a legal calling' in the sheriff's office, ran one of these. Interestingly, it was unlicensed but what brought her to the attention of the authorities in 1798 was that, in the dodgy tradition of Katherine Nicks and the Weltden women, she was also 'crimping' seamen who frequented the place. Because the Halls had a large family, they were allowed to remain in India on condition that they would 'not again be guilty of fraudulent practices'.[5]

After Plassey, another kind of enterprise for women appeared in the form of millinery shops. It was not, however, so much a military triumph nor any kind of administrative reform that opened up that kind of business venture so much as the eighteenth century itself. The three and a half centuries of Britain's connection with India unfortunately coincide with the most grotesque fashions in the entire sartorial history of western Europe and, of these, the eighteenth century easily saw the most bizarre. Over great, clumsy hoops made of cane, whale-bone, or osier were mounds of petticoats of varying materials—damask, velvet, heavy silk, chintz, and even ermine. Since women wore no underwear except a chemise, there was some relief from India's heat at least when a comforting breeze could be found. A woman's dress also required gloves, muffs, scarves, and jewellery.

Fans, often of delicate material such as gauze or painted silk, were also required for flirting, mourning, playing cards, drinking, chaise rides, and simply walking into church.

The eighteenth century has been called the 'age' of many things — the age of enlightenment, the age of aristocracy, the Baroque age, and one author calls it the 'Grand Century of the Lady'.[6] It might also be called the grand age of hats. Great wigs bearing flowers, feathers, gauzes, laces, and ribbons were topped by even more ponderous hats. The matter of getting into and out of a carriage or for that matter, any enclosure, without catapulting the monuments that a woman piled upon her head required a strategy perhaps as elaborate as that of any military operation. One might recall the famous picture of Georgiana Spencer, Duchess of Devonshire, with a four-foot long feather atop an enormous hat. In addition to fashion, given the importance of protecting one's complexion in order to make a good 'catch' in India, hats were worn whatever the weather.

India's climate was often blamed for the yellowing of women's complexions but the cosmetics that were applied to whatever parts of the body not covered by cloth were far more pernicious. Since they were often lead- or mercury-based, they could cause skin eruptions, gastric disorders, severe eye irritations, and the teeth and hair might fall out, and in some extreme cases, even death might result. The skin was doused in white paint, rouge, lip-salve, or the beauty patches imported from Louis XIV's court that were still fashionable. The cheaper version of the white paint base was made from whitening, flour, ground rice, and tallow soap. The more expensive variety was made of white lead, rice, and flour. Rouge was made from red lead mixed with vermillion or carmine.[7]

The managing of a millinery shop seemed to offer an obvious opportunity for a woman to either enhance her husband's income or to become financially independent. The millinery shops would specialize in all the accoutrements of a woman's dress—ribbons, gauzes, artificial flowers for the hair, jewellery, and dresses, and often the requisite cosmetics. The millinery business, however, was not lucrative. Besides competition from other milliners—and there were quite a number of them—they also faced extremely heavy competition from auction houses, or Europe shops. The millinery shops may have offered the advantages that a specialty shop does now—that is, they were smaller, goods could be made up to the customer's precise specifications, and prices on some articles may have been just a trifle lower, but the goods they had to offer were obtained from the same 'investments' as those purchased for sale in the Europe shops. The Europe shops had to be turned to for curling and pinching irons for the hair, more expensive jewellery and perfumes, powders, almond pastes for the hands, Hungary and Arquebusade water for the skin, and for tooth powders and tinctures. And they offered more besides— stationery, plate, cutlery, China, Wedgwood and Staffordshire ware, scales, weights, looking glasses, trunks, hosiery, carpets and mats, boots, every variety of furniture one could afford, and saddles and other tack. They also had glassware, blankets, musical instruments, bookcases and books, commodes, cabinets, liquor, hardware, uphol-stered goods, garden seeds, and an infinite variety of food.

Besides the competition from the Europe shops, a woman would also face some difficulty in obtaining the capital to invest in a shop. Loans from friends or relatives may have been a source. It would seem that Creighton, the owner of the Harmonic Tavern, supported his wife's venture in the millinery business, and an R.A. Balmanno, also a merchant in a wide variety of goods ranging from alcoholic beverages to pianos and violins, too probably supported his wife's millinery venture. The banians were about the only alternative source of aid a woman could turn to and most Anglo-Indians, men as well as women, hated to deal with them. Not only were they notori-ously unscrupulous but the 12 per cent rate of interest they charged must have seemed an awesome burden to take on for a business that was risky to begin with. In addition, a woman would require the assistance of a dressmaker and somehow her salary would have to be paid.

The greatest expense, however, would be the purchase of goods from a ship's investment. During a six-month voyage, a ship could be wrecked or have its entire cargo impounded either by pirates or by foreign, especially French, capture, and the Indiamen captains would have to raise the prices to balance the financial and personal risks they took on a voyage. Eliza Fay tells us the reason for the failure of her last venture in the millinery business and, in so doing, gives an insight into the perils other women in the same business must have faced. The ship itself had been detained so long for 'various causes' that her goods had come to what she calls a 'very bad market' and she was forced to sell some at retail, the rest at auction.[8] Still, despite the competition and the overhead, some millinery shops achieved an amazing longevity. Around the turn of the century, at least three shops in Calcutta had been in business for more than three years and Mrs Creighton remained in business for the astonishing length of twelve years, from 1791 to 1803.

In the early years of the nineteenth century, the advertisements for millinery shops dwindle and then almost entirely evaporate from the pages of the *Calcutta Gazette*. A rather typical case is a Mrs Mountain, who was married to a Calcutta merchant and left a widow in 1810. She had been running a millinery shop since 1803, but she found that the combined income from both her own and her husband's enterprises was rather meager. She was, therefore, forced to advertise that she had no means of procuring any stock whereby to continue her husband's business and, 'she humbly submits being employed by the Ladies in making up Dresses, &c. of their own Materials; until enabled to purchase an Investment by the unremitting attention she proposes paying to any orders she may be favoured with'.[9]

Other than the competition from Europe shops, there are two other possible reasons for the disappearance of the shops. First, although British women in India tended to be interested in copying fashions from home, the climate simply would not bear much of the frippery. Describing a ball at Madras in 1774, Alexander Mackrabie thought that 'if splendour accompanied Heat, a Ball in India ought to be uncommonly splendid. The appearance of the ladies even before Country Dances was rather ardent than luminous, when the Minuets are ended they go home with their Partners to undress, and after a little Refreshment [they] return again in the purest Innocence of Muslin and Simplicity of a Nightgown'.[10] There was one battle that India rarely lost—her climate trumped the demands of fashion, and while a woman may have tried to cope with the feathers, hoops, petticoats, rouges, and patches in public, in private, looser and lighter garments prevailed.

Secondly, the republican ideals of the age affected fashion after the French and American Revolutions, and women's clothing became more revealing and looser than it had been before. Colossal hats and wigs simply became passé. The eighteenth century of the hat gave way to the simpler nineteenth century of the bonnet. Dress also became simpler. An imitation of Greek drapery and line became apparent as early as 1793 in a gown falling straight from the waist-line to the ankles which were left uncovered. The waistline moved upward to just under the bosom and was girded by a ribbon or band. Hoops, stays, and the entire whalebone framework beneath went out for a brief decade or two leaving only one thin petticoat under the gown, allowing a woman more freedom of movement and no doubt more untrammelled breathing and better health than they had hitherto enjoyed or would have again following the Restoration. Sleeves were shortened to a little puff or cap on the shoulders, and the neckline was low and wide. Little underwear was worn and this was now washed frequently, a novelty introduced to Britain by the Empress Josephine of France. Materials were light and, for the most part, readily available in India—muslin, linen, poplin, cotton, and tulle. Corsets did come back into fashion after 1810, but they had little whalebone until 1821 when the fully boned corset appeared.[11]

The boarding schools met a need that was more universal than the millinery shops, and India itself provided an advantage of sorts. At any time, the dangers of the voyage home were enough to make the sturdiest adult tremble at the thought of a return, and the Napoleonic Wars made the voyage home downright suicidal. Many children were raised well outside the settlements under the care of a governess if one could be found but European governesses were expensive. Their passage from Britain had to be paid and there was always the possibility of their leaving the family in order to get mar-ried once they got to India.

In the early part of the century, Lady Mary Montague had lodged the first serious complaints against the prevailing system of educa-tion—or rather the lack of one—which kept women subordinate. Lady Mary then endured some social ostracism for merely giving proofs of her own intellectual prowess. By the middle of the century, however, the 'blue-stockings' had asserted the right of women to acquire as much knowledge as they pleased and to display it. Women of intellect and wit such as Sarah Jennings and Lady Suffolk, the confidante of Pope, Swift, Gay, Arbuthnot, and others, and Fanny Burney, Mrs Siddons, the actress, Georgiana Spencer, and, at the end of the century, Mary Wollstonecraft, by their very abilities argued for the right to a liberal education for all women.

Whatever thin prejudice remained against educating women was offset by the high mortality among both sexes, and the likelihood of a husband dying coupled with the difficulty of returning to Europe made preparation for a useful trade important. Like the taverns and millinery shops, boarding schools afforded an opportunity for a woman to support herself often in what must have been desperate financial circumstances. When Stackhouse Tolfrey died, his widow and three small children were left totally unprovided for and she was forced to keep a school, 'and that in a neighborhood where she had lived in the utmost splendour'.[12]

The boarding schools offered not only the same educational advantages as a governess but they also provided an opportunity for children to remain near their parents—an advantage the steamship would take from many Victorian children. Unlike the competition millinery shop owners faced, and despite the stigma that the Tolfrey advertisement might suggest, women in the boarding schools business had an area of enterprise uniquely their own, for while men also opened schools and taught a standard curriculum of reading, writing, and keeping accounts, women had an open field in the teaching of needlework, embroidery, and millinery where men normally would not be competent. The education was distinctively European; what was taught depended pretty much on the abilities of the people who ran the schools, and the curricula varied greatly from one school to another. Mrs Stuart ran a boarding school with her husband and a Mr Palmer, and taught her girls French and Latin which would have been positively useless in India but were prerequisites of good breeding and would be required in polite circles at home when—or if—they returned. But Mrs Stuart did not leave her young charges untutored in some practical skills for she also offered bookkeeping[13] in the event they married incompetent husbands or found themselves entirely on their own.

Besides practical skills, attention to moral development was also critical. Mrs Duncan whose boarding school was 'in an airy and retired pleasant garden on the banks of the river' offered millinery and mantua-making in addition to reading, writing, and record keeping, but she also was anxious to 'take the utmost care and pay the greatest attention to instilling into their young minds, virtuous and religious principles'.[14] A Mrs Murray opened a boarding school in Madras' Black Town in 1791 that offered reading, writing, the English language and arithmetic, music, French, drawing, and dancing, tambour, and embroidery and 'all sorts of Plain and flowered needle work'. She took some pains, however, to emphasize that her scholars would be 'genteelly Boarded, tenderly treated, carefully Educated, and the most strict attention paid to their Morals'.[15] Three years earlier, continuing a tradition begun in the late seventeenth century of recognizing rather than marginalizing interracial liaisons, Lady Archibald Campbell had founded the Asylum for Orphan Girls at Madras which took in, cared for, and educated legitimate as well as illegitimate girls.[16]

Education was normally sexually segregated, that is, boys would have male tutors and girls, women. In the case of a married couple opening a school, as the Stuarts did, children of both sexes could be accommodated. Yet, at least in one case, that of a Mr and Mrs Jarvis, only girls were taken in[17] and Mr Jarvis apparently did some teaching as well as superintending the management of the institution. When a man and a woman joined together in a school, the business was obviously more lucrative, but women who ran them alone could at least support themselves and perhaps make comfortable livings as well. Such an enterprise would not be enough to draw a woman to India but once there, for whatever reason, she might still give the pagoda tree a good shaking. Pearson speaks of one woman, a Mrs Hodges, who turned out girls described as 'vain, imperious, crafty, vulgar and wanton'.[18] But in return for inculcating these character traits, Mrs Hodges returned to England after only a few years in the teaching profession, 'with a snug fortune'[19] like some latter-day nabobess.

Like the millinery shops, the advertisements for boarding schools also tend to become fewer in the early years of the nineteenth century. The advent of steamship travel, coinciding closely with Britain's control of the seas following the Battle of Trafalgar, made the journey home shorter and far less dangerous than it had hitherto been. Thus, a child was more likely to be sent home for his or her education than residing in India. Orphaned Anglo-Indian children who had often been the clientele now could be taken in by mission schools, especially after the Charter Renewal Act of 1813 allowed missionary societies to operate freely in India and establish schools.

With the exception of Eliza Fay, the business women of the seventeenth and eighteenth centuries left no written records of their experiences. A lack of literacy is a possible but fairly remote explanation. They acquired and managed properties, and must have been literate at least enough to acquire rudimentary accounting skills.

Another possibility, however, suggests itself. One gets the impression that they were simply too busy. While the Victorians sketched and wrote and painted and collected artifacts, arranged gardens or tried to do good in India, they also complained chronically about being bored. Victorian women were also, however, often excluded from the administrative and military work of the Raj which gave purpose and meaning to the lives of their husbands. The women of the seventeenth and eighteenth centuries, on the other hand, had been able to share in the same kind of activity—trade—that had engaged their husbands. And it is almost inconceivable that they would not have made it a point to be at least aware of their husbands' business interests if they were not actively involved in them. Their own survival depended on what their husbands owned—or lost.

Although opportunities for women to engage in business enterprises would have evaporated in any case, by the end of the eighteenth century, the business woman did not quite 'fit' the scheme of things any more than did the merchants themselves. Both were involved in the kind of activity that was being increasingly disparaged. A woman had the questionable advantage of being 'forced' into business by 'unfortunate circumstances' and, as with Mrs Tolfrey, it was felt that she would not have been in those circumstances had Fate been a little kinder to her. In any case, it was government, not commerce or business, that set the tone in society. And government, especially after 1784, was becoming more regular, more ordered, and more careful of the interests of its Indian subjects.

In May 1784, Warren Hastings left India to face impeachment proceedings in the House of Commons.[20] Although he would ultimately be vindicated personally, the taint of corruption attached to the nabobs, seemed to cry out for correction. Coinciding with the Hastings impeachment, Parliament passed the Pitt Act of 1784 which centralized the government of India in a Board of Control in

London. Underlying the Pitt Act was the assumption that it had been the Company's servants who had heretofore wronged the Indian masses; thus, it was the Company's servants, now under the watchful eye of a disinterested and presumably more scrupulous Board, who would correct those abuses and guard against any further wrongdoing on the part of its servants.

After a twenty-month interregnum under Sir John Macpherson, Charles Cornwallis, his reputation unblemished after his surrender of the first British Empire at Yorktown, arrived in Bengal in September 1786, to begin the work of implementing the reforms envisioned in the Pitt Act. He was to be the first in a long line of governors who came to India with no prior experience or knowledge of the country they were to serve, but the Directors, stinging under the near ruin to which the nabobs had brought the Company's finances and suffering too under the burden of a righteous indignation at the vast wealth so speedily acquired on the sufferings of 'oppressed' Indians, were not looking for a man 'corrupted' by experience in India. They wanted honesty in the Company's government, someone capable—as the nabobs apparently were not—of assuming the burden of responsible government. And to Cornwallis, a man whose integrity, self-discipline, and capacity for hard work was, and still is, beyond reproach, they therefore gave what they had rarely given to Warren Hastings, or any other governor before him—their undivided and unequivocal support. With Cornwallis, the end of the vigorous, self-seeking, flamboyant days of the nabobs as well as those of merchants who had feathered their nests while doing the Company's service ended, and an age of high seriousness where corruption and mercantile extravagance would no longer be fashionable or tolerated began.

There is a certain irony in that the nation that was taking the lead in the Industrial Revolution—and would bring the fruits of that Revolution to India—and whose major source of wealth and international influence was trade was now embarrassed by it. Amal Chatterjee traces the transition like this: the trader 'travelled down a path which made him first hero, then the unrefined, over-wealthy disrupter of British society, next the greedy oppressor of "natives" and, finally, the despicable little peddler'.[21] Ironically, there was an Indian beneficiary. The banian who had been the object of opprobrium for almost two centuries now found his position taken by the Brahmin.

There were, of course, many merchants in British India and in fact their number grew as the British community itself grew. Among them the spirit of adventure, of commercial opportunism in the style of the old nabobs was far from gone. Their wealth was usually more stable than that of the nabobs had been but at the same time a growing division between the officers of the Company and the increasingly large community of free merchants became more marked. And it was that commercial spirit, with its easy-going, gift- and bribe-taking, social tolerance, and even indulgence in things Indian that stood condemned after 1784.

Among the casualties of the new moral tone at home were the wives of the nabobs.[22] The most prominent was the wife of the man who had come to epitomize the nabobs, Maria Hastings. Not only was her husband vilified but so was she. If Eliza Fay and William Hickey are to be believed (and there is no reason to doubt their testimony) Calcutta society, including Warren Hastings' most bitter enemy, Philip Francis, had embraced her. Not so, society at home. There were three strikes against her: (*a*) she had engaged in an adulterous liaison with Hastings while still married to Imhoff; (*b*) she was the wife of the man who seem to embody all that was 'wrong' with the nabobs, and (*c*) given that she was 'foreign' and not of aristocratic birth, she did not behave in a sufficiently subdued manner. The first strike might have been forgivable. Mrs Hastings was not the only wife to carry on an affair, and to do so quite openly. Indeed, Georgian society tended to be rather tolerant of both extra marital affairs and divorce. The second might possibly have been forgiven too, albeit with some difficulty, had it not been for the third. She dressed flamboyantly in shawls, jewels, and precious Indian fabrics. Instead of being reserved or reticent, she acted as she had in Calcutta, seeming to aim at being the most conspicuous figure in the room and having no apparent consideration for those whom she should have regarded as her social 'betters'.

In 1615, the Directors had envisioned that women could play only two roles in India, they could either get in the way or they could play a social and civilizing role. They had done both, and more besides. They had carved out commercial opportunities of their own. They had managed businesses and estates. They had invested and reaped the profits of their investments, and they had taken risks and lost much. By the end of the eighteenth century, marriage remained the only way a woman could advance economically. Empire, however, provided a variety of other roles in which she could flourish.

notes

1 Susan Stave, 'Investments, Votes, and "Bribes": Women as Shareholders in the Chartered National Companies', in ed. Hilda Smith, *Women Writers and the Early Modern British Political Tradition* (Cambridge: Cambridge University Press, 1998), 261.

2 Cited in Stave from 'Letters of Richard Barwell' in *Bengal Past and Present: Journal of the Calcutta Historical Society* (vols 8–13, 1914–16, no. 207, 2 October 1773), 273.

3 There are exceptions, notably Eliza Fay, who, after divorcing her husband on her first voyage out, then returned to India three more times with the intention of reviving her millinery business.

4 They were Eleanor French and a Mrs Chaplin. See Henry Davison Love, *Vestiges of Old Madras, 1640–1800*. Indian Records Series, 3 vols (London: John Murray, 1913), III, 502.

5 *Europeans in India*, Vol. 25, OIOC.

6 See Arthur Calder-Marshall, *The Grand Century of the Lady* (London: Gordon & Cremonesi, 1976).

7 Ibid., 41–2.

8 Eliza Fay, *Original Letters from India*, ed., E.M. Forster (London: The Hogarth Press, 1986), 263.

9 *Calcutta Gazette*, 15 September 1803 and 16 August 1810.

10 Philip Francis, *The Francis Letters*, ed., Beata Francis and Eliza Keary, 2 vols (London: Hutchinson and Co., 1901), I, 205.

11 Doreen Yarwood, *English Costume* (London: B.T. Batsford, Ltd., 1953), 204.

12 William Hickey, *Memoirs of William Hickey*, ed., Alfred Spencer, 8th ed., 4 vols (New York: Alfred A. Knopf, 1921), IV, 37.

13 *Calcutta Gazette*, 11 May 1786.

14 Ibid., 8 June 1786.

15 Love, *Vestiges*, III, 443.

16 Ibid., 352.

17 *Calcutta Gazette*, 1 February 1786.

18 R. Pearson, *Eastern Interlude* (Calcutta: Thacker, Spink, & Co. Ltd., 1954), 182.

19 Ibid.

20 The House of Commons had passed an earlier resolution to recall Hastings in May 1782 but, under pressure from the Company, that resolution had been withdrawn.

21 Amal Chatterjee, *Representations of India, 1740–1840: The Creation of India in the Colonial Imagination* (New York: St. Martin's Press, Inc., 1998), 7.

22 See Tillman Nechtman, 'Nabobinas: Luxury, Gender, and the Sexual Politics of British Imperialism in India in the Late Eighteenth Century', *Journal of Women's History*, 18, no. 4 (Winter 2006), 8.

part three

The age of improvement, 1805–1856

DEPENDING UPON ONE'S POINT OF VIEW, Britain's acquisition of India could not have happened at a more auspicious—or more unfortunate—time in her intellectual and spiritual history. It is hard to imagine that Henry V, having defeated the French at Agincourt, would settle down to the task of improving them or doing them any good. He might have been convinced that God was on his side, that God loved the English more than he loved the French, but there is no indication that he ever thought of improving them to make God love them as much as He loved the English. Nor had any of India's many previous conquerors been particularly interested in doing her any good. The Moghuls, India's latest conquerors, had been interested in efficiency and peace and quiet—which mainly meant organizing the collection of revenue and discouraging by any means necessary attempts at overthrowing them—but not in any kind of moral improvement. Even Clive, after Plassey, had not been particularly interested in improving anyone or anything in India.

The acquisition of empire and then, beginning in the late 1820s, the opening of steam travel,[1] gave women the hitherto unprecedented opportunity to explore India—an opportunity that many of them seized with a great deal of enthusiasm. Along with exploration came the happy burden also of describing and explaining India to their contemporaries at home.

As in the early years, when women had participated in the Company's commercial interests, so did they in the early nineteenth century share in the Company's mission to 'improve' India. Often this was understood as giving some kind of moral example that would have a beneficial 'effect upon the natives'. The decision to permit missionaries in India as of the Charter Act of 1813 gave other women a chance not only to provide moral example but also to participate in evangelizing India.

Ultimately, however, if one wants to 'improve' someone else, there is automatically an assumption of some sort of deficiency. The Conservative/Orientalist school which had thought Indian civilization had much that was worthy of preservation had been losing ground since 1813 and, by the early 1830s, under the impulse of Evangelicalism and Utilitarianism, the ideal of preserving and restoring India's past in order to renew her present had begun to be abandoned. Thomas Macaulay's *Minute on Indian Education* in 1835 accelerated a significant change in the attitude towards India. India would not only be improved, she would be fundamentally changed. As the *Minute* put it, Britain's objective in India would be to train a class of persons 'Indian in blood and colour, but English in taste, in opinions, in morals, and in intellect'.

Notions of class and race, which had hitherto been separate, now intersected and Indians, regardless of caste, fell to the bottom of the Anglo-Indian social ladder. By virtue of simple race, British women had a place on that ladder which they often vigorously defended. Others, however, were critical not only of the stratification itself but also of the treatment it accorded Indians. Indeed, through their eyes, it is possible to see the resentments that ultimately led to the Mutiny in 1857.

note

1 The first steam driven vessel, the *Enterprise*, arrived in Calcutta in 1825, after rounding the Cape, in 113 days. The familiar Peninsula and Orient, or the P&O, started its service to India in 1842. Before the opening

British Women in India

of the Suez Canal in 1869, the two most popular routes to India were the overland which involved going by steamer to Alexandria, taking a smaller boat to Cairo, then travelling overland to Suez and taking another ship for the final leg to India. The other route went around the Cape where there was a stop for re-outfitting and then on to India.

12

'in search of the picturesque'

THE CLEARING OF THE SEA LANES FOLLOWING Napoleon's defeat at
Waterloo, sandwiched as it was by the defeat of Tipu Sultan in 1799
on the one hand and then the defeat of the Marathas at Panipat in
1818 on the other, meant that travel both to and throughout most
of India could be carried on in much greater safety than had hitherto been the case. Thus, the number of women coming to India
increased but, more importantly, what they were able to experience
of India also was enhanced.

Peace on the high seas and in India coincided roughly not only
with the expansion of print at home but also with a much larger
readership among both women and men. Britain was becoming not
only a 'nation of shopkeepers' but also, according to Samuel Johnson,
'a nation of readers'.[1] The development of a culture of print also
coincided with the expansion of female literacy and, more significantly perhaps, the onus against women writing professionally, while
not completely disappearing, was loosening. Fanny Burney had 'vio-
lently' put away her book because she dreaded being thought 'studi-
ous and affected'[2] but went on to write charming novels and letters
which were well received. Before that, Mary Wortley Montague's

Turkish Embassy Letters in the early part of eighteenth century, and Mary Wollstonecraft's *Letters Written during a Short Residence in Sweden, Norway, and Denmark* at its end had catered to and at the same time created a demand for information about the strange, the foreign, the exotic. Travel books were widely read and passed around to friends and discussed at parties, and travel writers, both male and female, became central figures in the growing profession of letters.

The great bulk of the correspondence about India had been and would continue to be confined to official administrative, commercial, and military documents. The work of the Orientalists in the latter part of the eighteenth century as well as the enormous body of scholarship that would continue to expand throughout the Raj added another dimension to that correspondence, since that work, apart from its intrinsic intellectual value, was also important to carry out effective government.

Travel literature, however, was the oldest genre of writing about India. Beginning in the sixteenth century with the publication of Ralph Fitch's story of his adventures in Hakluyt's *Principall Navigations*, the genre had perforce remained largely a male preserve. Beginning with the publication of Jemima Kindersley's *Letters* in 1777, however, women began to shoulder a new and hitherto unprecedented role. Through their journals, letters, diaries, and articles they could convey a sense of India's people, geography, cultures, and religions that lay outside the realm of officialdom or scholarship. Hence, the explosion of writing by women about India that had begun shortly after Plassey, became in the nineteenth century a virtual torrent of prose, and it was a torrent supplemented by volumes of sketches, drawings, paintings, collections of artifacts, and, beginning in the late 1830s, photographs. Equipped with Romantic sensibility and often with some prior knowledge of India, they would wander about 'in search of the picturesque' as Fanny Parkes put it, and draw charming sketches of landscape and daily life, Indian people, history, religious practices, music and poetry, festivals, animals, vegetation, landscapes, and artistic and architectural wonders, and they would do so often with affability, warmth, and grace. And while many women continued to write letters and journals specifically for family and acquaintances, others, like Phebe Gibbes earlier, deliberately meant to shape opinion about India.

Far from withdrawing from India, many women reached out to India as far as their sex and race allowed, and embraced her with exuberant enthusiasm. They discovered that India could astonish, delight, exasperate, bewilder, puzzle, vex, and beguile them. They clambered up mountains, sailed up and down rivers, crossed streams on shaky rope bridges, got soaked in monsoon rains, tramped across dusty, hot deserts and through snake-infested jungles, were amused by jugglers, disgusted by fakirs, and terrified by tigers. They collected fables and legends and myths, and witnessed colourful weddings, *durbars*, local fairs, processions, and Hindu and Muslim religious festivals; they hunted wild game and puzzled out the meaning of the art they saw. They met the poorest and the richest of the Company's new subjects, they encountered Brahmins, rajahs and ranis, deeply poor Sindhis, fierce Sikh warriors, and spoiled princes and, far from improving any of them, they often simply wondered. They were conscious of empire but dominion was often not uppermost in their minds as they explored. Several of them learned Indian languages, some well enough to translate stories and even poetry into English. They liked Indian cuisine and wrote cookbooks. They bought carpets, shawls, fabrics, jewellery, and artifacts of all kinds for themselves and for friends at home.

Their perceptions were not mirror images of the men they accompanied nor, even though they shared an identifiable feminine perspective, were they mirror images of each other. The social circles to which they belonged and their own experiences coloured their reactions to the European as well as to the Indian community. Bessie Fenton's beloved first husband, Neil Campbell, had died within a year of their arrival in India, and thereafter her almost chronic melancholy pervaded everything and everyone she encountered in India. 'The misery of being the companion of vulgar people is one I never could become reconciled with',[3] she complained, and unhappily, many of the people of both races were not as cultivated as she might have wished. When she saw a tomb with the inscription 'To the Memory of Rose', even though she did not know who Rose was, she was oppressed by a 'kind of indefinable foreboding...There was, in the solemn radiance of the night, a saddening influence'.[4]

Others could be downright funny. The wit of Emily and Fanny Eden has been widely appreciated but there were others whose approach to India and their position in it was graced by a lively sense of humor. Harriet Tytler, for instance, advised her country-women that the best curries were made by Muslim women but they would have to be warned not to make it too hot 'for the English traveler does not consider it good manners to weep over his meals, especially just after giving thanks for what one is about to receive'.[5] Julia Maitland was told that every person in her household had a servant and even the horse had a man and a maid to care for it. The cat, however, was allowed to wait upon herself, whereupon Miss Maitland decided it might be wise to 'respect her accordingly'.[6] And Anne Katharine Elwood had trouble keeping a straight face when, upon meeting the 'managing person' of Bhorg, her ayah interpreted 'rani' as 'Mrs King'.[7]

They could also Romanticize India. Within the 'idol-caves' at Elephanta, Henrietta Lushington wondered at 'The awful faces, whose composure breathed/A calm like conscious power' and asked, 'Was not your fancy busy 'mong them there? Did you not seem to hear the hum of prayer?'[8]

They visited *zenanas* and, like Frances Benyon a century ear-lier, were often amazed at the wealth of the ladies there and, like Jemima Kindersley and Eliza Fay, pitied the residents whose lives seemed so bereft of meaning. While officials and policy-makers fretted about the zenana and sati, however, neither practice preoc-cupied these women writers as much as one might expect. The reason for that may be that, while India itself lay open to their exploration, the world of many Indian women, aside from their own servants, remained as closed as it had ever been. Except for Mrs Meer Hassan Ali who actually lived in a zenana and described its inhabitants and their activities in great and sympathetic detail, most British women dwelt on matters related to Indian women very little. Several scholars have suggested that the confinement of the zenana became an impetus for the female emancipation move-ment in Britain itself. While this is no doubt true, except for the missionaries, most of the women in the early nineteenth century seem to have been little interested in reforming the condition of women either in India or in England. When they do discuss it, it is usually perfunctory. Then, as if there are so many other interesting things to talk about, they move on.

If one could escape the sedate and often boring presidencies, India could offer much. There was in the *mofussil*, according to Marianne Postans, much more intercourse between European and native society than in the presidencies and 'this is always productive of good'.[9] For the most part, the exploration of India outside the presidencies was made in the company of a husband, brother, or other male companion. To a large extent, they traveled in a British vacumn, not so much *in* India as about it. Harriet Tytler was astonished that, as a girl of eighteen, she was able to travel alone for nine hundred miles through northern India 'alone'.[10] She really was not alone, however. In addition to her palanquin bearers, she often had the company of a British officer and her journey was broken by stays with British families.

But there were remarkable exceptions. Some of the most colourful descriptions of India come from the hands of women who were either single like Emma Roberts or, in the case of Fanny Parkes, moved about as if they were. For the most part, these women approached India with minds informed by at least a little knowledge of what to expect, or they acquired that knowledge once they arrived.

The third volume of letters about India to come from the hands of a woman is Maria Graham's *Letters on India* in 1814. Whether she had read *Hartly House* or not is unknown but, like Phebe Gibbes, Mrs Graham intended to deliberately shape opinions about India. Her purpose, she said, was to exhibit 'a sketch of India's former grandeur and refinement so that she could restore India to that place in the scale of ancient nations which European historians have in general unaccountably neglected to assign to it'.[11] Besides affording some entertainment and 'some matter of useful meditation ... to the reflecting reader', she wrote, she also hoped 'to direct the attention of those in whose hands so much of their destiny is placed, to the means of improving their moral and intellectual condition, as well as of securing them from political or civil injuries'.[12]

Born in July 1785, Maria Dundas sailed to India with her younger brother and sister in 1808 in the company of their father who had been appointed Commissioner for the Navy at Bombay. On board she met Lieutenant Thomas Graham whom she married in December 1809.[13] Because her first and longest residence was in Bombay, Mrs Graham's *Letters* and her *Journal*, unlike the letters of Jemima Kindersley and

Eliza Fay, provide an insight into Anglo-Indian life outside the capital. She is also the first woman to provide a glimpse of the much wider Indian experience that the empire would now make available to women, and to suggest that that experience was not uniform. While in Bombay, she made a point of visiting Indian families, talking with the women, eating with them, watching them work, and care for their children, activities that she suggests were not readily available in the other two presidencies. During a short stay in Calcutta, she regretted that 'the distance kept up between the Europeans and the natives, both here and at Madras, is such that I have not been able to get acquainted with any native families as I did at Bombay'.[14]

A child of the Scottish Enlightenment, she was keenly aware of the Orientalist scholarship begun a generation before her arrival in India and her *Letters* especially show a heavy reliance on their works, notably the historian, Robert Orme, as well as Henry Thomas Colebrooke, and Sir William Jones. Indeed, it might not be an overstatement to assert that she set the pattern for women not only using but also popularizing their works.

She studied Persian and apparently tried to learn as much as she could from both Indian and British scholars. Her *Letters* contains over a dozen chapters discussing India's languages, poetry, music, calligraphy, systems of geography, Hindu chronology, astronomy and astrology, castes, manners and customs, the history of the Muslims in India from the invasion of the Ghaznavids to the administration of Warren Hastings, Hindu mythology, tombs, and festivals. In an almost startling passage, she went beyond the earlier Orientalists, however. Given that she was in India before the final defeat of the Marathas, she related their history—and not unsympathetically—beginning with Shivaji who, 'although he employed treachery to forward many of his designs', yet 'his enterprises were always formed with sagacity, and executed with promptness and vigour'. She took her historical sketch down to the present *peshwa*,[15] 'whom the victories and intrigues of the English have placed on the Musnud'.[16]

Like Elizabeth Plowden, she delighted in Indian music, although she had an 'uncultivated ear'[17] and appreciated the *Sacontala*, the epic poem by the fourth or fifth century poet, Kalidasa, which had been translated by Jones, well enough to recount the entire story. She found a comparison between India's itinerant bards and those in the

Scottish highlands and even in Mexico and Peru, noting that the word 'bardi' was Hindi.[18] Echoing the earlier Orientalists, she found in Hindu civilization 'the maxims of the pure and sound morality which is founded on the nature of man as a rational and social being'.[19] She was not fond of the Hindu mythology, but 'I do not on the whole think worse of it than of that of the West, excepting indeed that its fictions have employed less elegant pens'.[20]

Again, like the earlier Orientalists, she shared the view that Hindu civilization had degenerated from a once glorious past. The sciences and arts she thought 'to be only slumbering and forgotten in India, and that to awaken the Hindus to a knowledge of the treasures in their own hands is the only thing wanting to set them fairly in the course of improvement with other nations'.[21] She concluded that the carvings at Elephanta 'must have been the works of a people far advanced in the arts of a civilized life, and possessed of wealth and power' but lodged in the hands of a 'crafty priesthood' who 'preached a miserable and degrading superstition to the multitude'.[22]

> We should remember that for centuries they have been slaves to hard masters, and that if by subterfuge they could not conceal their property, they had only to expect robbery and violence, thus falsehood became the only defence of the weak against the strong, and lost something, at least of its criminal character ...[23]

The caves enchanted her, however, and she carefully sketched them. Realizing that the sculptures 'would not be intelligible without at least a slight previous acquaintance with the principal gods of Hindustan', she proceeded to give what she called a 'brief', but what, in fact, was a lengthy and detailed account of them.[24] Like many of her contemporaries and like the earliest Orientalists of the Hastings era, she found in Hinduism parallels with ancient Greek, Roman, and Egyptian religions, and with Judaism and Christianity. In the 'superstitions of India, no less than in the lofty visions of Plato', she recognized 'the existence of those moral ties which unite the heart of man to the Author of his being'.[25]

Similarities with Christianity though there were, however, Mrs Graham was also quite capable of looking at India's religions as unique in their own right—and again in the tradition of the Orientalists—and as at Elephanta, the Jain shrine of Carli gave her a chance to explain that religion and to point out that while there were similarities with Hinduism, there are no personifications of deities at Carli nor separate cells for secret rites, and she nicely separated Jainism from Hinduism.[26] Her residence in Bombay gave her a chance to investigate the Parsis and, as Anna Leonowens would do about twenty years later, give a thorough account of their Zoroastrian creed, religious festivals, marriage, family, and burial traditions, the history of their expulsion from Persia and their coming into India, and their ingenuity in accumulating wealth.[27] A side trip to Ceylon (Sri Lanka) and a visit to a Buddhist temple gave her a chance to discuss Buddhism, again as a unique religious experience unrelated to Christianity.[28]

Mrs Graham was, however, not uncritical of Indians. There was nothing of a Romantic or philanthropic spirit in her but there was nothing either of disdain for Indians. If Indians, she said, 'have the virtues of slaves, meekness, forbearance, and gentleness, they have their vices also. They are cunning, and incapable of truth; they disregard the imputation of lying and perjury, and would consider it folly not to practice them for their own interest'.[29]

What makes Maria Graham so attractive is that, to her, vulgarity and stupidity as well as gentleness and kindness were human not racial traits. Indians could indeed be liars and cheats but Englishmen could be petty, narrow-minded, and vulgar. She found the lives of Indian women dull, but she also found the lives of many English women and men intolerably dull and insipid. The 'small number of rational companions', she thought, 'make a deplorable prospect to one who anticipates a long residence here'.[30]

The most prolific of all women writers before the Mutiny was Emma Roberts, who like Maria Graham, deliberately wrote for a public audience. She accompanied her married sister to India in 1828, and then, following her sister's death in 1830, moved to Calcutta where, until her departure in 1833, she contributed to a number of periodicals and edited the *Oriental Observer*. Her three-volume *Scenes and Characteristics of Hindostan*, published in 1835, was a compilation of articles she wrote for the *Asiatic Journal*. Four years later, in 1839, her *East India Voyager or Ten Minutes Advice to the Outward Bound* appeared, and two years after that, *Notes of an Overland Journey through France and Egypt to Bombay* was published. By then, in 1840, she had died in Poona, but works under her name continued to appear. The two-volume *Hindostan: The Landscapes, Palaces, Temples, Tombs; The Shores of the Red Sea; and the Sublime and Romantic Scenery on the Himalaya Mountains* (1845–47) was a collection of sketches and drawings but with her descriptions, and in 1841, John Murray published the sixty-fourth edition of a book of domestic cookery which she had edited and included a couple of recipes for curries and other Indian dishes.

There is in her work some of Maria Graham's Orientalism but, unlike Mrs Graham, Miss Roberts was less certain that there was much in India that needed to be improved. Calcutta was still a 'city of palaces' for her as it had been for Eliza Fay, although 'a certain want of keeping and consistency, common to everything relating to India, injures the effect of the scene'.³¹ Delhi, however, was an unqualified delight. Mosques and minarets glittering in the sun, 'some garlanded with wild creepers, others arrayed in all the pomp of gold', superb edifices, and luxuriant gardens rendered it an 'Eden of delight' were it not for the suffocating, choking, stifling, blinding, smothering dust. She was captivated by the wide and handsome main street, the Chandery Chauk, with its tree-shaded canal running down the centre, the cries of street vendors, the discordant songs of itinerant musicians screamed out to the accompaniment of the tom-tom, the shrill cries of camels and trumpeting of richly caparisoned elephants, the neighing of horses and grumbling of cartwheels. She described cheetahs and hunting leopards being led hooded through the streets, along with beggars, idle loungers, 'insolent retainers of great men', Mussulmans of 'lazy, dissipated, depraved habits, gaudily decked out in flaunting colours', and 'fine, tall, splendid-looking men' who brought all kinds of merchandise from Kashmir, Persia, and Tibet and whose 'noble aspect' contrasted with the 'squalidness' of their attire.³² The Taj Mahal was 'a fairy place'; Benares, an Indian Venice; and the *ghat*s even in the small villages along the Ganges, often made of granite but more frequently of polished *chuman*, were 'superb and spacious'.³³

Like Emma Roberts, Fanny Parkes was indifferent to the Sanskritic view of India's past and seemed unaware that much of anything had degenerated. She was the daughter of a Welsh army officer, Captain William Archer, and his wife, Anne. In 1822, when she was twenty-seven years old, she married Charles Parkes who had returned home on leave from a year at the Company's East India College at Haileybury. In June that year, the pair returned to India where Charles was posted as a Collector of Customs first at Calcutta and then at Allahabad. Charles appears very seldom in her diaries but when he does he seems to be a kindly, quiet man, generous especially to his wife, hard-working but not overly ambitious, content with the life of a Collector. Fanny, on the other hand, was temperamentally quite the opposite. She did not remain at Allahabad but moved all over northern India, travelling up and down the Ganges between Allahabad and Calcutta, moving cross country, visiting Lucknow, Delhi, Meerut, Fatehgarh, Agra, and into the Himalayas. Defying—or, more likely, ignoring—social convention, these travels were without Charles.

In one respect, Fanny Parkes was simply a rather plump busy-body with enormous energy who regularly rode eight or ten miles before breakfast.[34] She went tiger-hunting and hog-hunting and had a penchant for archery—Indian style—and for taxidermy, and collecting butterflies.[35] She acquired a very large collection of trinkets and images of all sorts—gold, silver, bronze, black and white marble—paintings, ornaments, and Persian and Hindustani proverbs and sayings which she then had cut onto seals.[36] When she received the gift of a sitar she learned how to play it.[37] She acquired a taste for betel, and polished gems for bracelets, snuff-boxes, and brooches. She could give her readers instructions on washing the hair in the Indian manner,[38] on lacquering boxes, and arranging a turban.[39] She could give the mythology behind sati by quoting from the Shasters,[40] and give a competent account of Lachmi, goddess of beauty.[41] She went to a Ram Leela festival and then gave a fairly detailed account of Ram and his winning of Sita. So eagerly did she study the customs of the Indians that her friends would laugh at her and tell her they expected to see her someday at *pooja* in the river.

Her approach to India, however, like Maria Graham's, was not uncritical. There were Indian customs that annoyed her. Indian ladies were shocked that British women dined with men 'and that too with uncovered faces'. An British woman going out on horseback was considered 'monstrous' in some areas of India[42] and some of her Indian acquaintances could not comprehend Fanny galloping about on her horse. Her not being afraid to sleep in the dark 'without having half a dozen slave girls snoring around me' surprised them. Her remaining alone in a room and not being unhappy when alone allowed them to look upon her as a 'very odd creature'.[43]

Mrs Parkes' deep involvement with Indian people was not only personally satisfying, at one point it also gave her a diplomatic role to play. A queen of Gwalior, the Baiza Bai, had been ordered from her residence in Fateghur into exile either in Benares or somewhere in the Deccan. That understandably distressed her, although she spoke on the subject 'with a command of temper and a dignity' that Fanny admired. Called upon to deliver an opinion as to what the queen ought to do, Fanny found it 'an awkward thing to tell an exiled Queen she must submit'.

> I hesitated; the Bai looked at me for an answer. Dropping the eyes of perplexity on the folded hands of despondency, I replied ... 'Jiska lathi ooska bhains,'—i.e., he who has the stick his is the buffalo! The effect was electric. The Baiza Bai and the Gaja Raja laughed, and I believe the odd and absurd application of the proverb half reconciled the Maharaj to her fate.

> I remained with her Highness sometime, talking over the severity of the orders of the Government, and took leave of her with great sorrow.[44]

As with Eliza Fay earlier, for Fanny Parkes India was personal. It was not a distant 'Other' nor was it a place of work and sacrifice and pain and responsibilities and the display of good example, nor was it a place to be improved but a place of joy. Her exuberant openness often made her seem rather crude and tasteless. Her compassion for another woman's grief and the sharing of techniques of horseman-ship were very little things and like so many other little things they would not at all alter the course of British Indian history nor have any sort of lasting 'effect upon the natives'.

Perhaps the best assessment of her role in Anglo-Indian affairs was the criticism that her book, *Wanderings of a Pilgrim in Search of the Picturesque*, won from the *Calcutta Review*.

> It would seem as if she had no higher aim, and had reaped no better fruit, during twenty-four years in India, than the gratification of a restless curiosity, and the pleasure of describing what she had seen, in the spirit of the clever exhibit or fararee-show.[45]

Further, the *Review* complained that, although her descriptions 'are truth itself', 'the pilgrim has lived so long away from her own land, that she appears to have forgotten the dignity and delicacy of a woman in any grade of respectable British society; for we cannot suppose that the kind of notoriety, won by such coarse and questionable expedients, could have any charm for a mind so gifted and accomplished'.[46] Her opening invocation to Ganesha, the Hindu patron of literature, was 'in the worst possible taste'.

> When she steps out of her own natural and better self for the poor affectation of displaying her familiarity with the proverbs and superstitions of the natives, or of repeating stories that other women would shrink from, her levity becomes profane, and her Amazonian tone coarse and indelicate.[47]

That criticism is sad. As important and interesting as the revealing of India might be, the official mission of Britain was ultimately not merely to understand or to enjoy or to explore but to improve her.

notes

1 Cited in Brian Dolan, *Exploring European Frontiers: British Travellers in the Age of Enlightenment* (New York: St. Martin's Press, Inc., 2000), 11.

2 Madame d'Arblay, *Diary and Letters of Frances Burney*, ed., Sarah Chauncey Woolsey, 2 vols (Boston: Roberts Brothers, 1880), I, 15.

3 Bessie Fenton, *Journal of Mrs. Fenton* (London: Edward Arnold, 1901), 263.

4 Ibid., 49–50.

5 Harriet Tytler, *An Englishwoman in India: The Memoirs of Harriet Tytler, 1828–1858*, ed., Anthony Sattin (New York and Oxford: Oxford University Press, 1986), 23.

6 Julia Maitland, *Letters from Madras during the Years 1836–1839, by a Lady* (London: John Murray, 1846), 19.

7 Anne Katharine Curteis Elwood, *Narrative of a Journey Overland from England, By the Continent of Europe, Egypt and the Red Sea to India, including a Residence There, and Voyage Home in the Years 1825, 26, 27, and 28*, 2 vols (London: Henry Colburn and Richard Bentley, 1830), II, 224.

8 Mrs Stephen [Henrietta] Lushington, 'The Isle of Elephanta' in *The Sea Spirit and Other Poems* (London: John W. Parker, 1850), 157.

9 Ibid., 86.

10 Tytler, *Englishwoman in India*, 58.

11 Maria Graham, *Letters on India* (London: Longmans, 1814), 2.

12 Ibid., vii.

13 In 1827, she accompanied her husband on a cruise to South America during which he died. She later married the painter Augustus Callcot. Her writing career continued, including children's literature although she had no children of her own. Her most popular work was *Little Arthur's History of England* published in 1835, a patriotic history of England which nowhere acknowledged the imperial dimensions of British power.

14 Maria Graham, *Journal of a Residence in India* (Edinburgh: Printed by George Ramsay, for Archibald Constable and Company, 1812), 136.

15 The office of *peshwa* had been created by Shivaji's grandson, Shahu, in the early eighteenth century. Originally, the peshwa was a prime minister but, in the face of weak lineal descendants of Shivaji, the office soon become hereditary rather than appointed and its holder the virtual ruler of the Marathas.

16 Graham, *Journal*, 80–4. The *musnud* is the throne.

17 Graham, *Letters*, 50.

18 Ibid., 47.

19 Ibid., 87.

20 Ibid., 339.

21 Ibid., 87.

22 Graham, *Journal*, 58.

23 Graham, *Letters*, 7.

24 Graham, *Journal*, 45ff.

25 Ibid., *Journal*, 53.

26 Ibid., 65.

27 Ibid., 37ff.

28 Ibid., 90.

29 Ibid., 27.

30 Ibid., 28.

31 Emma Roberts, *Scenes and Characteristics of Hindostan, with Sketches of Anglo-Indian Society*, 3 vols (London: W.H. Allen, 1835) I, 1–3.

32 Ibid., 171–6.

33 Ibid., II, 295–7 and I, 224–9.

34 Fanny (Parlby) Parkes, *Wanderings of a Pulgrim in Search of the Picturesque, during Four and Twenty Years in the East*, 2 vols (London: P. Richardson, 1850), I, 62.

35 Ibid., I, 243.

36 Ibid., I, 134.

37 Ibid., II, 501.

38 Parkes, *Wanderings*, II, 503.

39 Ibid., I, 94.

40 Ibid., I, 206.

41 Ibid., I, 108–9.

42 Ibid., I, 451.

43 Ibid.

44 Ibid., II, 38–9.

45 'Wanderings of a Pilgrim in the East', *Calcutta Review*, XVI (January–June, 1851), 500.

46 Ibid., 476.

47 Ibid., 475.

13

burdens of empire

ALTHOUGH THERE MAY HAVE BEEN A GOOD BIT of arrogance, ethnocentricity, and ignorance of Indian cultures, nonetheless, for the first time in history perhaps, there were conquerors who thought their task was not merely to exploit but to improve, and the impulse to improve was often completely genuine, and for its own sake. Nor was it specifically related to empire. Throughout the nineteenth century, England's own working classes would be improved far more vigorously than any of her colonies would. Nonetheless, a good argument might be made that, among all of Britain's colonies, none was to be subjected to such ferocious improvement as India would be.

Granted, as in Britain itself, there was much to improve. By the standards of the early Industrial Revolution, India was backward technologically, and by any Western standard, she also seemed backward socially and morally. In many cases, Indians had indeed been poorly served by rulers whose ostentatious wealth existed next to the dreadful squalor of ordinary people who often had fewer rights than cattle. For generations, *zamindars* had unmercifully squeezed their *ryots* or peasants, tax revenues were collected arbitrarily at best, and law courts served the whim of the local ruler. Punishments were cruel, frequent, and levied with caprice. Enemies could be flayed alive. In dynastic quarrels, brothers, fathers, and sons gouged out the eyes of rivals. Criminals could be tied to the hind legs of an elephant and dragged through the streets, and if that failed to kill the victim, his head would be placed upon a stone for the elephant to crush. Wives and daughters could be taken off the streets by force and sent to a ruler's harem. Fights to the death between animals were common but so were they in England. In India, however, fights to the death between wrestlers, often drugged with opium or *bhang*, were also common. Until Colonel William Sleeman penetrated the cult and began the process of suppressing it[1] bands of marauders and robbers, commonly known as Thugs, devotees of the dark goddess, Kali, preyed on travellers, murdering them, and seizing their wealth. Organized thieves called dacoits roamed the countryside unmolested.

Apart from dacoity and Thuggee, there were four practices that seemed most to cry out for intervention: (*a*) the idolatry, superstition, and 'indecent' ceremonies of the Hindus, (*b*) female infanticide, (*c*) the *zenana*, and (*d*) sati. There was, however, some ambivalence about the first of these. For one thing, it is manifestly impossible to legislate the beliefs that give rise to religious practices. Secondly, practices such as the Churruk Poojah or the Juggernaut or extreme penances and fasts harmed no one but the devotee himself.[2] Third, the company had been receiving complaints about Catholic padres and their Indian converts parading about with 'bell, book, and candle' from the earliest settlements in the seventeenth century, and there was a parallel in contemporary Europe. As Anne Katharine Elwood observed, the 'dreadful tortures' of the Indian Sunyasi and the 'multifarious mythological beings of the Hindoo Pantheon' both resembled Roman Catholic penitential practices and honouring of saints.

> ... for what are the canonization and the worship of saints, but the deification of Men? And can the disciple of St. Bruno, whilst practicing severities that make the blood run cold, blame the fanatic Yoguee, who imagines immortal bliss will be the reward of the crueltie he inflicts on himself?[3]

The latter three practices had no such parallels in Europe, were specifically related to women, and engaged reformers of both sexes far more zealously than the matter of idolatry. One might wonder why, with a rather large array of basic rights denied to women in India, the zenana and sati came in for particular attention. Why, for instance, until the latter part of the century, was there no comparable agitation for the right of an Indian woman to be educated, to have access to legal redress, to sue for divorce, or any of a myriad host of legal rights? The answer might lay in the fact that there was a parallel at home where British women also lacked legal equality.

There were, however, no parallels for the zenana and sati at home. Yet, the rather one-dimensional approach to both practices is an indication of how little they were understood, and how little it was thought necessary to understand them in order to 'improve' them out of existence. Both were confined to a relatively small portion of Indian society; the vast majority of Indian women were affected by neither practice. The zenana was a Muslim, not a Hindu, invention, was often confused with purdah,[+] and had no uniform practice. One differed from the others as much as a single family differs from other families. Most women, like Frances Benyon and Jemima Kindersley, found the lives of the women boring and pitied them. Fanny Parkes, on the other hand, thought a zenana 'a delightful place for private murder'. She had heard of a wealthy Indian finding two of his wives with another man. The man escaped, but he killed both the women, and Fanny exploded:

> A man may have as many wives as he pleases, and mistresses without number;—it only adds to his dignity! If a woman takes a lover, she is murdered, and cast like a dog into a ditch. It is the same all the world over; the women, being the weaker, are the playthings, the drudges, or the victims of the men; a woman is a slave from her birth; and the more I see of life, the more I pity the condition of the women.[5]

Unlike those earlier visitors, however, and in a vein that was by now becoming familiar, most of them blamed both the confinement of the zenana and sati on 'Brahminical tyranny'. Because it was something beyond political influence, as Marianne Postans put it, 'the emancipation of Eastern women from their present mental and personal imprisonment, would require that the prejudices of their forefathers should be laid low'.[6] She believed that whatever improvements might be made would have to be gradual.

Others, however, had different experiences. Anne Katharine Elwood encountered a rani at Bhoorg who had successfully set aside her husband 'from his habits of inebriety'.[7] And Anna Harriette Leonowens was aware that purdah and the zenana did not tell the entire story of Indian women. She discovered the 'startling fact' that historically, Indian women had distinguished themselves almost as much as men.[8] At least one of the six Marathi ranis that Frances Duberly visited appeared to be not only 'an unusually intelligent woman' but also literate. She was well informed about the royal families of Europe and familiar with the leading events of the Crimean campaign, and questioned Mrs Duberly, who had been the only officer's wife to accompany her husband there, about it. Mrs Duberly thought her information came from a Persian newspaper which she received weekly.[9]

Like the zenana, sati was also rare. Horrific as the custom was, sati was regarded as an honour and might have been preferable to the living death to which a widow was often subjected. As Eliza Fay had done earlier, several women saw a connection between sati and English custom. Fanny Parkes observed,

> The laws of England relative to married women, and the state of slavery to which those laws degrade them, render the lives of some few in the higher, and of thousands in the lower ranks of life, one perpetual sati, or burning of the heart, from which they have no refuge but the grave, or the cap of liberty,—i.e., the widows, and either is a sad consolation.[10]

Interestingly, in 1829, when the Governor-General, William Bentinck, abolished sati it was not because of a tremendous public outcry by English women. Nor, for that matter, as Mrs Postans might have predicted, did his prohibition entirely end either that practice or Thuggee which was prohibited at the same time.

The attitude towards both institutions would seem to be part of the perception of the 'Other' that Edward Said marks as a part of the imperial consciousness. On the other hand, the imperial relationship may have had little or nothing at all to do with that focus. There were few travellers before the nineteenth century who did not comment upon them. Moreover, the Brahmo Samaj, founded by Ram Mohan Roy in 1828, was just as concerned as any Englishman about eradicating both evils. The difference, of course, was that neither those earlier travellers nor the Samaj was in a position to make them targets of legislative action. Nor had earlier travellers drawn the conclusion from the practices that Hindu civilization at its root was degraded.

Several scholars, most notably Catherine Hall and Kathleen Wilson, have pointed out that a society's treatment of women was frequently held up as evidence of its degree of civilization, with 'rude' or 'uncivilized' societies cruel to their womenfolk and 'advanced ones respectful of them'.[11] Philippa Levine also argues that the behaviour, the demeanour, and the position of women became a fulcrum by which the British measured and judged those they colonized. Women became an index and a measure less of themselves than of the men and societies among whom they lived. Thus, despite their relative infrequency, the zenana and sati more than any other customs related to women or even to men seemed convincing arguments that Indian civilization was degraded and needed to be improved.[12]

It was not only the institutions affecting women, however, that seemed in need of change. Most of what was 'wrong' with Indians was that they were not British, or at least they were not what the British thought the British were. They were not hard-working, masculine, sober, honest, or Christian. In describing Indians generally, several terms recur over and over again—indolent, devious, effeminate, cunning, supine, servile, and, of course, idolatrous. Such qualities could not, obviously, be legislated. If Indians were to be really improved, therefore, it was felt that the example of British men and women would be the best prod. To either her credit or her blame, cultivating the moral qualities by which she had merited India would become Britain's major justification for ruling her.

There was, however, a Sisyphean element to improvement. Unlike the working classes in Britain who had not been conquered by a foreign power, the military victories in the late eighteenth and early nineteenth centuries had seemed to 'prove' the primitivists correct in their assessment of Indian character. If there had been no glorious past from which India had degenerated, if Hindu culture had always been degraded, could it then be improved by anyone, even Englishmen? Two of the leading primitivists, Charles Grant and Sir John Shore, had come away from their service in India utterly convinced of the depravity of the Indian character. In 1797, in a tract entitled *Observations on the State of Society among the Asiatic Subjects of Great Britain, Particularly with Respect to Morals and on the Means of Improving It*, Grant had argued that Indian society, laws, and arts were degraded and the Hindus depraved, and that it was Britain's mission to educate Indians out of their bondage to Hinduism. Grant's argument, as Ainslee Embree puts it, was 'that the only possible excuse for British rule in India was the possession of a superior truth and the willingness to use it to transform Indian life'.[13]

Sisyphean or not, transforming Indian life would have to go beyond administrative, legal, and technological reforms, and women as well as men now had to think about what 'effect upon the natives' their behaviour might have. Helen Mackenzie was one of many women who worried that the conduct of Europeans was such as to make the natives 'despise and abhor' them, for although the Indians were worse themselves, 'yet they expect those above them to be better than they'.[14]

Within Anglo-Indian society, there was also a sharp change. The flamboyance, casual amorality, and dissoluteness that had made the nabobs seem like extremely lucky merchants rather than cunning thieves were now not only frowned upon for simple moral reasons, they also seemed vaguely un-British, unpatriotic. Extravagance in dress, possessions, and behaviour could still be found, but since it was now associated with the ill-gotten wealth of the upstart nabobs, it became prudent to be not quite so obvious about displaying wealth, if indeed one had it.

Attempts to eradicate vice in the Company's services were as old as the Company itself. Now, however, improvement placed new burdens upon British women. The fact that they had never been much of an uplifting force did not convince many people that women could not and should not be such a force. Behaving well on behalf of trade was one thing; indeed, one could become a partner in a husband's mercantile work, even when, as with Katherine Nicks or the Weltden women, it might involve a bit of larceny. Behaving well on behalf of an empire was quite another. Indeed, far from being the encumbrance that Thomas Roe had complained of two centuries earlier, it was assumed that women now had a distinct role to play not only in counteracting the immorality of British men—their husbands, sons, and brothers—but serving also as exemplars of that higher moral purpose that now came to justify Britain's empire in India.

The higher moral tone made life frankly a bit duller. Lavish masked balls were still popular, but after 1786, Cornwallis greatly curtailed the entertaining at Government House, and completely discontinued the customary Christmas dinner, ball, and supper.[15] More than any other entertainment, the balls carried a political overtone. Besides the two in honour of the king's birthday and New Year's Day, there were, for a number of years, anniversary balls in honour of Wellesley's victory over Tipu Sultan on the fourth of May. Interestingly, however, there never were anniversary balls given in honor of Clive's victory at Plassey, a marked indication of the desire to distance the new rulers of India from the nabobs.

There was nothing at all like a witch-hunt for sinners but, while Anglo-Indians had always quarrelled and complained and bickered with and about each other with tremendous enthusiasm, there was now a new moral edge to their scrutiny and criticism of each other. In 1788, a paper complained about 'a very general depravity of con-versation and manners, both in mixed and male societies'[16]—a com-plaint that would have elicited at best an indifferent shrug a century, even a half century, earlier.

While the manners of women had, in general, resembled those of men both at home and in Anglo-India, it was the behaviour of women that was now expected to rise to a standard that hitherto had not been expected of them. About a decade after the 1788 complaint, the *Calcutta Gazette* carried an advertisement concerning 'a certain per-son' whose behaviour at the Wheeler Theatre on the opening night of a performance was apparently so offensive that the theatre desired 'that in future she will not be permitted to remain in the house should she be so ill advised as to repeat her visit'.[17] And in 1807, a small scan-dal occurred when the schoolmistress of one of the boarding schools was brought to trial on a charge of 'prostituting one of her scholars for money'. She was acquitted when it was discovered that the indict-ment had been laid against the wrong person, but the Chief Justice, not wanting to miss the occasion for a lesson on the sins of the flesh, lectured her on the great 'infamy of her conduct, and the scandalous abuse of the character she had assumed—the mistress of a public school'.[18] And this to an apparently blameless woman.

Dancing was a particularly touchy matter. Indeed, when the British scrutinized relations between the two races, they very often touched upon feminine dancing as a cause for the strained racial relationship. Because the only Indian women who danced in public were hired specifically for the purpose of entertaining Indian men, the appearance of British women dancing in public would have seemed to Indians that the wives of British gentlemen were simply professional courtesans, and that British men in India were not socially good enough to marry respectable British women. The Englishwoman Mrs Meer Hassan Ali, who had ignored social convention long enough to marry a Lucknow nobleman, took it up again on the matter of dancing. She observed that since it was considered indecorous in either sex among Indians to practise music, singing, or dancing in public, they could never reconcile themselves to the propriety of the Sahib Logue 'figuring away in a quadrille or country dance...and I have often been asked why I did not persuade my countrywomen that they were doing wrong'.[19]

On the other hand, the 'effect on the natives' may have had more to do with British sensitivities warmed by Evangelicalism than with any real Indian prejudices. The introduction of the waltz about 1812 requiring its male and female participants to embrace each other made dancing seem particularly risqué, not only in India but in Britain, and its seeming indecency appeared to be particularly out of place where the British role was a civilizing and improving one. For religious reasons, Mary Sherwood gave up dancing altogether. In fact, she resolved to give up going out in public at all so that she might 'do good'.[20] However, an Anglo-Indian custom dictated that single women could not dance unless the ball had been opened by a married one. And poor Mrs. Sherwood who happened to be the only married woman at a ball at Cawnpore where no Indians at all were present had to forego her holy resolve and open it.[21]

Happily, Mrs Sherwood was something of an exception. Most British women ignored Indian prejudices and since they needed partners for dancing, so, apparently, did British men. If Indians found British women dancing offensive, they also found the English taste for wine and beef offensive. That did not induce Englishmen to stop consuming alcohol and meat any more than Indian tastes prevented anyone from dancing. When Fanny Parkes went to an entertainment at the Residency in Lucknow, the women were not allowed to dance after dinner because the king of Oudh would have thought they were quadrilling for his amusement like nautch girls.[22] But she found other Indian prejudices working against her country-women as well.

> You cannot roam in India as in Europe, or go into places crowded with natives, without a gentleman; they think it so incorrect and so marvelous that they collect in crowds to see a beebee sahiba who is indecent enough to appear unveiled. A riding-habit and hat, also, creates much surprise in unfrequented bazaars, where such a thing is a novelty.[23]

Nor was dancing necessarily an insurmountable barrier to contact with Indians. The Eden sisters made a point of inviting forty natives to every dance they gave at Calcutta.[24] Some women travelled as much as sixty miles to a station where it was not unusual for a few rajahs in splendid dresses and jewels to appear. Emily Eden observed that they really did think the ladies who danced were 'utterly good for nothing, but seemed rather pleased to see so much vice'.[25] She tried to persuade the ladies of Simla to agree to dance at a ball to which several Sikh envoys had been invited and, after quite a series of delicate negotiations, eventually succeeded in getting all but three to come to the ball and to dance. Two of the envoys had seen British dancing before and were aware that the ladies were ladies and not nautch girls, and Emily hoped they explained that fact to the others.

The connection between English women dancing extended to the nautch. Captain Charles Mundy suggested that European ladies who attended these 'spectacles' be warned beforehand that they would only witness a 'sufficiently stupid display'. Sensitivity to the feelings of his female companions would make the situation of a gentleman 'irksome and uncomfortable', he thought, for he would sit 'in constant and not unfounded dread lest these fair liberals in morality should commit some, perhaps unintentional, solecism against decency'.[26] The saintly Bishop Heber, however, thought there was more for a rigid moralist to condemn in one Italian ballet than in all the nautch-es he had ever witnessed in India. And Reverend William Tennant, who was just such a rigid moralist, simply found them insipid.[27] By the late 1840s, however, a contributor to the *Asiatic Journal* found that the 'more respectable' portion of the British community scru-pulously avoided them, and those given by Indian gentlemen were attended only by 'such less reputable Europeans as have little or no character to lose'.[28]

Male prejudices aside, British women usually reacted to the nautch in the same way that Englishmen did—some of them liked it and some of them did not. Sir Charles d'Oyly's watercolour, *Nob Kishen's Nautch Party* (see the frontispiece to this volume), done between 1825 and 1828, shows Europeans of both sexes along with Indian men cavorting merrily on chairs while several Indian women, presumably nautch girls, mingle among them. Satirical though the painting was, the *Nautch Party* is a fair indication that moral considerations often had little to do with the judgement anyone of either sex made of the nautch. Emily Eden found the dresses and attitudes of the dancers 'graceful' and was always extremely amused by it but she thought the singing 'dreadful and very noisy'.[29] Fanny Parkes, on the other hand, could not admire the dancing but 'some of the airs the women sang were very pretty'.[30]

The reaction among women to that other Indianism, the hookah, also remained as varied as it had ever been. There had always been complaints about it—but not on moral or racial grounds. There were simply men and women who could not tolerate the taste, and the stale, putrid odour it left in a room, especially a room where dancing was supposed to take place, must have been extremely offensive to people who so highly valued fresh air. Not only was there some expense involved in its use, but what may have been worse, the hookah could have been associated with the vulgar and corrupt nabobs.

Some Anglo-Indians never did lose their taste for it. Even at its height, however, the hookah had competed in fashion with ordinary pipes and cigars. Any abandonment of the hookah seems to have depended more on one's individual taste and his ability to afford the expense than on his or her sex or religious inclinations. But the idea that the presence of women inhibited smoking—or at least should have inhibited it—was beginning to have some currency because there were suggestions that for ladies to smoke the hookah was in dubious taste.[31] When half her husbands' guests arrived at a public breakfast in 1812 armed with their hookahs, Lady Nugent resolved to set her face against the 'odious custom 'of young men smoking.[32]

Lady Nugent's disgust was not universal. Unfortunately, some ladies had a most indelicate taste for hookahs and some also developed an equally indelicate taste for cheroots. Bessie Fenton was astonished when a young lady at her hostess' house in Calcutta deliberately sat down before breakfast each morning to smoke a cheroot, and a formal dinner she attended ended in everyone but Mrs Fenton herself smoking cheroots.[33] Since there were other ladies present it was plainly not only men who enjoyed smoking. Still the idea persisted that women should disapprove of smoking and drinking and so they were usually turned out of the room after a dinner so that 'unrestrained by the presence of the fair sex, the majority of those who remain will drink and smoke in earnest, and the chances are, there will be several rows'.[34]

Most women accepted the burden of improving the folks around them, British as well as Indian. Most of the time. Perhaps. Lady Nugent had no inhibitions whatever in making the attempt to reform two Englishmen whose immense whiskers rather horrified her, and the fact that they ate neither beef nor pork seemed to her to render them as much Hindus as Christians. Facial hair came to be associated with Indians and with Europeans who had 'gone native' —that is, Europeans, like the discredited nabobs, who had not been interested in improving Indians.[35] Although they seemed to have formed opinions and prejudices more 'native' than British, it was decidedly the whiskers of Lady Nugent's acquaintances that seem to have distressed her most.[36]

Nonetheless, as in the earlier factories, assaults upon vice, whether in Indians or Englishmen, were often futile. Mrs Sherwood was mortified by the levity among the soldiers of her husband's regiment and would abruptly leave a conversation she considered 'frivolous' but she thought women, especially younger women, were also inclined toward vice.[37] Helen Mackenzie agreed that although the gentlemen in India were far above the average, morally, the ladies fell far below. She did not blame India or Indians, however. Her reason was precisely because they picked up their husbands' bad habits. Deprived of a mother's care, she argued, they were brought out and married far too young, before their education 'in the present deficient system' was finished. So they had no standard of manners or taste by which to test those among whom they were thrown. Married at sixteen or eighteen, they would adopt 'the strangest phraseology' from their husbands and their husbands' friends. It is common, she complained, to hear ladies speak not only of their husbands by their surnames, 'a thing unpardonable, except of a peer!', but of other gentlemen in the same manner, and to talk of 'our kit' and use such terms as 'jolly', 'pluck', 'a cool thing', 'lots', 'rows', and 'no end of things!'[38] Like Reverend Patrick Warner in the seventeenth century, the Reverend Tennant was dismayed that religious and moral duties were never enforced among the British in India resulting not only in the loss of virtue but the ruin of many youthful fortunes as well.[39]

Drinking also thwarted efforts at improving anyone. Thomas Pitt would have found that his countrymen—and women—could still consume a 'damnable amount' of alcohol. Harriette Ashmore heard of a woman in Calcutta who used to *restrict* herself to a dozen bottles of ale a day. She admittedly could not vouch for the accuracy of the statement but she did see women consuming four, five, or six glasses of champagne at dinners or ball suppers.[40] More beer was consumed in the *mofussil* and, according to Mrs Ashmore, a mofusilite was known by his or her partiality for that brew.[41]

Attempts to 'improve' India would last as long as the Raj itself but Sir Thomas Munro who served as Governor of Madras in the late eighteenth century saw the early contradictions that would ultimately undermine any such efforts. 'We are working against our own designs,' he wrote. 'The improvement of the character of the people, and the keeping them, at the same time, in the lowest state of dependence on foreign rulers...are matters quite incompatible with each other.'[42] If improving Indians amounted to providing some sort of example of British manners and morality, then some women did indeed serve, or at least try to serve, the role the Directors in 1615 had envisioned—they were a kind of support for the official, public role the Company now had assumed. On the other hand, there seems to have been, among many of them, both men and women, a sense that Munro's criticism carried much weight and that whether they danced or did not dance, smoked hookahs or smoked nothing, behaved badly or well, in the long run, mattered to India very little. In that sense, as far as serving the larger, and fairly futile, purposes of the Company, they really had become, as Thomas Roe had characterized them two centuries earlier, 'incumberances'.

notes

1 Sleeman became superintendent of operations against the Thugs in 1835 and commissioner for the suppression of Thuggee and dacoity in 1839.

2 In the Churruk Poojah, a rope attached to a pole in passed through iron hooks inserted into the devotee's back just below the shoulder blades. He is then lifted and swing about the pole for several minutes before being lowered to the ground. In the Juggernaut, pilgrims would throw themselves under the wheels of a cart carrying heavy idols that often resulted in fatalities.

3 Anne Katharine Curteis Elwood, *Narrative of a Journey Overland from England, by the Continent of Europe, Egypt, and the Red Sea to India, including a Residence There, and Voyage Home, in the Years 1825, 26, 27, and 28*, 2 vols (London: Henry Colburn and Richard Bentley, 1830), II, 26.

4 The word 'purdah' comes from the Persian word for curtain or screen, and refers to the practice of keeping a person out of public view. A zenana (the word is also derived from Pension) is where women are kept in purdah, but purdah can also include restrictions that apply to an individual woman.

5 Fanny (Parlby) Parkes, *Wanderings of a Pilgrim in Search of the Picturesque, during Four and Twenty Years in the East*, 2 vols (London: P. Richardson, 1850), II, 56–7.

6 Marianne Postans, *Cutch; or Random Sketches Taken during a Residence in One of the Northern Provinces of Western India; Interspersed with Legends and Traditions* (London: Smith, Elder, and Co., 1839), 57.

7 Ibid., 251.

8 Anna Harriette Crawford Leonowens, *Life and Travel in India: Being the Recollections of a Journey before the Days of Railroads* (Philadelphia: Porter and Coates, 1884), 202.

9 Frances Isabella Duberly, *Campaigning Experiences in Rajpootana and Central India, during the Suppression of the Mutiny, 1857–58* (London: Smith, Elder, & Co., 1859), 39–41.

10 Parkes, *Wanderings*, II, 420.

11 See Kathleen Wilson, 'Empire, Gender, and Modernity in the Eighteenth Century' and Catherine Hall, 'Of Gender and Empire: Reflections of the Nineteenth Century' in ed. Philippa Levine, *Gender and Empire* (New York: Oxford University Press, 2004), 14 and 46 respectively.

12 Philippa Levine, ed., *Gender and Empire* (New York: Oxford University Press, 2004), 7.

13 Ainslee Embree, *Charles Grant and British Rule in India* (London: George Allen and Unwin, Ltd., 1962), 157.

14 Helen [Mrs Colin] Mackenzie, *Life in the Mission, the Camp and the Zenana; or Six Years in India*, 2 vols (London: Richard Bentley, 1854, 2nd ed.), I, 278.

15 William Hickey, *Memoirs*, ed., Alfred Spencer, 8th ed., 4 vols (New York: Alfred A. Knopf, 1921), III, 306.

16 Cited in William Carey, *The Good Old Days of Honorable John Company*, 2 vols (Calcutta: R. Cambray & Co., 1906) I, 457.

17 *Calcutta Gazette*, 23 February 1797.

18 Carey, *Good Old Days*, I, 458.

19 Mrs Meer Hassan Ali, *Observations on the Mussulmauns of India*, 2 vols (London: Parbury, Allen, and Co., 1973 reprint from the 1832 edition), I, 196.

20 Mary Sherwood, *The Life and Times of Mary Sherwood, (1775–1851) from the Diaries of Captain and Mrs. Sherwood*, ed., F.J. Harvey Darton (London: Wells, Gardner, Darton, & Co., Ltd., 1910), 294.

21 Ibid., 312–3.

22 Parkes, *Wanderings*, I, 73–5.

23 Ibid., I, 115.

24 Emily Eden, *Up the Country*, 2 vols (London: Richard Bentley, 1866), I, 187.

25 Ibid., I, 23.

26 Godfrey Charles Mundy, *Journal of a Tour in India* (London: John Murray, 1858), 44.

27 Reverend William Tennant, *Indian Recreations*, 3 vols (London: G. Steward, 1804), I, 56.

28 'The English in India' in *Asiatic Journal and Monthly Miscellany*, ser. 3, v. 4 (London: William H. Allen & Co., 1845), 352.

29 Eden, *Up the Country*, I, 176.

30 Parkes, *Wanderings*, I, 40.

31 *Bengal Gazette*, 28 April–5 May 1781.

32 Maria Nugent, *Lady Nugent's Journal*, ed., Frank Cundall (London: Adam & Charles Black for the Institute of Jamaica, 1907), 360.

33 Bessie Fenton, *Journal of Mrs Fenton* (London: Edward Arnold, 1901), 18.

34 John Lang, *Wanderings in India* (London: Routledge, Warner and Routledge, 1861), 24.

35 The lack of facial hair to many Indians, on the other hand, was an indication of effeminacy.

36 Nugent, *Journal*, 372–3.

37 Sherwood, *Life and Times*, 330.

38 Mackenzie, *Life in the Mission*, II, 268.

39 Tennant, *Indian Recreations*, I, 97.

40 Harriette Ashmore, *Narrative of a Three Month's March in India; and a Residence in the Dooab: By the Wife of an Officer in the 16th Foot* (London: R. Hastings, 1841), 81. The *mofussil* was any station outside the presidencies.

41 Ibid.

42 John Bradshaw, *Sir Thomas Munro and the British Settlement of Madras Presidency* (Oxford: Clarendon Press, 1894), 181.

14

pilgrims in petticoats: the evangelicals

AS THE COAST FADED FROM SIGHT DOROTHY CAREY, probably sensed that she would never see England again. It was May 1791, Eastertide, the loveliest of seasons. The daffodils and forsythia would have been fading but the tulips, hyacinths, buttercups, periwinkle, and pansies would have been in bloom, and the lilac and spirea would have been budding. The Revolution in France was two years old but it had not yet threatened England directly; thus, she had no reason to worry that the voyage to India would be any more dangerous than Nature's own storms and winds could make it. Nonetheless, apart from the length and discomfort of the journey, did she not then wish in that season of resurrection and new life that God had left her husband, William, alone and that he had been content to spend the rest of his life as a shoemaker, the trade he had originally pursued?

Dorothy would not have heard of Thomas Roe—she was illiterate— but surely, if any woman bound for India had cause to be considered an 'incumberance' and who no doubt had reason to consider herself one, that woman was Dorothy Carey, now nursing her sixth child born less than a month earlier. Although leaving England in the spring must have been wrenching, at least her husband had waited until she had given birth. When William had first received the call to evangelize India several months earlier, he had felt that God's summons had to be answered immediately, and had made preparations to leave Dorothy and his large family behind, and spend the remainder of his life in India. Now, did she thank God that at least William had been persuaded to wait until the birth of this child and then to take his family with him rather than abandoning them altogether? Did she worry that, although their passage to India was paid for, William and his colleague, John Thomas, would be working without a license to preach the Gospel? Was she even aware that, at that moment, the East India Company opposed missionary activity in India among Indians?

Once in India, Carey found that the allowance of fifty rupees a month, which he received from the newly formed Baptist Missionary Society was inadequate for the maintenance of Dorothy and his family and he accepted the offer of a Mr Udny at Malda to take charge of an indigo factory at Mudnabatty on a salary of two hundred rupees a month.[1] He remained there for over five years, combining missionary work, the study of Sanskrit and Bengali, and the translation of the Scriptures with indigo planting. In 1799, four other Baptist missionaries arrived to support Carey. One of them died three weeks after landing and another, a ship's surgeon, died about twenty months after his arrival. But the other two, Joshua Marshman and William Ward, remained to carry on missionary work in Bengal for over thirty years outside the Company's jurisdiction at the Danish settlement of Serampore about sixteen miles north of Calcutta.[2]

The work that Carey had been called to do took a heavy toll on Dorothy. Ill with dysentery and perhaps mentally ill for many of the thirteen years that she lived in Bengal, she also lost a son. Carey's biographer hints at the high price Dorothy Carey paid for her husband's zeal.

> … all the strain she had lived through reacted upon her, till her brain became the haunted chamber of morbid fancies and tormenting fears. She grew the opposite of all she naturally was. Those whom she most tenderly loved, the most she turned against. Her spirit passed into a permanent gloom. 'Twas the price she paid for daring to India in those unsheltered years. None, knowing the facts, will cast stones.[3]

She died in December 1807 and in May of the following year Carey remarried. His biographer speaks the sentiments that were perhaps those of Carey's colleagues. 'The earliness of the engagement was its possible offense. But had he not for ten years been lonelier than a celibate?'⁴ Many years later, even another woman, also the wife of a missionary, would give Dorothy Carey scant sympathy. Without mentioning the reasons for it, Martha Weitbrecht noted that Carey's wife was unwilling to accompany him, though she was 'led at last to give a reluctant consent'.⁵

Carey's second wife, like Dorothy, has no perceptible identity or personality of her own except in relation to Carey. She was an invalid, the daughter of a Schleswig nobleman, the Chevalier de Rumohr. She had arrived in Serampore the same year as the mission there was founded by Carey and his colleagues, in 1799. Carey taught her English and baptized her, and her knowledge of Danish, Italian, and French enabled her to assist him in his translation work. Her literacy, like that of Mrs Marshman and Mrs Ward, allowed her to take an active share in her husband's work in a much more concrete way than Dorothy Carey had been able to do.

The chief mark of the Evangelical was an earnestness born of an intense, consuming religious conversion, often felt in real mental and sometimes physical pain in the terror of sin and the joy of spiritual rebirth. Evangelicalism transcended religious sects and social classes, nor was there a clergy. Indeed, the leading Evangelicals— William Wilburforce, Thomas Clarkson, Zachary Macauley, and Hannah More, the 'old bishop in petticoats'—were lay men and women. The labours of such people for humanitarian reforms such as the abolition of the slave trade reflect the two-fold duty once conversion had come. First, it was necessary to preserve the soul in the state of grace through prayer and work. The second aspect was more far-reaching. It was the duty of the convert to evangelize, primarily by preaching. Initially, evangelization was targeted at already baptized but lukewarm Christians at home, nor were the earliest evangelicals interested in changing the social order so much as sanctifying it.

Britain acquired empire in India just as Evangelicalism came to England, and initially there was no necessary connection between the two events. The French Revolution, however, coinciding as it did with major conquests in India, not only accelerated the spread of Evangelicalism within Britain itself, but it also changed its direction to target 'heathens' outside Britain. Both the atheism of the Revolution in its glorification of Reason over Faith, and Hinduism's polytheism stood in sharp contrast to the 'vital religion', the uniquely British religion, of the Evangelicals. Thus, there was a blurring of what was moral and what was patriotic and both were intensely emotional.

For many Englishmen, religion in the eighteenth century had rarely been an inconvenience. Discussions of virtue and vice, salvation and damnation, redemption, conversion, time, and eternity had excited little heat, nor even, in many circles, much interest. Clerical office was less a vocation than a prudent investment, and keeping the Sabbath holy had less to do with prayer than maintaining the social order. Similarly, in India, the repeated exhortations of the Directors about daily prayers and appearing at church on Sunday had more to do with commerce than with God for, as they had noted in their debate about Anne Keeling, a curse could befall those who thwarted the Divine will, and it was understood that that curse could be economic. When, however, wealth could be had without any particular reference to piety, religion became simply an inconvenience or, as Alexander Mackrabie had noted earlier, 'the fear of God had not been the kind of Wisdom most in Request in Bengal'.[6]

There had long been some interest in evangelizing in India but such activities had often been directed not at Indians, but at Anglo-Indians themselves. When the Company's charter had come up for renewal in 1793, the efforts of individuals chiefly connected with the Clapham Sect to obtain government support for missionary enterprise in India had met with opposition from the Company itself, still largely under the influence of the Orientalists. Nonetheless, proselytization among Indians had already begun with such ferocity that, in 1807, the Governor-General, Lord Minto, complained of the missionaries at Serampore, and particularly of William Carey, in a dispatch to the Directors. Their preaching, he said, 'contains no trace of argument or dispassionate discussion, but consists almost exclusively of denunciation and reproach directed against that class [Brahmins] which is revered as sacred by the whole body of the Hindoos'.[7] Minto's reproach had a sympathetic audience for the Court of Directors agreed that sending missionaries to India was 'the most wild, extravagant, expensive, unjustifiable project that was ever suggested by the most visionary speculator, and that it would affect the ultimate security of our Eastern possessions'.[8] By 1813, however, when the Charter came up for renewal again, the French Revolution had spawned Bonaparte, vast new territories had been added to the Company's holdings in India, and the government recognized that India was too important to be left to traders. Missionary work in India was formally inaugurated and Reginald Heber was appointed the first bishop of Calcutta.

Evangelicalism did not in the long run provide an instrument by which the fundamental status of women could be changed, but it did open another avenue for them to participate in what the Company was about. The influential Reverend Tennant thought that every European, man or woman, should lend a hand in 'suppressing the vices' of the Hindus since, even if they failed to improve the lot of the natives, they would promote their own virtue. What, exactly, a woman's role should be in either improving anyone or in even promoting her own virtue could be somewhat problematical, however, for, although the Evangelical stressed the importance of the individual's relationship with God, there was still clearly a difference between the individual who was a man and the individual who was not. No matter how spiritualized and committed to God each of the members of his family, including his own wife or daughters, were, the Evangelical did not drop the Hebraic notion that the order of society was grounded in the subjection of wives to their husbands. Thus, a Dorothy Carey would be expected to subordinate her own needs to those of her husband. It was a spiritual support rather than a physical or intellectual adornment that she was to strive to become. Thus, we find the missionary Henry Martyn unable to admit to a woman that any qualities other than those of her soul prompted him to propose marriage. He wrote,

> My principal desire in this affair is, that you may promote the kingdom of God in my own heart, and be the means of extending it to the heathen. My own earthly comfort and happiness are not worth a moment's notice... I can only say that if you have a desire of being instrumental in establishing the blessed Redeemer's kingdom among these poor people, and will condescend to do it by supporting the spirits and animating the zeal of a weak messenger of the Lord who is apt to grow very dispirited and languid, 'Come, and the Lord be with you'.[9]

While rejecting the fashions of the world, including those having to do with women, Martyn also erased her flesh, and the woman still remained a thing—a spiritualized object, not a unique human being.

The Company's opposition notwithstanding, the 1813 Charter Renewal Act changed its purposes in India, and that also changed the nature and degree of participation in which women could share in those purposes. As they had formerly entered into the commercial activities of the Company so would they now, with those opportunities largely closed, participate in its proselytizing mission. Like the mission to 'improve', however, the matter and manner of proselytizing were extremely complex and diverse. While many Dorothy Careys undoubtedly entered India with a good bit of reluctance or even dread, many others, like the women of the seventeenth century, saw in India a chance to expand their own personal agendas. And those agendas, while influenced by Evangelicalism to one degree or another, often were not confined to simply being spiritual supports of male missionaries.

Besides adorning mission churches with flowers, their own needlework, handicrafts, or other delicate refinements, they also were called upon to organize and run girls' schools,[10] care for orphans and the sick, and become actively involved in their husbands' work, even to the point of preaching and, if necessary, conducting religious services. Whether they were conscious of it or not, they were, in fact, early feminists in that their labours to save souls often involved saving bodies as well, from sickness, from child marriage, and above all, from the ignorance that kept Indian women confined in purdah. Thus, an elementary literacy and some understanding of hygiene were required if not before the departure for India, then as soon after arrival as possible. In addition, they normally had their own children and households to manage and, because the income of a missionary was often sparse, they had to do these things without the army of servants that a civil servant's wife, for instance, possessed. If a missionary's wife did not come to India possessing a good degree of resilience and resourcefulness, she would perforce have developed those qualities with some haste.

One of the best known missionaries was Margaret Cooke, the first woman to be sent from England specifically for the teaching of Indian girls. Her subsequent marriage to Isaac Wilson of the Church

Missionary Society strengthened her position in India, but she had an independent energy of her own as well. Her first concern was to become fluent in both Hindustani and Bengali and then propose to parents that their daughters would benefit from her instruction as servants, mothers, and mistresses of schools themselves. Her first efforts were a number of bazaar schools in Calcutta which did not live up to her expectations. Her next venture was a large school which she named the Central Female School. It had an 'excellent' house, with accommodations for teachers, school rooms, and a suitable place for a class of female orphans, to be educated entirely as Christians.[11] Unless the child was an orphan, however, Mrs Wilson usually was not able to keep a day-scholar after she was six or seven years old.[12] Emily Eden met Mrs Wilson after she had been working for twenty years in India. By then she was a widow and had moved her entire establishment to a location seven miles from Calcutta. She had collected about 160 orphans after a great flood in 1833, some even rescued from pariah dogs. She took any orphan that was sent to her, including the two little girls Miss Eden had purchased for three pounds from a drunken Muslim father who had abused them.[13] The poor woman was apparently always short of funds and 'in a position which would justify a weaker person in sitting down and taking a good cry, but she was as cheerful and as happy as if she had not a care on her mind'.[14]

At the very best, the results of the labours of missionary women were likely to be rather discouraging. For a start, it was often difficult to convince Indians, either men or women, that they needed saving, or that there could be only one true religion. The Indian prejudice against the education of girls presented formidable barriers, and the few girls who did enter their schools often left about the age of nine to be married. In the initial stages too there were no Indian women available to serve as teachers so the entire burden fell upon the English women themselves.

There was another handicap in that even the meager equipment necessary for teaching the rudiments of a number of useful occupations such as needlework was often difficult to obtain.[15] Finally, their only converts were likely to be low caste or untouchables, the so-called rice Christians whose conversion often had less to do with saving their souls than winning sustenance for their bodies. Most heartbreaking must have been the harassment their new converts, particularly women, often suffered from their own families and neighbours.

More often than any other single group, missionaries, especially missionary women, often bore the opprobrium of having 'gone native' from their fellow Europeans. And with good reason. They had access to a level of Indian society that few other women had or sought. Not surprisingly then, very seldom does one find a missionary woman referring to either sati or the *zenana*. These were customs belonging to a class of Indian women that missionaries rarely encountered. Rather, it was the middle or lower castes with which they identified, those restricted by purdah but not in a zenana, and the injustices and cruelties that individual women and girls in their acquaintance endured with which they most sympathized. They encountered parents casting sick children into the Ganges and saw family members stuff mud into the mouth, nose, and ears of a dying relative to hasten his or her demise. Having become aware that women of lower castes were required to bare their breasts in the presence of higher caste men, missionary women devised a little jacket to cover the upper body. To regard that as Victorian prudery is simplistic; the custom degraded more Indian women than the zenana, and degraded them more profoundly.

Like the Orientalists, many of the missionaries took a deep interest in Indian cultures, languages, and history. They had to learn India's languages, not only to preach and translate the scriptures, but to communicate with the people among whom they lived. In his zeal to learn Indian languages, William Carey himself set a remarkably high standard for such scholarship among both scholars and missionaries. His command of Bengali, Sanskrit, Marathi, and Assamese induced Wellesley to appoint him professor of Sanskrit and Bengali at the new Fort William College, founded in 1800 to prepare civil servants for service in India, where he remained until the College itself was abolished in 1831. Many women also became fluent enough in Indian vernaculars to teach Indian girls simple literacy in both English and often in an Indian language, and to teach them crafts such as needlework, cooking, and basic hygiene. Even if she had had access to a *munshi*, or teacher, however, a missionary woman was often too busy with unscholarly matters to give much time or attention to the cultivation of a language's finer points, especially if that language was Sanskrit.

There were several fundamental differences between the missionaries and the Orientalists, however. First, the knowledge the missionary acquired had as its purpose a complete transformation of India, a total uprooting of Hinduism. The Orientalists, on the other hand, had felt that whatever reforms were needed in India would have to be grafted onto existing social and religious structures, flawed though they might have become. Although many of the Orientalists, Sir William Jones in particular, had been devout Christians, their sympathetic engagement with Indian cultures often struck the missionaries as somehow tepid at best or totally flawed at worst. Martha Weitbrecht voiced that distrust this way: 'Many learned men had been allured to India, and had found an absorbing subject for study and metaphysical research, in her ancient literature and venerable religion; most of those individuals were, however, instigated by no love for the truths of the Bible, but rather by a desire to discover something that might invalidate its Divine authority.'[16]

A second major difference was the source of the knowledge about India itself. The Orientalists often were able to employ well-educated Indian scholars as their mentors. The missionary, on the other hand, was likely to rely on far less erudite teachers whose own knowledge of the classic Sanskritic texts was likely to have been narrow if it existed at all. That mattered a great deal because it limited the understanding and appreciation for classical Hinduism that might have given a missionary a more sympathetic view of its canonical sources. On the other hand, the Indians among whom he or she worked also normally would have shared that limited knowledge. While their empathy for Hinduism itself might have been imperfect, and their mission to transform India itself would remain largely unabated, missionaries often knew individual Indians and were more sympathetic to them than many scholars, administrators, or soldiers.

Even the most militant missionaries might have been somewhat gentled by contact with Hindu people. In 1856, Martha Weitbrecht met a Mr Bomwetch at Santipur, not far from Calcutta, who seems to have been rather zealous, for she says that he had abandoned the 'cautious policy' of his predecessor. Nonetheless, Mr Bomwetch had won the respect of at least one Brahmin businessman. While one might guess that the Brahmin's decision had more to do with business than theology, there is also the suggestion of mutual respect. 'The Hindus delight in discussion', she said, 'and have no objection to speak of Christianity, or any other religious faith, in an open, friendly way ... surely it is men ... [who are] honest, loving, faithful, who have the confidence of the natives, and if there be any European they will love and trust, it must be the missionaries.'[17]

Her observation suggests that the mission to transform India was hardly uniform or monolithic, not only as policy but even for the individual Evangelical. Indeed, one can imagine many men and women, Indian and British, finding themselves in quiet conversations about God, as well as a host of other matters, where there was neither 'ruler' nor 'subject', neither Christian nor Hindu, but simply seekers of the Divine. As Susan Thorne points out, the kingdom the missionaries sought really was of God, not Man. Their motivations were primarily theological, not nationalistic, and certainly not imperialistic. The presence of missionaries was essentially more destabilizing to the European community itself, rather than to any Indian community. The missionaries were often contemptuously dismissed as fanatics and they, in turn, were quick to expose their fellow countrymen's abuse and exploitation of Indians along with their other 'sins',[18] a practice not designed to win friends.

Evangelical Christianity provided an avenue by which secular women not formally connected with an individual male missionary or a missionary society could also share actively in what had now become one of Britain's cardinal roles in India. Since the late seventeenth century, especially with the founding and managing of orphan societies, women had long played active roles in charitable and philanthropic works. The wider scope Evangelicalism gave to women, however, provided an avocation for many women who otherwise would have had little outlet for their energies. Rather often, that work fused Christianity with a genuine attempt to alleviate suffering. There was a sense that the mere fact of becoming a Christian brought not only spiritual benefits but physical good as well. As a six-year-old, Harriet Tytler witnessed her father's attempt to help a number of men, women, and children who, on the verge of death from starvation, had come to the banks of the Ganges to be able to die at the holy river. When he offered them food, however, they refused since it had not been cooked by a Brahmin. She determined that when she grew up she would 'save all the little starving children and bring them up as Christians'. Thirty-three years later, she founded her Himalayan Christian Orphanage, later known as the Mayo School, at Simla.[19]

Similarly, Maria Graham encountered a Mrs A., the wife of a rice and sugar-cane owner at Salsette, who had 'the face and the heart of an angel', and who took in the poor and the wretched to whom she gave medical help since there was no medical man within many miles. She had rescued an Indian boy from starvation and was raising him as a mechanic. She was also instructing the daughter of a friend along with her own two children. In addition, 'her drawing is that of an artist; her judgment in music is exquisite; and her taste correct in both ancient and modern literature'. Her manner was 'gentle and unembarrassed' and Maria wished that there were a few more such European women in the East, 'to redeem the character of our country-women, and to shew the Hindoos what English Christian women are'.[20] She did not, however, think missionary activity was necessary to that end. Missionaries, she thought,

> are very apt ... in order to place our religion in the brightest light, as if it wanted their feeble aid, they lay claim exclusively to all the sublime maxims of morality, and tell those they wish to convert, that their own books contain nothing but abominations, the belief of which they must abandon in order to receive the purer doctrine of Christianity. Mistaken men![21]

Work such as that of Mrs A. would often, but not always, be among Indians. Mary Sherwood included both races in the schools she ran in the *mofussil* at Cawnpore, Dinapore, and Meerut. Lady Loudon, the Marchioness of Hastings, was responsible for the creation of the Calcutta Free Book Society 'for the promotion of the moral and intellectual improvement of the natives, by the diffusion among them of useful elementary knowledge'.[22] She was also responsible for the founding of a school at Barrackpore for some eighty Indian boys and sixteen European and Eurasian girls[23] and for an asylum in Calcutta for white orphan girls.[24] Usually, however, women were the beneficiaries rather than the founders or managers of philanthropic societies. They would organize balls or sell subscriptions to other kinds of 'assemblies', but, like the Indians, they were set normally in the role of receiving, if not charity, then the benefits of the foresight and prudence of a husband who took care to provide for them in the event of his death.

A critical method for converting Indians, however, was felt to be the moral example the British themselves could provide—and write about. Indeed, women writers played a significant role in providing something of a new genre, a kind of hagiographical or 'conversion' novel detailing the progress of a Hindu, guided by the example of a worthy Christian, toward Christianity. The main purpose of conversion stories was not merely to edify or entertain, but as Tony Ballantine points out, critiques of Hinduism were primarily intended for a British, not an Indian, reading public, and with a twofold purpose. First, by emphasizing Hindu polytheism, idolatry, and licentious, Evangelicals would be able to secure financial, spiritual, and political support from home for the proselytization of India. The second aim was political; the Evangelicals were questioning the Company's 'toleration' of Hinduism and the place of religion in the colonial public sphere.[25]

The first of these conversion stories, Elizabeth Hamilton's *Translations of the Letters of a Hindoo Rajah*, appeared in 1796. Miss Hamilton never went to India herself but her brother, Charles, did in 1772, under the patronage of Warren Hastings. He returned to England in 1786 and, with Elizabeth's assistance, translated a code of Muslim laws from Persian and worked on a history of the Rohillas. By the time he died in 1792, Elizabeth had come to share not only his genuine love for India and its people, but a hope that they could be converted. The hero of the *Letters*, Charles Percy, modelled after her brother, dies at the beginning of the narrative but it is his influence that induces the rajah, Zāārmilla, to become a Christian. In Zāārmilla's letters to his friend, Kisheen Neeay, however, Hamilton takes the opportunity to criticize many British customs, including its religious indifference, the continuance of the slave trade, and the treatment of women. Although India and Indians are treated gently, there is an interesting contrast with *Hartly House* where it is the English Christian, Sophia Goldborne, who submits to instruction from a Brahmin. In Hamilton's book, it is not only the Englishman who influences the Brahmin, but one who is not an official, nor a merchant, nor a missionary, but an ordinary layman and a soldier, the stout defender of empire, God's as well as Britain's.

More influential than Hamilton was Mary Sherwood whose *Indian Pilgrim* placed Bunyan's *Pilgrim's Progress* into an Indian context and was translated into Hindustani. Her main character, also an Indian Brahmin, is led through a number of religious experiences with Hinduism, Islam, and Catholicism and, after rejecting all of these as unfulfilling, he finally accepts Evangelical Christianity as the source of Divine Wisdom. Mrs Sherwood came to India in 1805 with her husband and for the next ten years moved about India from one military post to another. She wrote a number of books dealing with the themes of Indians being converted to Christianity by English example or preaching. Much of her writing was directed at children. She wrote short stories and catechisms for them, as well as longer works such as *Little Henry and His Bearer, Little Lucy and her Dhaye,* and *The Last Days of Boosy.* The Henry stories describing how Henry came to a true understanding of Christianity, how he died, and his influence on his bearer, Boosy, became quite popular in Anglo-Indian circles as well as England, and were translated not only into Hindustani but several other languages.

About the mid or late 1820s one perceives the rift not only between Evangelicals and Orientalists[26] but also between missionaries and secular evangelicals. While both groups shared a belief in the depravity of Hinduism as a social and religious system, contempt for Indian people came more often from secular evangelicals than from missionaries and often had less to do with the gospel than with values that were secular. Cleanliness, industry, and thrift which for most of the Christian era had had little or nothing to do with Christianity were now found to be not far from godliness, and the Indian, regardless of how thoroughly baptized he or she might become, quite often fell short. Helen Mackenzie found that, without constant prodding, native Christian women would lapse into 'idleness, extravagance, love of dress, bad management of their children, and the absence of all exertion for the souls of others'.[27] In fact, she knew of one woman, the wife of an Indian catechist, who, although she had been brought up in an orphan school 'in the most simple manner', yet dressed in clear muslin and ran her husband into debt by buying bear's grease and perfumes. There was another in her acquaintance who would not carry a plate in her own hands from one house to another and several who always hired tailors to make their own and their children's clothes while they sat idle.[28] Such lack of industry and thrift was clear evidence to Mrs Mackenzie of the ultimate inability of the Indians, even when Christianized, to absorb the essence of Christian virtue after all. Bessie Fenton also thought Indians an 'abject and contemptible race', proof of which was that 'even their wealth seems to contribute as little to *their own* gratification as that of *any other* person'.[29] Indians were indolent to excess and, from habit and constitutional temperament, careless of promises or engagements. 'They present a mass of obstinate inertness; there exists not in the heart of these degraded beings any spirit of emulation or self-respect to supply the place of bodily energy'.[30]

Unable to obtain moral maturity, Indians were like children. Not only were they childlike, but they were vicious children at that. Helen Mackenzie and her husband whose zeal earned him the soubriquet, 'Mullah' Mackenzie, one day passed a little girl singing at the top of her voice and her husband told her that the words of the song were so detestable and vile 'that hardly any man among the worst in London could sing such, unless previously intoxicated'. And Mrs Mackenzie immediately associated the vileness of the song with Hinduism itself. 'Muhammedans are practically as bad as the Hindus, though their religion is far better', she thought, 'for nothing, it is said, can equal the abominations of the Hindu deities and modes of worship.' And then she added, 'Think what must be the state of a nation, when children are systematically trained in wickedness, and their acts of worship consist of crimes.'[31]

For Mary Sherwood, the evil effects of Hinduism actually could be seen in the countenances of Hindu women. Coupling Christianity with an oblique attack on concubinage, she found the women of Madras 'fearful to look upon':

Their skin is shriveled and hanging loose, the lips thin and black, and the whole expression that of persons hardened by misery and without hope, having in youth exhausted all that life can give, and, through this rapid exhaustion, having grown old before the youth of an honourable English wife could have begun to face: ... all this evident misery, without counting the many secret cruelties which abound in every heathen land, in every dark corner of the earth, being the effect, either direct or indirect, of those abominable creeds which we think it an act of charity not merely to tolerate but to patronize. If a long residence in heathen and Mahometan countries renders a European blind to these symptoms of misery and degradation in the natives of India, well may we regret the feelings of grief and horror with which the English lady or gentleman first visits a native bazaar.[32]

While she felt that it would have been unjust to persecute Indians on account of their religious principles she could not understand how anyone could 'contemplate the miserable effects of a false religion' and make no effort to deliver such people 'who are groaning under these horrors of darkness'.[33] Shortly after her arrival in Calcutta she saw an English gentleman riding through the square with his *sais* or groom running along beside his horse. Mrs Sherwood thought it was 'a monstrous and unchristianlike piece of tyranny for a white man to come all the way from Europe to make some poor black wretch run by his horse, and in a climate so hot, too; the black man was much slenderer and weaker, of course, than his white tyrant'.[34] But she met the 'tyrant' shortly thereafter and found him then a 'gallant captain' and after a longer residence in India concluded that 'the English in India are universally kind masters, and that the coming of the English to Hindustan is the greatest blessing which ever descended on the poor Hindu'.[35] Indeed, it was a blessing that she thought should be thrust upon India and was horrified when it was not. 'Few people at home', she complained, 'know that the British authorities still countenance idolatrous ceremonies by their presence.' She had been told of 'that most degrading saturnalia', the Holi festival, in Nagpur, when the resident Sir Henry Pottinger allowed himself to be sprinkled with the red powder used by the celebrants. 'No Mussulman Government', she fumed, 'ever degraded themselves thus.'[36]

Perhaps the most unusual English woman to encounter an Indian religion and to do so on a uniquely personal level was Mrs Meer Hassan Ali through her marriage to a Muslim nobleman from Lucknow. Whether she ever actually converted to Islam is unclear. If her husband had been a *sayyed*,[37] he could not have legally married her at all. Assuming he was not, he still would have had to insist on some kind of conversion, but she does not mention any such ceremony. In any case, she certainly violated every single tenet of Evangelicalism by marrying him. She wrote one of the most complete descriptions of Islam that had hitherto appeared in English, from the apparition of the angel Gabriel to Mohammed to the Shi'a/Sunni schism. Her detailed and sympathetic account of Sufism, including an explanation of the difference between Majub and Saalik Sufism, brought her into a discussion of the great Persian Sufi poets, Hafez and Sa'idi, as well as the poet Ferdowsi. And while she does not appear to have read any of them in the original, she exhibited credible knowledge of the content of several of their works. She explained Muslim prayers, the distinction between the Quran and the Christian Bible, Islamic views on marriage and polygamy, wedding customs, and the major festivals in Islam.

In the long run, if Indians were so innately depraved that even Christianizing them would not necessarily change them much, one has to wonder why, apart from elevating one's own spiritual lot, anybody would bother to try. In reality, some Englishmen and women simply relinquished the effort, and not because they were either bad Christians or bad Englishmen. As prevalent and powerful as Evangelicalism was, it did not always prevent Englishmen or women from viewing India through kind eyes. Maria Nugent was persuaded to give up the idea of converting her *sirkar* only when she was told that such an attempt might lead to 'unpleasant circumstances'.[38] Like many Europeans, she found the Churruk Poojah 'shocking' and it was 'melancholy indeed to think that human beings should so torment and degrade themselves, from a false idea of religion'.[39] Yet about seven months earlier, she had concluded, 'Whenever I see them in the water, with their eyes lifted up to heaven, and their hands clasped, I cannot avoid giving them credit for real feelings of religion; and I am certain, that whatever their mistakes or superstitions may be, such prayers, offered in purity of heart, are acceptable to the Almighty.'[40] Mrs Nugent was not the most tolerant British woman to ever set foot in India but her small generosity is some indication that the open-minded sympathy for India which had often characterized the previous age had not been entirely forfeited.

The Orientalists' view that Indian institutions, including her religions, did have an inherent validity, that hers was a rich and highly developed civilization, still provided the philosophical context through which many British men and women approached India and India's religions. Indeed, the body of knowledge about India's religious life that had begun to accumulate in the time of Warren Hastings was vastly expanded and enriched by the Victorians. Translations by both women and men of religious works and sacred texts from both Islam and Hinduism, of sacred and profane poetry, of legends, stories, and fables from both religious traditions, appeared in European languages, along with commentaries, critiques, and textual analyses.

Nor was it simply scholars and eccentrics that could see India and her religions through sympathetic eyes. There was still an inclination, carried over from the Enlightenment, to see an underlying unity in all human religious experience, a tendency towards 'Why, they are just like us, after all!' Like Maria Graham earlier, Marianne Postans, Emma Roberts, and Anne Katharine Elwood also sympathetically described the religious festivals and beliefs of Hindus and Muslims and found parallels between the different sects in each with Catholic and Protestant divisions in Europe.[41] Not only did these women explore Indian religions, they also were critical of the behaviour of their own Christian countrymen. Fanny Parkes was 'much disgusted' by the Churruk Pooja[42] but it was not Hinduism itself that bothered her; rather, it was excessive religious enthusiasm of any kind, for if she thought Hindoos gullible, Englishmen were not much more virtuous. 'People think of nothing but converting the Hindoos; and religion is often used as a cloak by the greatest schemers after good appointments. Religious meetings are held continually in Calcutta, frequented by people who hope to pray themselves into high salaries, who never thought of praying before.'[43]

Emma Roberts was only a little less tart than Fanny Parkes about evangelizing or improving India. While the British had an opportunity to introduce a 'better code of morals', she thought it would also be unwise to 'stigmatize a whole race as inimical to all improvement'. Her countrymen, she thought, had thrown more odium on the natives than they deserved, and

> in our reprobation of crimes and follies, which we have little or no temptation to commit, we forget how often we err on the score of benevolence, justice, courtesy, and charity, towards those who have so much right to expect all the Christian virtues at our hands. Never, perhaps were the lines of Hudibras more strongly exemplified than in India, since most certainly there,
>
> > we Compound for sins we are inclined to,
> > By damning those we have no mind to.[44]

Evangelical Christianity is often regarded as causing a new chasm between the British and Indians, or rather widening one that had existed from the earliest entry of Europeans into India. That is not quite true. The disdain with which nineteenth-century Christians regarded Indians, both Muslim and Hindu, had an earlier antecedent in the pattern of contempt with which *mustees* and *castees* who had a partial Christian, albeit Catholic, identity, had been regarded in the seventeenth century. And individuals on both sides of that chasm had been able to bridge it. Similarly, in itself, Evangelical Christianity probably had less to do with developing the rift between the two races than is commonly thought, and for two reasons. First, the vast majority of Indians never saw an English man or woman, let alone an Evangelical, and least of all a missionary. Despite the translations of Mary Sherwood's works and that of the missionaries who put the scriptures and other Christian writings into Indian languages, there is a good chance that most Indians who could read did not read these materials.

Emma Roberts provides a second consideration: that in close contact with Hinduism or Islam, Christianity itself might lose some of its militancy. In describing the festival of Muharram in Lucknow, she gave a fascinating glimpse into how Islam had been changed by India. The feast commemorates the martyrdom of the Prophet's grandsons, Hassan and Hussein, at Karbala in the seventh century, an event that marks the beginning of the Shi'ite/Sunni schism in Islam. It is an event normally marked by lamentations and re-enactments of the violent and tragic events, either symbolically or often, quite realistically and, with self-flagellations, bloodily. What Miss Roberts witnessed, however, was pageantry, spectacle, colour, and gaiety. She described the gaudy banners, streamers, and umbrellas, the processions to heavily ornamented 'tombs' of the martyrs, grandees distributing money, and crowds of people, Muslim and Hindu, joining in the festivities. Mullahs, she said, recited the 'oft-told, but never tiring story' of Karbala, and then the tragic scene was enacted by young men expert at broad sword exercises. The entire spectacle would be esteemed scandalous in Persia or Arabia, she thought, but what she encountered in India was 'a blending between the two religions, which could scarcely be expected from the intolerant disciples of Mahomet and the exclusive followers of Brahma; ... Their zeal has relaxed, and they have become vitiated by the examples around them'.[45] Touching on India's ability to absorb and to 'Hinduize' any and all religious experiences, not excluding perhaps Christianity, she observed, 'Hindoos have found it advantageous to their interests to assist at Mussulman ceremonies, and the faithful have not been backward in the sacrifice of religious principles upon occasion of great importance. Conversions have also been extremely imperfect ...'[46] Maria Graham also touched on the universality of some religious observances. Muslims participated in the Holi as fully as Hindus participated in Muharram, she noticed, because of 'the disposition all men feel to rejoice with those who rejoice'.[47]

There is a certain irony in that Britain should consider evangelizing a country that was home to one of the oldest communities in Christendom—and to a community that could trace its origins to an Apostle, no less. In addition, it was a community that had never been particularly zealous about converting or reforming its non-Christian neighbours but, rather, had long since learned to live in their midst in relative calm.

The identification of Christianity as an essentially Western creed that imperialists sought to force upon India is at least inaccurate if not somewhat patronizing. People have traded in India for the last ten thousand years, and many have brought their creeds with them. A few, not only Christians but also Muslims, Buddhists, and Jews, have proselytized. If one wants to look for zealotry in the pursuit of converts in India, the Jesuits and particularly the Portuguese Jesuits who had persuaded new converts to remain steadfast in the faith through the encouragement of the Inquisition, make the religious fervour of the British evangelicals in India, both lay and ordained, appear positively flaccid.

In the long run, it may have been neither Christianity even in its evangelical form, nor Christian missionaries as such, that offended Indians so much as the notion that anything European was superior to anything that was Indian. And there would have been many Indians (and not only Brahmins) who, had they been asked, might have reciprocated with the notion that there was nothing European that was superior or even equal to anything Indian.

notes

1 William Carey, *The Good Old Days of Honorable John Company, Being Curious Reminiscences during the Rule of the East India Company from 1600 to 1858*, 2 vols (Calcutta: R. Cambray & Co., 1906), II, 39.

2 Kathleen Blechynden, *Calcutta Past and Present* (London: W. Thacker & Co., 1905), 225–6.

3 S. Pearce Carey, *William Carey* (London: Hodder and Stoughton, 1923), 162.

4 Ibid., 274.

5 Martha Weitbrecht, *Missionary Sketches in North India with References to Recent Events* (London: James Nisbet and Co., 1858), 20.

6 Philip Francis, *The Francis Letters*, ed., Beata Francis and Eliza Keary, 2 vols (London: Hutchinson and Co., 1901), I, 233.

7 House of Commons, *Parliamentary Papers*, 'Papers Relating to East India Officers', Vol. VIII (1812–13), 324.

8 Cited in Weitbrecht, *Missionary Sketches*, 24.

9 Reverend John Sargent, ed., *Life and Letters of the Reverend Henry Martyn* (London: Seeley, Jackson, and Halliday, 1862), 418.

10 For a discussion of the work of individual missionary women, see Kenneth Ingham, *Reformers in India, 1793–1833* (Cambridge: Cambridge University Press, 1956).

11 Reverend William Buyers, *Letters on India, with Special Reference to the Spread of Christianity* (London: John Snow, 1840), 157.

12 Violet Dickinson, ed., *Miss Eden's Letters* (London: Macmillan and Co., Ltd., 1919), 283.

13 Emily Eden, *Up the Country*, 2 vols (London: Richard Bentley, 1866), II, 89–90.

14 Dickinson, *Miss Eden's Letters*, 283.

15 Ibid., 86–9.

16 Weitbrecht, *Missionary Sketches*, 23.

17 Ibid., 141.

18 Susan Thorne, 'Religion and Empire at Home', in Catherine Hall and Sonya Rose, eds, *At Home with the Empire* (Cambridge: Cambridge University Press, 2006), 145.

19 Harriet Tytler, *An Englishwoman in India: The Memoirs of Harriet Tytler, 1828–1858*, ed., Anthony Sattin (New York: Oxford University Press, 1986), 10.

20 Maria Graham, *Journal of a Residence in India* (Edinburgh: Printed by George Ramsay for Archibald Constable and Company, 1812), 115.

21 Maria Graham, *Letters on India* (London: Longman, 1814), 88.

22 'Free Schools in India', House of Commons, *Parliamentary Papers*, Vol. LX (1831–32), 406.

23 Ingham, *Reformers in India*, 60.

24 Mary Sherwood, *The Life and Times of Mrs Sherwood (1775–1851) from the Diaries of Captain and Mrs Sherwood*, ed., F.J. Harvey Darton (London: Wells, Gardner & Co., 1910), 397.

25 Tony Ballantyne, *Orientalism and Race: Aryanism in the British Empire* (Houndsmills, Basingstoke, Hampshire and New York: Palgrave, 2002), 99.

26 See Thomas Trautman, 'The Missionary and the Orientalist', in *Ancient to Modern: Religion, Power, and Community in India*, eds, Ishita Bannerjee Dube and Saurabh Dube (New Delhi: Oxford University Press, 2008).

27 Helen [Mrs Colin] Mackenzie, *Life in the Mission, the Camp and the Zenana, or Six Years in India*, 2 vols (London: Richard Bentley, 1854, 2nd ed.), II, 283.

28 Ibid.

29 Bessie Fenton, *Journal of Mrs Fenton* (London: Edward Arnold, 1901), 41. Her italics.

30 Ibid., 199.

31 Mackenzie, *Life in the Mission* , I, 109.

32 Sherwood, *Life and Times*, 253.

33 Ibid., 252.

34 Ibid., 264.

35 Ibid., 265.

36 Ibid., 272.

37 Sayyeds are direct descendants of the Prophet and strictly endogamous; that is, they may marry only other sayyeds.

38 Maria Nugent, *Lady Nugent's Journal*, ed. Frank Cundall (London: Published for the Institute of Jamaica by Adam & Charles Black, 1907, 360.

39 Ibid., 380.

40 Ibid., 365.

41 See Marianne Postans, *Cutch; or Random Sketches Taken during a Residence in One of the Northern Provinces of Western India; Integrated with Legends and Traditions* (London: Smith, Elder and Co., 1839), chapter 10.

42 Fanny (Parlby) Parkes, *Wanderings of a Pilgrim in Search of the Picturesque, during Four and Twenty Years in the East.* 2 vols (London: P. Richardson, 1850), I, 28.

43 Ibid., I, 145.

44 Roberts, *Hindostan*, 54–5.

45 Emma Roberts, *Scenes and Characteristics of Hindostan, with Sketches of Anglo-Indian Society.* 3 vols (London: W.H. Allen and Co., 1835), II, 187.

See also William Dalrymple's discussion in *The Last Mughal: The Fall of a Dynasty—Delhi, 1857* (New York: Vintage Books, 2006), chapter 2. Dalrymple also points out that there was strong opposition to that synthesis among leading Muslim clerics, especially in Delhi.

46 Roberts, *Scenes and Characteristics*, 188.

47 Graham, *Letters*, 323.

15

of clay and porcelain

Here all are grasping at rank and superiority, with an eagerness propor-
tioned to the conscious want of it, and to the obscurity of their former
condition. This has brought to the subject so great an interest, and so
much perplexity, that even the ingenuity of the ladies, who are commonly most deeply versant in this science, is often unable to unravel it.[1]

SO COMPLAINED THE REVEREND WILLIAM TENNANT. Since the establishment of the first factories, quarrels about rank had been frequent,
often violent, and, as Reverend Tennant suggested, the presence of
women had done nothing at all to mitigate the rancour. Indeed, they
had quite often exacerbated it.

The year 1818 was significant not only for the defeat of the
Marathas at Panipat but for the publication of the *East India Register
and Directory*. The Civil List, as it simply came to be called, also
contained an Army List and Non-official Directory. Every man
connected in any way with India, either at home or in India, from
members of the Asiatic Society, East India Company stockholders,
and the Court of Directors down to the lowest private, serving or
retired, civil servants, judges—all were listed in order of their rank.[2]
It quickly provided ammunition for more feuds among civilized

English people than any other written work of the nineteenth century, with the possible exception of Darwin's *Origin of Species*.

As several scholars have noted, the empire in India was as much about class as it was about race but exactly when or how the two intersected is difficult to pinpoint. It had long been an article of social faith among Europeans as well as Indians that societies had ranks and orders, varying degrees of subordination and authority, which were rarely questioned since good order was assumed to be the foundation of 'politeness' as well as of peace. Well into the nineteenth century, there was a vaguely Chartist or trade unionist smell about assuming manners and airs not befitting one's station. Even among the most radical Whigs, there was the sense that 'place' was something to be granted by those in authority rather than assumed by the 'lower orders'.

Thinking about race lay outside theories about social order, however. In the sixteenth and seventeenth centuries, in view of the fragile position English factories had occupied vis-á-vis Indian authorities, it would have been the height of absurdity to view native peoples as inferior. In addition, Englishmen in the earlier generations also would have recognized that Indian society closely resembled their own: a carefully graded hierarchy of status, extending in a seamless web from chiefs and princes at the top to less worthy figures at the bottom. Moreover, these two essentially hierarchical societies were seen as coexisting, not in a relationship of (English) superiority and (Indian) inferiority, but in twin structures of equivalence and similarity: princes in one society were the analogues to princes in another, and so on and so on, all the way down two parallel social ladders.[3]

In the early nineteenth century, the natural chasm was increasingly marked by racism. Coinciding with the Civil List was the publication of James Mill's *History of India* in 1817 with its negative assessment of Hindu civilization. The two taken together created a hierarchy in which, no matter how low one ranked on the Civil List, Indians, regardless of caste, even regardless of how Anglicized or Christianized they might become, ranked lower.

Clamouring for rank was as old as the first factory at Surat. There, rank had been more fluid than at home since it was determined not by birth but largely by one's function in regard to commerce. The necessity of providing for a military presence had muddied the problem further by raising the question of how military rank compared with civilian rank. Matters had become even more awkward in the mid-seventeenth century when men had begun to arrive in India whose ranking by birth had not matched their commercial importance within the Company.

What made the clamouring for rank peculiar among Anglo-Indians and between that community and India in the early nineteenth century was that it now was at variance not only with the mercantile wealth engendered by the Industrial Revolution, but also with the egalitarian impulses of the French and American Revolutions which were eroding the social orders within Britain itself. The Revolutions had challenged status and the traditional barriers of birth and fortune, and insisted upon the assertion of human rights rather than a mere acknowledgement of duties. In Europe, most men were becoming citizens. In India, those same citizens were dealing with peoples who would be subjects. There was therefore an artificiality, a brittleness about the entire thing, an awareness that the Britain they were dedicated to keeping alive in India was not quite the Britain they had left.

The concern with rank and protocol in India was more excessive than would have been tolerated in England and was a bit of a trial to both men and women. One Anglo-Indian described the system in somewhat artistic terms. He remarked that there were three sets of Europeans at every station, two of blue porcelain and one of clay. The blue porcelain were the civil and military people and the clay were the planter and mercantile elements.[4] The designation, he granted, had nothing whatever to do with their social standing at home, for clay could be found in the porcelain sets and vice versa. The leaders were the well-paid and important members of the civil services. The civilians regarded themselves as solely responsible for the destinies of India but then, so did the military who were of second rank in the blue porcelain set and, regardless of what was said in public, the army knew it was inferior in rank and in salary to the civilian services.

The distinction between 'civil' and 'military' stations, namely, stations where one authority or the other was predominant, often brought on terrible feuds in small stations where there was a subordinate element of one or the other, and both would then contend for supremacy. The feuds rarely went beyond cold nods, exclusion from dinner parties, and pompous commands about trifles, but it could happen that the question of supremacy would actually be referred to higher authorities. Between the army and the civil service was a vague, ill-defined region in which military men acted like administrators and civilians directed military operations, but everyone knew his 'set' and if he temporarily forgot it, the rest of the community would exercise sufficient pressure to bring him back. As Emma Roberts wryly observed, 'The struggle for precedence was carried on with a spirit and perseverance worthy of colonial warfare.'[5]

As they would have done at home, women took precedence according to the rank of their husbands. The distinction between civil and military and the jealousies between the two had nothing to do with women at all. Nevertheless, most of them did their conjugal duty and encouraged their husbands' enmities and divisiveness. An occasional woman, however, would get tired of the entire quarrel. During a dinner at Madras, an officer told one lady, 'Now I know very well, Mrs. __, you despise us all from the bottom of your heart; you think no one worth speaking to in reality but the Civil Service. Whatever people may really be you just class them all as civil and military—civil and military; and you know no other distinction. Is it not so?' The lady replied, 'No; I sometimes class them as civil and uncivil.' Still the same author had to confess that there was a difference between civil and military wives.

> The civil ladies are generally very quiet, languid, speaking in almost a whisper, simply dressed, almost always lady-like and *comme il-faut*, not pretty, but pleasant and nice-looking, rather dull, and give one very hard work pumping for conversation. The military ladies, on the contrary, are always noisy, affected, showily dressed, with a great many ornaments, *mauvais* for chatter incessantly from the moment they enter the house, twist their curls, shake their bustles, and are altogether what you may call 'Low Toss.' While they are alone with me after dinner they talk about suckling their babies, the disadvantage of scandal, 'the officers' and 'the Regiment', and when the gentlemen come into the drawing-room, they invariably flirt with them most furiously.[6]

If wives were boring on the subject of rank, however, their husbands were equally dull.

As soon as three or four of them get together they speak about nothing but employment and promotion. Whatever subject may be started they contrive to twist it, drag it, clip it and pinch it, till they bring it round to that and if left to themselves they sit and conjugate the verb 'to collect'! 'I am a Collector—He was a Collector—We shall be Collectors—You ought to be a Collector—They would have been Collectors.'[7]

On the other hand, for the first time in the history of British India, women expressed a great deal of discomfort about a situation over which they could have no control. Maria Graham found the women of Bombay 'under-bred and over-dressed, and, with the exception of one or two, very ignorant and every grossiere'.[8] The men in the company were what a Hindu would call of a higher caste than the women but not terribly more impressive. She thought the merchants were the most rational companions. 'Having, at a very early age, to depend on their own mental exertions, they acquire a steadiness and sagacity which prepare their minds for the acquisition of a variety of information, to which their commercial intercourse leads.' But the young civil servants were so taken up with their imaginary importance that 'they disdain to learn, and have nothing to teach'. The military were not much better for although she met with many well-informed and 'gentleman-like' persons, still the small number of rational companions made a 'deplorable prospect' to anyone who anticipated a long residence in India.[9]

Since planters, tradesmen, and merchants, even the wealthier ones, were extraneous to what the British were now about in India, everyone in the civil and military services was a 'better' to the clay who were not. Clay consisted of covenanted members of the commercial and administrative services, such as surgeons and civilian technical specialists. Socially, they were at best merely tolerated and not quite fit for a young lady of 'breeding' to be married off to without incurring enormous social burdens. Clay was not actually denied access to Government House or to any of the lesser social privileges but porcelain made it very difficult to accept them. The upper orders of clay, however respectable or wealthy, could not even venture on to the Calcutta Course for the ritual evening ride, 'without the experience of many galling slights and mortifying embarrassments'.[10]

Beneath even the level of clay were members of the uncovenanted services, what P.J. Marshall has called a 'largely silent presence'.[11]

These were men who were employed by the Company's government but who had not agreed to a contract or covenant such as that entered into by the military and civil servants. The respectable 'unofficial' European element of merchants, planters, technical specialists, or professional people grew but their numbers were still limited until the greater penetration of the Indian economy by private British enterprise in the 1860s and 1870s.[12] A considerable number of 'poor whites' was another silent presence.

The trouble with the uncovenanted was that many of them were Eurasians, and it was upon this community that class and race intersected. Eurasian wives of civil and military officers were not fully accepted in European society or if they were accepted they were treated, according to Reverend Tennant, 'with such caution and ceremonious reserve, as must continually put them in mind of their degradation'.[13] Nonetheless, the breach was never quite absolute. Lord Hastings observed the 'excessive depression' in which the half-castes were held by the Company's servants, and it was not until his wife, Lady Loudon, privately hinted that colour would never be noticed that Eurasian ladies were admitted to Government House. Prior to her arrival, when there had been no Governor's lady since the departure of Maria Hastings, such women, even though of the best education and married to men in prominent positions, had not been admitted there.[14]

Lady Loudon's generosity may not have been typical of all Englishwomen, but her contemporary, Maria Graham, showed something of the same spirit. She agreed that Eurasians should be discouraged from going to Europe in order to permanently settle there, but her reason pointed blame not at them nor miscegenation per se but rather that 'their complexion must subject them to perpetual mortification'.[15]

While never unbridgeable, the breach did widen. Bessie Fenton who came to India in 1826 expressed the chasm between Englishmen and Eurasians, albeit unwittingly. She thought the prejudice against half-castes was 'very strange' and blamed the presence of European women for it, 'since formerly, when European ladies were rarely met with, [Eurasian women] held a place in society which they have now entirely lost'.[16] But when she heard that her cousin had married a Eurasian girl she was 'a little mortified'.[17] When she and another woman attended a nautch, they were careful to keep walking about the room since 'the benches were filled by half-castes, and not liking to seat ourselves with them' they took the alternative.[18] A bit later, in the mid-1830s, Emily Eden described their status thus:

> The 'uncovenanted service' is just one of our choicest Indianism, accompanied with our very worst Indian feelings. We say the words just as you talk of the 'poor chimney-sweepers,' or 'those wretched scavengers'—the uncovenanted being, in fact, clerks in the public offices. Very well-educated, quiet men, and many of them very highly paid; but as many of them are half-castes, we, with our pure Norman, or Saxon blood, cannot really think contemptuously enough of them.[19]

She thought the prevalent attitude regrettable since some of them were 'thorough gentlemen' and she never saw 'better behaved people'.[20] About a generation later, Madeline Wallace-Dunlop noticed that 'those with the slightest taint of half-caste are ignored completely, and in India the eye gets educated to detect the least trace with a celerity that is astonishing'.[21]

The trouble with Eurasians was that more than any other single factor, more than British ladies dancing or smoking hookahs or behaving in ways that might have a 'bad effect upon the natives', the presence of Eurasian children belied the moral, and with it, the political authority upon which the British had established their claim to rule India. Any attempt to directly attack such a widespread and ingrained practice would have been ludicrous in the extreme but now it struck a fundamental nerve that was not specifically moral nor at all related to the feelings of British women on the subject.

While trade had prospered and, as long as salaries remained modest and even after they had been raised, the factors had normally preferred concubines to British wives. Indeed, an argument might be made that concubines had done as much, if not more, to quiet British men's souls. Nonetheless, the idea persisted that British families signalled stability, a moral 'rightness', a signal that Britain's—or the Company's—work was not far removed from God's.

Two centuries later, not much changed. The British wife who had been a sign of stability and morality against 'whores' who were 'popish Christians' in the seventeenth century, now represented that same stability and morality against the Indian concubine, and concubinage extended from the lowliest soldier in the ranks to the very highest offices in India. John Shore himself, before he was a Governor-General and long before he had presided over the Bible Society, had baptized an illegitimate son at St John's Church.[22] So pervasive was it that Lady Falkland told of a gentleman newly arrived from England who, upon visiting a school for Eurasian orphans, was accosted by a small boy who ran up to him, clung to his legs, looked imploringly into his eyes and cried 'Papa! Papa!'[23] The young Samuel Sneade Brown thought that only the intervention of a Higher Power could sway his countrymen from the charms of Indian women, and observed 'that a person, after being accustomed to their society, shrinks from the idea of encountering the whims or yielding to the fancies of an Englishwoman'.[24]

Precisely because it was so pervasive, British women could not have been unaware of the practice; yet not a single one of them ever mentions concubines directly. Nonetheless, their concern for the offspring of interracial liaisons had spawned any number of orphan societies and schools as early as the late seventeenth century and, although they were below the level of clay and porcelain, Eurasians had been a constant presence in Anglo-Indian social circles as well. Eurasian men occupied the lower ranks of the covenanted services, and Eurasian daughters were often sent to ladies' seminaries in the presidency towns to be educated, then to England to be 'finished' and then returned to India to marry fellow officers.[25]

Englishmen, administrators, collectors, soldiers, planters, could not be faulted for the spawning of Eurasian children so it became the Hindu woman who was 'degraded'. Like prostitutes at home, Indian women now were often derided as uneducated, jealous, and physically as well as morally dirty. In India, Hindu mothers were also responsible for the presumed submissiveness and timidity of their sons. 'However speculatively or ruminatively wise,' thought Colonel William Sleeman, '[they are] quite unfit for action, or for performing their part in the great drama of life.'[26] Unable to obtain moral maturity, then, Indians remained like children. Honoria Lawrence spoke of the 'obstinate childishness, so often seen in native character' but chided her husband for scarcely ever addressing an Indian without an abusive epithet even when he was not angry.[27]

Below Eurasians, at the bottom of the social order, were Indians themselves. While British women had always found it difficult to develop real friendships with Indian women, it had been possible, as Phebe Gibbes' *Hartly House* illustrated, to at least imagine deep affection and possibly even sexual attachments between British women and Indian men. It now became difficult, if not impossible, to develop a connection with the Indian world, male or female, based on mutual respect and understanding, and the chasm was deliberate official policy which was committed to restricting the British community in India to a body of temporary residents, assimilated as closely as possible not to India but to home.[28] In 1830, the East India Company forbade its employees to wear Indian clothing on official occasions, thus reinforcing a prevalent attitude noted by Emma Roberts that 'while less elegant native customs have found universal favour in European eyes, the greatest possible distinction in dress has been thought necessary'.[29] An Indian costume, pajamas, which had been a common dress in the eighteenth century, now became something Englishmen slept in rather than wore during the day.

Mrs Fenton was amazed to find it 'the extremity of bad taste to appear in anything of Indian manufacture—neither muslin, silk, flowers, or even ornaments, however beautiful'.[30] And the profusion of paintings and sketches that in the eighteenth century had shown British women, and men, in elements of Indian dress or in Indian social settings now evaporated.

When an older lady was asked what she had seen of the 'natives' during her years in India, she replied, 'Oh, nothing! Thank goodness, I know nothing at all about them nor I don't wish to; really, I think the less one sees and knows of them the better.'[31] Helen Mackenzie thought it very wrong for Europeans to treat Indians like brutes, to abuse and beat them, and she was horrified that 'the most vulgar parvenus treat native gentlemen as the dirt beneath their feet'.[32] When her husband told her that Hindus had no eye for beauty and would prefer tom-toms to Mozart, however, Mrs Mackenzie agreed that indeed their artistic tastes were inferior.[33] She was also convinced that Hindu mythology was far beneath that of the ancient Romans and Greeks and that, instead of being an entity in itself, Indian architecture and sculpture were proportionately debased.[34] The magnificent remains of the Moghuls, the glories of the old forts, mosques, the marbled vaults, the tombs, and gem-encrusted walls all astonished her, not because of their great beauty but because such beauty had been erected by heathens.

Especially in the last decade or perhaps even decade and a half before the Mutiny, ignorance of and distaste for India became *de rigueur* for many Anglo-Indians. Madeline Wallace-Dunlop had been born in Bombay in 1824 and then returned with her family to England. In February 1856, she and her sister, Rosalind, journeyed to India to visit their brother, a magistrate stationed at Meerut. Although she had grown up in a home filled with artifacts from India, she went expecting to hate India. And she did. Travelling from Calcutta to Meerut, she saw only 'groups of weird, impish-looking figures' and swarms of 'little, naked, bronze children'.[35] The Indians were 'hot, dirty' and her brain was 'racked by the intricacies of a language difficult of comprehension, and nasal in the extreme'. [36]

Even Indian princes were made to feel like *persona non grata* at Government House. On going to a station in the *mofussil*, Europeans would seldom call on the Indian notables of the district and that had once been done as a matter of course since the survival of the merchant and his trade had depended on the good will of such people. Now, certificates of respectability were often required of the notables before they could be guaranteed a chair when they visited an office. No sitting accommodations were provided in the courts for spectators or for any officials of the court except the judges. In Calcutta, many writers expected every Indian to salute them and many were so ignorant of Hindustani that they could not count beyond twenty. As Percival Spear puts it, 'So the garden was watered by thin sprays of efficiency from small watering-cans of duty instead of by the streams and fountains of cooperation and common ideals, until in our own days, instead of the rose trees and lotus flowers that had been looked for, came up stubborn cactuses of criticism and bitterness.'[37]

That changed relationship with India is reflected in a term that now came into use to refer to British women, 'memsahibs'. The term is related to the masculine, 'sahib', meaning lord or companion. The 'mem' was a corruption of 'ma'am' or 'madam', thus, the British wife and all other British women were the sahibs' ma'ams. At least in written records, the term is not used until the 1790s. Before that, 'bibi', a term of respect for Indian women, was also used and continued to be used for Englishwomen. 'Memsahib', however, referred exclusively to European women. Neither Indian nor Eurasian women could be memsahibs, even when they were concubines.

The term 'memsahib' indicated not merely a separation from India, however. It also contributed to a painful charade. People who might have come from the very bottom of society at home became lords and ladies, sahibs and memsahibs, in India. Unfortunately, as soon as they left India, they would again be painfully ordinary. Bessie Fenton put her finger on the precise source of the entire farce. 'Perhaps it is that those whose pretensions and place in society are not fully established attach that import to observances and omissions which persons who feel themselves in their proper sphere never question or remember, and either adopt or reject at pleasure.'[38]

Like many British men and women, however, Helen Mackenzie could draw a line between her general view of Indians and her dealings with individual Indian things or people. She liked Afghans in general very much, for instance, and she drew a lively image of an Afghan scout named Suleyman Khan who possessed those qualities normally associated only with British men—that is, boldness, intelligence, and determination. These qualities pleased Mrs Mackenzie and had actually raised Suleyman high in the confidence of his employers. Even Suleyman Khan, however, was an appendage, an 'interesting' figure on a British landscape of India, for he was 'just the kind of man you read of in a novel, who guides the hero through unimaginable dangers'.[39] It is the Englishman who is the hero. The native, no matter how noble and capable, serves.

While the British would often be condescending and both sexes were capable of grand thoughtlessness, however, many could also still live with Indians on terms of mutual respect and affection, and become caustic about their countrymen who would not. Fanny Parkes, who 'could no more jest or indulge in levity beneath the dome of the Taj, than I could in my prayers' was appalled to find a band playing on the marble terrace of the Taj Mahal and Englishmen dancing quadrilles in front of the tomb.[40] She also became extremely angry upon hearing in 1831 that the Governor-General, William Bentinck, had sold a beautiful piece of Moghul architecture, the Muti Masjid at Agra, for 125,000 rupees (then about £12, 500) and that it was being pulled down. About the same time, she also heard that the Taj itself was being offered for sale.

> The present king might as well sell the chapel of Henry the Seventh in Westminster Abbey for the paltry sum of 12,5000: for any sum the impropriety of the act would be the same. By what authority does the Governor-general offer the taj for sale? To sell the tomb raised over an empress, which from its extraordinary beauty is the wonder of the world? It is impossible the Court of Directors can sanction the sale of the tomb for the sake of its marble and gems.[41]

Like Fanny Parkes, there were many who noticed and regretted the increasing withdrawal of their countrymen from India. Lord Hastings thought the English too negligent of the 'little winning attentions which operate strongly on the feelings of the natives' but he also went on to say that he felt that the Indians just could not comprehend the 'simplicity of our address and habits' and ascribed English manners 'to our holding the natives too cheap to care what they may think with regard to us'.[42]

Those 'little winning attentions' are a part of what, in Persian, is called *tarofe*. At its worst, tarofe is no more than a worthless or insincere compliment.[43] Normally, however, it is a stylized, often rather elaborate system of polite discourse still used to smooth political, diplomatic, financial, and even personal affairs. Without tarofe, what Westerners would understand as simple, straightforward, blunt speech is taken for mere rudeness and boorishness. While it might still have been employed in oral discourse, rarely, after 1818, is there any written record from an English administrator containing tarofe. Indeed, there might be an argument that the reason the British became so hated was not because of Evangelicalism but because of the lack of that respect that tarofe entails.

The story of the British Raj, however, is not simply about domination but about criticism of that domination by women as well as men. Anna Harriette Leonowens complained that the viceroy and the officials around whom the whole Indian empire revolved were often ignorant of the Indian languages, races, religious and social prejudices, and she had often heard gentlemen of great intelligence in other respects speak of the people of India with profound contempt, classing in one indistinguishable mass Brahmans, Hindoos, Parsees, Mohammedans, Arabians, Persians, Armenians, Turks, Jews and 'other races too numerous to mention'.[44] Emma Roberts thought that Indians could be most easily managed by kindness 'by those who endeavour rather to humour than to force them out of their prejudices; a practice to which the scornful European is rather too strongly addicted'.[45]

Julia Maitland, the wife of a district judge, described an incident where an old Brahmin visited the house of a Captain Price. Upon hearing the Brahmin's voice, Price sauntered out of the next room, his hands in his pockets and, planting himself directly in front of the Brahmin and without any *salaam* or other compliments, loudly and rudely asked, 'Well, old fellow, where are you going?' Although the Brahmin answered with the utmost respect, Mrs Maitland saw an angry scowl come over his face, and observed, 'A little politeness pleases them … The upper classes are exceedingly well bred, and many of them are the descendants of native princes, and ought not to be treated like dirt.'[46]

Well before the Mutiny, the scowl on the old Brahmin's face revealed how hated the English could be. Emma Roberts also noticed it and, almost prophetically, worried that retaining the possession of India would depend mainly upon conciliating a class of persons whom, she said, 'it appears to have been hitherto the policy to depress and neglect, if not to insult'.[47] Because her countrymen were so careless of pleasing or offending the people amid whom they resided, she worried that, however respected the government may have been for its good faith, still, they 'usually contrive to make themselves hated wherever they go'.[48] She was fearful of the 'haughty superciliousness, arrogance and contemptuous conduct, too characteristic of Anglo-Indians'.

> Instead of exerting the superior knowledge, virtue, wisdom, science, &c., of which we make so great a vaunt, in gaining the respect of, and affording an example to the less fortunate people of India, we disgust them by the display of all our bad qualities, while they cannot possibly, by intuition, know that we have any good ones.[49]

Anna Leonowens also noticed it. She attended a dinner where, in spite of all the laughter and merriment, the exaltation of British power and British supremacy in India, she had a feeling of 'reserved force pervading those mute, motionless figures around us'. The conversation turned on theories of home government and how it should be administered. She was then too young to understand that discussion, but what she did comprehend was that 'no one seemed to mind those dark, silent, stationary figures any more than if they had been hewn out of stone.'[50]

More ominously perhaps was a story written by Elizabeth Elton Smith who came out to India in 1828, with her husband, a major in the Company's Madras army. Her *East-India Sketch Book* is a collection of twenty-seven stories about Anglo-Indian life, one of which, 'The Punishment', tells of the revenge taken by a Rajput sepoy, Cassee Sing, whose commander, an inflexible person named Ferrarton, orders him flogged before his regiment for theft. Cassee Sing deserts and then by infiltrating the household of the colonel through the children's ayah, slays both his sons and is about to do the same to his daughter but for the intervention of the ayah who had nursed the child. Fiction though it is, the story, published in 1833, is an eerie foretelling of the events of 1857. On Saturday, May 9, eighty-five sepoys who had refused to use cartridges which they (mistakenly, as it turned out) thought were greased with animal fat were paraded before the garrison at Meerut, stripped of their uniforms and shackled with leg irons. The exercise, like Ferrarton's flogging of Cassee Sing, was designed more to humiliate than to inflict physical pain. The next day, the sepoys at Meerut mutinied. Like the Hindu whose angry scowl Julia Maitland observed, the sepoys tended to be Brahmins, the caste so often blamed for what was 'wrong' with India.

Beneath the level even of those 'dark, silent, stationary figures' were those rare British women who actually had physical, emotional contact with Indians. There is some evidence that some British women did go into prostitution but there is a record of only one woman, Mrs Meer Hassan Ali, actually marrying a native. Biddy Timms had been a milliner in the household of Princess Augusta, a daughter of George III. Sometime between 1812 and 1816, she met her husband who was then a professor of Hindustani at the Company's military college, Addiscombe. She married him in March 1817 and then accompanied him out to India where, according to Honoria Lawrence, she was 'much respected' by both natives and Europeans. Unable to tolerate her husband's polygamy, however, after twelve years, she returned to England where she became the matron of a boys' school. What is interesting is the comment about her marriage from Honoria Lawrence who was a rather open-minded woman, that one would long to know how 'a woman with her cultivated mind and seemingly right principles, came to wed the Meer'.[51] Presumably, marrying an Indian man would require either an uncultivated mind or no 'right principles'—or both. Mrs Meer Hassan Ali's *Observations*, with her careful surveys of both Hindu and Muslim beliefs and her sympathetic view of life within a *zenana*, were published in 1832, but did not see a reprint until 1973.

The protocol attached to rank was heavy, elaborate, and burdensome. How or why it had evolved, no one seemed quite sure. Lady Amelia Falkland was to find that even the wife of a governor had very little power against the custom attaching to rank. She thought ladies in India were more tenacious of rank than people were in England.[52] They would carry their 'burra bibi-ship', as she called it, into the steamers when they went home to England. Like Maria Graham, however, she found that the men were every bit as bad. One of her friends who had travelled with several other men from Calcutta tried to persuade them that whatever their social importance had been in Calcutta they would be 'small folk' in London but apparently with very little response. The son of a peer had received an East India Company appointment and came out with an officer in the Company army, both of them enjoying equivalent rank. On leaving England, Lady Falkland's aristocratic friend took precedence at dinner since he was a peer, but at Aden, the first place belonging to the Company, the Company's officer said to her friend, 'Now sir, I take rank of you', which he promptly did by virtue of his very slight seniority as a military man, and displaced her friend at table.[53]

Adherence to the minutiae of protocol was of such importance primarily because the maintenance of an illusion depended upon it. And it was not only the illusion upon which empire rested, but the personal illusions about self that were at stake. Mrs Colin Mackenzie thought it must be a sad letdown for a woman who had been the 'burra bibi' at some station, or even of a presidency for a number of years to return home and find that a civilian ranked somewhere between a merchant and a police magistrate and his wife was placed after any captain's wife.[54]

After four years in India, Emily Eden reflected that hers had been 'essentially an artificial life'.[55] Social intercourse in Victorian England was very often exhilarating. The pages of Dickens sparkle with scintillating wit, profound human insights, and a noticeable display of individuality. One can imagine Pickwickian characters and conversations abounding in real life England, but not in India. It was of both sexes that a newcomer to Calcutta remarked, 'The tone of society is artificial, the manners of its members cold and formal, and their feelings blunted and unrefined.'[56]

'It is a gossiping society,' declared a weary Emily Eden.

> They sneer at each other's dress and looks, and pick out small stories against each other by means of the Ayahs, and it is clearly a downright offence to tell one woman that another looks well. It is not often easy to commit the crime with any regard to truth, but still there are degrees of yellow, and the deep orange woman who has had many fevers does not like the pale primrose creature with the constitution of a horse who has not had more than a couple of agues.[57]

notes

1 Reverend William Tennant, *Indian Recreations*, 2nd ed., 3 vols (Edinburgh: Edinburgh University Press, 1808), I, 58.

2 Douglas Dewar, *In the Days of the Company* (London: W. Thacker & Co., 1920) 103–14.

3 See David Cannadine, *Ornamentalism: How the British Saw Their Empire* (New York: Oxford University Press, 2001), 7–8.

4 An Old Indian, 'Social Life in Bengal Fifty Years Ago,' *Calcutta Review*, LXXIII (October 1881), 380. A few years later, Florence Marryat initially divided the residents of Madras into 'roast' and 'boiled', then changed that to three categories, the gay, the religious, and the inane. The highest god worshipped by the men was 'Rupee' and for the women it was 'Rank'. See Florence Marryat, *'Gup': Sketches of Anglo-Indian Life and Character* (London: Richard Bentley, 1868), 62.

5 Emma Roberts, *Scenes and Characteristics of Hindostan, with Sketches of Anglo-Indian Society*, 3 vols (London: W.H. Allen, 1835), III, 76.

6 Quoted in Dennis Kincaid, *British Social Life in India, 1608–1937* (London: George Routledge & Sons, Ltd., 1939), 153.

7 Quoted in ibid., 154.

8 Maria Graham, *Journal of a Residence in India* (Edinburgh: Printed by George Ramsay for Archibald Constable and Company, 1812), 28.

9 Ibid.

10 'The Evening Ride', *Calcutta Magazine and Monthly Register* (1831), I, 291.

11 See P.J. Marshall, 'British–Indian Connections. 1780 to c. 1830: The Empire of the Officials', in Michael J. Franklin, ed., *Romantic Representations of British India* (London and New York: Routledge, 2006), 50.

12 Ibid.

13 Tennant, *Indian Recreations*, I, 72.

14 Francis Rawdon, Marquess of Hastings. *Private Journal of the Marquess of Hastings* (Allahabad: The Panini Office, 1907), 158.

15 Graham, *Journal*, 128.

16 Bessie Fenton, *Journal of Mrs. Fenton* (London: Edward Arnold, 1901), 38.

17 Ibid., 69.

18 Ibid., 242.

19 Emily Eden, *Up the Country*, 2 vols (London: Richard Bentley, 1866), I, 199.

20 Ibid., 200.

21 Madeline Wallace-Dunlop, *The Timely Retreat; or a Year in Bengal before the Mutinies*, 2nd ed., 2 vols (London: Richard Bentley, 1858), II, 149.

22 Christopher J. Hawes, *Poor Relations: The Making of a Eurasian Community in British India, 1773–1833* (Richmond, Surrey: Curzon Press, 1996), 4.

23 Viscountess Amelia Cary Falkland, *Chow-Chow: Being Selections from a Journal Kept in India, Egypt, and Syria*, 2 vols (London: Hurst and Blackett, 1857), I, 26.

24 Samuel Sneade Brown, *Home Letters Written from India between the Years 1828 and 1841* (London: Printed for Private Circulation by C.F. Roworth, 1878), 17.

25 Ibid., 10.

26 Lieutenant Colonel William Henry Sleeman, *Rambles and Recollections of an Indian Official*, 2 vols (London: J. Hatchard and Son, 1844), I, 332. On the other hand, Sleeman witnessed the sati of a very old grandmother, who, despite the protestations of her family, had freely gone to her death with a dignity that impressed him. 'There is no people in the world,' he said, 'among whom parents are more loved, honoured, and obeyed than among the Hindoos; and the grandmother is always more honoured than the mother.' Ibid., 72.

27 Cited in *Honoria Lawrence*, ed. Maud Diver (Boston: Houghton Mifflin Company, 1936), 119.

28 P.J. Marshall, 'British–Indian Connections', 51.

29 Roberts, *Scenes and Characteristics*, III, 291–2.

30 Fenton, *Journal*, 82.

31 Cited in Michael Edwardes, *Bound to Exile: The Victorians in India* (London: Sidgewick and Jackson, 1969), 41.

32 Helen [Mrs Colin] Mackenzie, *Life in the Mission, the Camp and the Zenana*, 2 vols (London: Richard Bentley, 1854, 2nd ed.), I, 364.

33 Ibid., 205.

34 Ibid., 139.

35 Wallace-Dunlop, *The Timely Retreat*, II, 110.

36 Ibid., 211.

37 Percival Spear, *The Nabobs* (London: Humphrey Milford, Oxford University Press, 1963), 137.

38 Fenton, *Journal*, 175.

39 Mackenzie, *Life in the Mission*, 255.

40 Fanny (Parlby) Parkes, *Wanderings of a Pilgrim in Search of the Picturesque, during Four and Twenty Years in the East*, 2 vols (London: P. Richardson, 1850), I, 355–6.

41 Parkes, *Wanderings*, I, 220.

42 Rawdon, Hastings, *Private Journal*, 60.

43 An example of tarofe comes from a letter addressed by John Russell, then president of the factory at Fort William, to a successor of Aurangzeb, Shah Farucksir, in 1713.

> The request of the smallest particle of sand, John Russell, President for the English East India Company (with his forehead at command rub'd on the Ground), and reverence due from a Slave amongst those that make their request to your Throne which is the Seat of Miracles your Lord of the world, and the present age, a Support and shade to all that inhabits the world you equallize [*sic*] the great Darius your Throne Resembles that of Solomon's, you'r [*sic*] a second Cyrus, a Conquerour of Countrys, a Strengthner [*sic*] of the root of justice, and an eradicator of violence and oppression. (See Charles R. Wilson, *The Early Annals of the English in Bengal* [London: Thacker & Co., 1900], II, part 1, 111).

44 Anna Harriette Crawford Leonowens, *Life and Travel in India: Being Recollections of a Journey before the Days of Railroads* (Philadelphia: Porter and Coates, 1884), 321.

45 Emma Roberts, *Hindostan: Its Landscapes, Palaces, Temples, Tombs; The Shores of the Red Sea; and the Sublime and Romantic Scenery of the Himalaya Mountains* (Delhi: Oriental Publishers, 1972), 13.

46 Julia Maitland, *Letters from Madras, during the Years 1836–39, by a Lady* (London: John Murray, 1843), 157–8.

47 Roberts, *Scenes and Characteristics*, III, 86.

48 Ibid., I, 187.

49 Ibid., *Hindostan*, 34.

50 Leonowens, *Life and Travel*, 35.

51   *The Journals of Honoria Lawrence, India Observed 1837–1854*, ed., John Lawrence and Audrey Woodiwiss (London: Hodder and Stoughton, 1980), 139.

52   Falkland, *Chow-Chow*, I, 91.

53   Ibid., 92–3.

54   Mrs Colin Mackenzie, *Life in the Mission*, II, 26.

55   Eden, *Up the Country*, II, 176.

56   'The Calcutta Belle', *Calcutta Magazine and Monthly Register*, 1832, 645.

57   Violet Dickinson, *Miss Eden's Letters* (London: Macmillan and Co., Ltd., 1919), 281.

16

'for the quiet of his mind and the good of his soul'

IN THE CHURCH OF ENGLAND CEMETERY AT CAPE TOWN, a simple obelisk bears the inscription, 'Underneath this stone reposes all that could die of Lady Sale.'[1] Not much is under that stone.

Florentia Sale was an exceptional woman, an exceptional human being. Victorian India produced not just Florentia Sale but a number of other women of great energy, intellect, wit, and courage.

England was the birthplace of the ideologies that coloured British thinking about India. Victorian England was also, however, the birth-place of an increasingly alert and aware group of women who were not about to stifle their abilities and intellects under poke bonnets and crinolines. It was the Victorians, after all, and not the Georgians, who produced Jane Welsh Carlyle, the Bronte sisters, George Eliot, Harriet Martineau, Christina Rosetti, Elizabeth Barrett Browning, Florence Nightingale, and the Queen herself. Although the 'rights of women' were rarely mentioned in polite circles, a 'woman's place' was no more to be taken for granted than the 'place' of the 'lower orders'.

The 'helpmate' theory of women widened the woman's sphere and justified her education and instruction. Her charitable and philanthropic works, her 'doing good' such as caring for children and the poor, teaching and caring for the sick began to become professionalized. As they did, women had to ask for more than favours or privileges—they would have to begin to ask for rights, although that was still in the distant future. Curiously, some of the most articulate and intellectually active women were ardently opposed to what eventually became the Women's Rights Movement. They normally saw their own accomplishments rather as a freak of nature and not as the expression of a new social force. Queen Victoria was one of these. In her own person she combined the duties of a wife, mother, and sovereign but she detested the idea of women's rights and actively fought to keep the professions closed to women. She had her own brand of feminism, however, and would often complain about the exploitation of 'us poor women' by their husbands. Even Prince Albert was not exempt from 'that despising of our poor degraded sex (for what else is it, as we poor creatures are born for Man's pleasure & amusement) [which] is a little in all clever men's natures'.[2]

It was a rare woman who argued for equality but when Englishwomen came to India, they carried in their intellectual baggage the growing sense that there could be more to life there than chits, gossip, marital arrangements, and porcelain. They honoured and respected their husbands, fathers, brothers, and Britain. But there was more. Beyond respect and conjugal or filial loyalty, not only missionary women but several other women, like the four discussed in this chapter, and like Anne Keeling two centuries earlier, accepted and expected to play the role, not merely of spiritual supports but of full partners with their husbands or brothers in their work in India.

That work lay at the four levels of Anglo-Indian society. Emily Eden's brother was at the very highest level of the civilian service, Florentia Sale's husband was in the military service, Marianne Postans' husband was also in the military but his work was more academic than military, and Lena Login's husband, John, a surgeon, belonged to the uncovenanted service. Two of them, Emily Eden and Lena Login, were born into the aristocracy, Florentia Sale, the granddaughter of a governor of Madras, belonged to the Anglo-Indian aristocracy, and Marianne Postans, although not of aristocratic birth, belongs to the category of writers that includes Maria

Graham and Fanny Parkes, but unlike them, she partook of her husband's work rather than branching out on her own.

Because all four of these women had a habit of respecting themselves, they had no need to demand subservience of Indians or of anyone else. They did not need empire to give them security or social status, and they were used to approaching other human beings with that charm, grace, and, often, wit, which they were accustomed to receiving themselves.

There is a good chance that Emily and Fanny Eden brought more charm and wit to India than any other people, men or women, did before the Mutiny. They and their nephew, William Godolphin Osborn, accompanied their brother, George, Lord Auckland, when he came out to assume the Governor-Generalship in 1835. Not that Emily wanted to come to India. She most certainly did not. She thought that a sentence to Botany Bay would be a joke compared with being sent to India. 'There is a decent climate to begin with, and the fun of a little felony first. But to be sent to Calcutta for no cause at all!'[3] Neither she nor Fanny had ever married but they took great delight in their nieces and nephews. Moreover, they were accustomed to moving in the highest Whig circles, a milieu in which Emily shone, for politics had been part of the air she breathed since her childhood. Her father had been Postmaster-General and a president of the Board of Trade. Her eldest sister, Eleanor, had been the one true love of the younger Pitt, and Emily herself counted the likes of Lord and Lady Melbourne among her closest friends.[4] Devoted to her brother, she did not think of India as a 'fishing' ground or a place to improve. She was thirty-eight when the call to India came, well past the age when the idea of some romantic adventure or two would have excited a girlish fancy. However, she felt 'of use' to George and that 'I am in my right place when I am by his side'.[5]

William Dalrymple quite rightly characterizes her as witty and intelligent, but waspish, haughty, and conceited.[6] At times she was also arrogant, sardonic, condescending, droll, crusty, clever, and entertaining. She grumbled a good bit about India and counted every day that would bring her closer to leaving it. She particularly detested Calcutta but it was not the Calcutta of India that she hated. Rather, it was the artificial contrivances of the capital. 'I never could take to Calcutta society,' she declared, 'even if there were any, but there is not.'[7] She found their Calcutta house and household 'very magnificent' but 'I cannot endure life there'.[8] As Lady Falkland, the wife of a governor of Bombay, would a decade later, the Eden sisters were to find that even a position at the pinnacle of society was not enough to enable a woman to break with customs she found tedious.

On 21 October 1837, the Eden sisters and Auckland left Calcutta for a tour through the Northwest Provinces. The tour lasted until March 1840 and became the subject of a two-volume account by Emily, *Up the Country*, published twenty-six years later. Although Emily often found it dull, the tour was done in a grand style. Along with the wagons full of baggage, the camels, elephants, and several hundred horses, the caravan included the Governor-General's staff and their families, a bodyguard, the regiment that escorted them and camp followers—about 12,000 people in all.[9] They followed the Ganges from Calcutta to Fategarh and then to Bareilly, Meerut, Delhi, and Simla. Along the way they met with delegations of local dignitaries and emissaries from Indian princes, and with British officials, and there were constant entertainments and official presentations. There was much panoply and majesty and diplomacy and dignity, not much of which impressed Emily, who was rather used to majesty and diplomacy and dignity after all. She hated camp life and she suffered frequently from headaches, fevers, 'spasms', and the delay of mail from home. She quickly discovered that the heavy and formal entertaining required at every stop could make camp life as tiresome as public life in Calcutta. Shortly after the tour began, she complained, 'We have had such a fatiguing day—just what we must have at every station—but still it is fatiguing.'[10] Between the bouts of entertaining, she expressed fear that they might all be getting quite dull. Sitting in front of their tents, having tea before breakfast one morning, Emily mused, 'X. and Z. sneeze at each other; W.O. smokes a double allowance; F. suffers from hunger; I yawn; G. groans and turns black; the doctor scolds C. because the road was dusty, and A. rushes off to business.'[11] Part of Emily's boredom on the tour was due to the fact that she herself was not dull or obsequious or self-pitying or earnest. Consequently, when she found these qualities in her countrymen, male or female, she could become rather tart. She and Fanny endured a long speech at Kurnaul about them, 'what we had done for society—added to its gaiety, and raised its tone, &c.,

&c., I should have thought it was all the other way—that society had lessened our gaiety, and lowered *our* tone, but who knows? There is a change somewhere, it appears'.[12] At Simla, when she encountered five women whose husbands were in Afghanistan living together in a small house for six months and who declared that they never had quarrelled, she gently skewered the hypocrisy and pettiness of many of her countrywomen with 'I can hardly credit it—can you?'[13] At the same time, she could be gentle with three married ladies at Baulyah.

> One lady has had bad spirits (small blame to her), and she has never been seen; another has weak eyes, and wears a large shade about the size of a common verandah; and the other has bad health, and has had her head shaved. A tour [toupe?] is not to be had here for love or money, so she wears a brown silk cushion with a cap pinned to the top of it.[14]

When a 'very pretty, and a good little thing' named Mrs Thomas James came to her attention, Emily observed that 'if she falls into bad hands, she would soon laugh herself into foolish scrapes' for 'a girl who marries at fifteen hardly knows what she likes'.[15] This 'merry unaffected girl' became one of the most notorious women of her time under the name of Lola Montez whose chequered career involved scandals with, among many others, Franz Liszt and King Ludwig I of Bavaria.

Religious enthusiasm of any sort, Christian or non-Christian, was an affront to Emily Eden's own calm reason.

> The Hindus convey a pig carefully cut up into a Muhammedan Mosque, whereupon the Mussulmanns cut up the Hindus. Then again the Mussulmanns kill a cow during a Hindu festival, and the Hindus go raving mad. Then an *un*sensible man like Sir P. Maitland refuses to give the national festivals the usual honours of guns, drums, etc., which they have had ever since the English set foot in India. In short, there is an irritation kept up on the plea of conscience, where the soothing system would be much more commendable and much easier.[16]

Her own rationality and tolerance characterized her perception of Indians. She was not at all careful about the spelling of Indian words in English, she never bothered to learn Hindustani, and she avoided asking questions because 'I hate information'.[17] She was quite unable to perceive Indians as a species of beings separate and unlike the English species. The Indians she encountered were usually noble or princely and they interested her very much. Some of them she found tedious but rarely was she patronizing about any of them, or for that matter, about Indians who were not princely. At Bullgha, Auckland decided rather suddenly to bring his steamer ashore and pay an informal visit to a horse fair. His staff was 'half mad at the idea' since they had not been previously consulted, but Emily encouraged her brother to make the visit even though 'the Governor-General should never appear publicly without a regiment and there was no precedent for his going to Bullgha fair. I told him we had made a precedent'.[18]

Among the princes Auckland interviewed on the tour was Ranjit Singh, king of the Sikhs and Lion of the Punjab. He was then one of the most powerful men in northern India and controlled affairs between the Indus and Afghanistan. Auckland visited him in state and Ranjit reciprocated with gorgeous pageantries. The matters they discussed were grave, and the decisions they made were momentous, but Emily watched it all with a rather detached amusement. Ranjit and especially Auckland were laying the groundwork for what would turn out to be an utter tragedy for the British in Afghanistan. Because she was so close to her brother, Emily was informed of the daily progress of the negotiations with Ranjit and she was fully aware of what was transpiring in Afghanistan, but she was accustomed to matters of state, after all, and it was the details of the negotiations and of the individuals involved in them that attracted her notice. She noticed, for instance, that when he was due to receive Auckland in a *durbar*, Ranjit would go off hunting to give the impression of being missing whenever he was to have a meeting with anyone important. 'He is generally caught in time, but it is a matter of etiquette that neither party should appear to wait for the other, so if Runjeet goes out hunting G. must stop to shoot or fish.'[19] Etiquette also dictated that Auckland be fetched by an 'istackball' or embassy and he 'cannot stir from his tent, if he starves there'.[20] For Emily, Ranjit was neither enemy nor ally nor heathen nor incurably depraved, but 'a very drunken old profligate, neither more nor less. Still he has made himself a great king; he has conquered a great many powerful enemies, he is remarkably just in his government; he has disciplined a large army; he hardly ever takes away life, which is wonderful in a despot, and he is exceedingly beloved by his people'.[21]

Once 'caught' for a durbar, Emily noticed that Ranjit 'had no jewels on whatever, nothing but the commonest red silk dress. He had two stockings on at first, which was considered an unusual circumstance; but he very soon contrived to slip one off that he might sit with one foot in his hand, comfortably'.[22] She thought Khurruck Singh, Ranjit's son and then heir-apparent, stupid, a bore, and a nothing, but she did not mind flirting with him.[23] She and Fanny met the thirty-two 'Mrs Runjeets' on rather a basis of equality for 'they laughed at our bonnets, and we rather *jeered* their nose-rings.'[24] She could be terribly condescending, as when she observed of Indians, 'They are civil creatures, and I am very fond of the natives',[25] but she also thought it rather shocking when the camp ate ham and drank wine in an Agra mosque even though it had been 'desecrated'.[26]

Emily Eden had a keen sense that the British were changing India profoundly and that India would never be the same again. At Delhi, she observed, 'Stupendous remains of power and wealth passed and passing away—and somehow I feel that we horrid English have just "gone and done", merchandised it, revenued it, and spoiled it all. I am not very fond of Englishmen out of their own country.'[27] Her sister, Fanny, concurred,

> These people must have been so very magnificent in what they did be-
> fore we Europeans came here with our bad, money-making ways. We
> have made it impossible for them to do more, and have let all they ac-
> complished go to ruin. All our excuse is that we do not oppress the na-
> tives so much as they oppress each other, a fact about which I have my
> suspicions.[28]

In June 1841, Emily played chess with a 'very kingly sort of per-son' named Dost Mohammed. He kept inventing new rules which she somehow thought 'if he were not a Dost it was not quite fair'.[29] Six months later the British garrison at Kabul was being evacuated under the gaze of Dost Mohammed's son, Akbar, and British soldiers and civilians, including women and children, began a forced march back to India that would leave only one survivor. The First Afghan War would go down as one of the great tragedies in British India before the Mutiny. To Emily, the disturbances in Afghanistan would furnish 'one of those pretences for interference England delights in … and when once we begin I know (don't you?) what becomes of the country we assist—swallowed up whole'.[30] Yet when the full horror of the retreat from Kabul became known and her brother had been recalled to England under a storm of outrage, Emily's opposition to 'swallowed up whole' was muffled in her loyalty to her brother. Auckland's successor, Lord Ellenborough, indicated at the outset that it would be no part of British policy to meddle further in Afghan affairs and the Cabinet in London agreed to thank him. According to Charles Greville, however, Emily Eden, 'who is a very clever and wrong-headed woman, was furious, and evinced great indignation against all their Whig friends, and especially Auckland himself, for being so prudent and moderate, and for not attacking Ellenborough with all the violence which she felt and expressed'.[31]

Auckland's terrible mistakes regarding Afghanistan involved another woman, Florentia Sale, the wife of General Robert 'Fighting Bob' Sale. In his *Flashman* novels, George Macdonald Fraser refers to 'dear, dreadful' Lady Sale as a 'dragon' and a 'raw boned old heroine'.[32] Whether the soubriquet is appropriate or not, and while the First Afghan War produced many victims, Lady Sale proved herself to be every bit the soldier that her husband was and, arguably, its only real hero.

There is a good chance that if Emily Eden and Lady Sale had ever met in India, they would have wasted precious little love on each other. Yet, in addition to their aristocratic background, the two women had much in common. Like Emily Eden, Lady Sale came to India because it was her duty to do so but, again like the Eden sisters, once there she concerned herself not at all with improving Indians or guarding a bungalow. Like Emily Eden, she apparently knew very little, if any, Hindustani. If she ever collected facts or things about India, it is not so indicated in her journal. Both women were rather prone apparently to 'hate information', and neither betrayed much knowledge of Indian history, art, literature, religions, or science. Equipped with a cool rationality, tolerance, and aristocratic grace, neither woman was inclined to prejudge Indians, to categorize or to stereotype them, but instead to draw their ideas of India and Indians from what they experienced there.

The First Afghan War grew out of the fact that, after Napoleon's agreement with Tsar Alexander at Tilsit in 1807, Russia had replaced France as Britain's most serious rival for influence in Asia. The threat of Russian imperialism through a subservient Persia made

Afghanistan a particularly vulnerable point through which British India might be breached. In 1837, Persia, with Russian support, besieged the city of Heart, then the stronghold of the old Afghan dynasty headed by Shah Shuja, now a company pensioner, who had been overthrown by Emily Eden's chess partner, Dost Mohammed. Dost Mohammed meanwhile controlled the city of Kabul, south of Herat.

Lord Auckland's position when he came out to succeed William Bentinck in 1836 was an extremely delicate one. The Persian–Russian threat at Heart necessitated a strong British ally in Kabul. In congratulating Auckland on his appointment, however, Dost Mohammed complicated matters by asking for assistance not only against Persia and Russia but also against Britain's staunch ally, Ranjit Singh, who could provide a formidable barrier against Russian expansion on the northwest frontier. Ranjit had previously threatened Afghanistan's territorial integrity by seizing the city of Peshawar. Pressured partly by London and partly by his own advisors, Auckland embarked on a perfectly disastrous plan. To allay any fears Ranjit Singh might have that Britain would support or tolerate Afghan retribution for the seizure of Peshawar, Auckland ordered the capture of Dost Mohammed in 1839. He was replaced with Shah Shuja. Ranjit, however, had skilfully avoided any direct involvement in Afghanistan after Peshawar and then had died some months prior to Dost Mohammed's capture. The British therefore found themselves holding Kabul without any Sikh support. Then, because of Shah Shuja's unpopularity, it was necessary for the British to occupy the country.

Unfortunately, the British fear of Russian imperialism, more fancied than real, ignored the Afghan's own love of independence. Mohammed Akbar Khan, Dost Mohammed's son, was able to bring together a loose alliance of Afghan tribes. The threat that Akbar Khan represented, however, was not taken seriously by Auckland at first. When the Court of Directors ordered him to make an immediate retrenchment on the grounds that there was no longer any need for such vast expenditures in Afghanistan, Auckland instructed his agent in Kabul, Sir William Macnaghten, to reduce expenditure in every possible way. Essentially this meant withdrawing large bribes to chieftains whose main occupation in life was plunder. Macnaghten had been in the east long enough to know what the effect of that would be but, under Auckland's orders, he had no choice but to obey. He summoned the chiefs together and informed them that the flow of British gold was being cut back to a trickle. Shah Shuja would now have to be responsible for his own treasury and safety. The chieftains salaamed respectfully and went off to stir up trouble against the British and Shah Shuja under the leadership of Akbar Khan. Despite his experience in the east, Macnaghten was certain that the troubles were temporary and his dispatches to Auckland conveyed that impression.

Incredibly, just as the subsidies to the chiefs were cut, the British garrison in Kabul was also reduced. The bulk of the army under General Sale was moved in October 1841 to Jelalabad, about 75 miles east of Kabul. The man left in charge of the Kabul garrison was General William George Keith Elphinstone who, in 1841, was sixty years old, amiable, gouty, and altogether unwell. Lady Sale, who had stayed in Kabul, calmly observed in October that if there were a rising in there, 'we should be entirely without the means of defense'.[33] Throughout the autumn, Duranis, Ghilzais, and other for-midable tribes continued to raise the standard of revolt against Shah Shuja and the British. Macnaghten, however, continued to ignore repeated warnings from every quarter, and Lady Sale concluded that he lacked 'sufficient moral courage' to stem the current of decep-tion concerning the quiescence of the chiefs. She felt that the state of supineness and fancied security of those in charge of the Kabul garrison was the result of deference to the opinions of Auckland. 'In fact, it is reported at Government House, Calcutta, that the lawless Affghans are as peaceable as London citizens; and this being decided upon by the powers that be, why should we be on the alert? Most dutifully do we appear to shut our eyes on our probable fate.'[34]

The day she wrote those words, 2 November 1841, the British Agent in Kabul, Sir Alexander Burnes, was murdered by a Kabuli mob.[35] A massacre of British officers and their families followed. The army was only a half hour away but Elphinstone wrote to Macnaghten, 'We must see what the morning brings, and then think what can be done.'[36] As Elphinstone and his troops looked on, the Kabulis stormed the Bala Hissar, the fort where the commissariat was stored.

The responsibility for the failure to move, according to Lady Sale, rested not with Elphinstone alone. His vacillation was most provoking, but his judgement at least was good. It was the 'cold cautiousness' of two subordinates, whose 'doubts on every subject' induced Elphinstone 'to alter his opinions and plans every moment'.[37] By early November, Lady Sale herself would 'never doze now till daylight' but sat up to watch from a housetop. By mid-December, she would muse, 'How strangely military matters are conducted at present.'[38]

On 11 December, Macnaghten was forced to conclude a humiliating treaty by which he agreed to withdraw British forces from Afghanistan. Several days later, enticed to a conference, Macnaghten himself was shot, presumably by Akbar Khan himself.[39] As the price of a new and worse treaty, the British were to be given safe conduct to Peshawar, hostages were to be surrendered, individual chiefs were to be paid large sums, and Jelalabad and all forts inside the Afghan border were to be evacuated.

On 6 January 1842, the terrified, shivering, hungry defenders of Kabul set out on a retreat that was to give a grim and terrible climax to the tragedy. There were roughly 16,500 people in the procession— about 700 Europeans, 3,800 Indian soldiers, and the rest were camp followers and their families. There were horses, bullocks to pull the carts, camels, mules, and ponies. Most of the European women and children travelled in camel-panniers.[40] To reach their destination in Jelalabad, they had to travel through desolate mountain country, deep in snow, held by Ghazis and Ghilzais whom no treaty would have kept from plunder even under the best of conditions. As the Kabuli mob poured into the cantonment in order to plunder and destroy what had been left behind, it became evident that the Afghani chiefs had no intention of honouring the treaty. Frost-bitten, without fuel, shelter, food, or ammunition, the procession was easy prey to marauders. Having survived the awful night of 6 January, Lady Sale awoke on the morning of the 7th to find several men had frozen to death.[41]

> Snow still lies a foot deep on the ground. No food for man or beast; and even water from the river close at hand difficult to obtain, as our people were fired on in fetching it. Numbers of unfortunates have dropped, benumbed with cold, to be massacred by the enemy; yet, so bigoted are our rulers that we are still told that the Sirdars are faithful, that Mohammed Akbar Khan is our friend!!!&c., &c., &c., and the reason they wish us to

delay is that they may send their troops to clear the passes for us! That they will send them there can be no doubt.[42]

The following day, 8 January, Akbar Khan agreed to protect the column of refugees in return for 15,000 rupees, Eldridge Pottinger, George Lawrence, and Helen Mackenzie's husband, Colin ('Mullah') Mackenzie, as hostages, and the condition that Sale's force at Jelalabad be evacuated. 'These disgraceful propositions were readily assented to; and the three officers went off to the Sirdar.'[43] The negotiations over, the column was then attacked. The sufferings of the women travelling with the baggage were extreme. Several women as well as the youngest child of a Mrs Boyd were carried off. A Mrs. Mainwaring was carrying her infant, less than three months old, when an Afghan asked her to mount his horse behind him. Fearful of treachery, she declined the offer. Shortly after, the Afghan snatched the shawl from her shoulder. The poor woman had to walk 'a considerable distance' through deep snow, picking her way over the bodies of the dead, dying and wounded, frequently crossing streams of water 'wet up to the knees, pushed and shoved about by men and animals, the enemy keeping up a sharp fire, and several persons being killed close to her'.[44] The pony upon which Lady Sale's daughter, Alexandrina Sturt, was mounted was wounded in the ear and neck, and Sturt himself was later to die of wounds he received in the attack. As for Lady Sale, she had 'fortunately only one ball in my arm; three others passed through my poshteen near the shoulder without doing me any injury'.[45] Later, she calmly reported, Dr Bryce 'kindly cut the ball out of my wrist, and dressed both my wounds'.[46]

The following day, shortly after Lawrence, Pottinger, and Mackenzie arrived at the Khoord Kabul fort, the Sirdar proposed that married men and their families be put under his (Akbar Khan's) protection and given safe conduct and honourable treatment to Peshawar.[47] Since there clearly now was only the faintest hope of ever reaching Jelalabad alive, Lady Sale, her now widowed daughter, Lady Macnaghten, and Mrs Alexander Burnes together with a number of other hostages were taken to the Khoord Kabul forts. In all, there were twenty men, nine women, and fourteen children.[48] What happened to the caravan they left is well known. The route to Jelalabad was littered with frozen, bloody reminders of the retreat.

On 17 January, the hostages learned that only one survivor, Dr Bryden, had walked into the fort at Jelalabad.

Lady Sale's captivity would last until 13 September. On 19 January, they were allowed for the first time since the retreat had begun to wash their faces. 'It was rather a painful process, as the cold and glare of the sun on the snow had three times peeled on my face, from which the skin came off in strips.'[49] There was something to eat—greasy sheep skin and bones, cooked with rice and served on chapattis. She and her daughter were not yet covered with crawlers by the end of January but they were 'in fear and trembling' of them.[50]

Given half a chance, Lady Sale would have delighted in a most painful death for Akbar Khan but she could admit that for his own political purposes, Akbar had done as he had said he would do—he had destroyed the British army in Afghanistan. And then, 'he has ever since we have been in his hands, treated us well:—that is, honour has been respected'.[51] The common comforts that they would have liked, she admitted, were unknown to Afghan women and in any case, they were prisoners and as captives, well treated. They suffered from filth, but 'the Affghans are not addicted to general ablution … Here again is a difference between their tastes and ours, who so enjoy bathing twice a day'.[52] The greasy and 'disgusting' food again was a matter of taste. 'One person likes what another does not. By us, a strong cup of coffee is considered a luxury; whilst an Affghan the other day, who had some given to him (he had never tasted any before), pronounced it bitter and detestable.'[53]

A soldier's wife even in extremity, she observed in May that the people of Afghanistan had been ruined by the 'perfect stagnation of trade'. Now was the time to strike, she thought, for they would probably side with the British were they to show in force.

> But I much dread dilly-dallying just because a handful of us are in Akbar's power. What are *our* lives compared with the honour of country? Not that I am at all inclined to have my throat cut: on the contrary, I hope that I shall live to see the British flag once more triumphant in Affghanistan: and then I have no objection to the Ameer Dost Mohammed Khan being reinstated; only let us first show them that we can conquer them, and humble their treacherous chiefs in the dust.[54]

Through her letters to General Sale, word of her captivity had reached the newspapers and what they wrote very much amused her.

'Nothing can exceed the folly I have seen in the papers regarding my wonderful self.'[55] But a small controversy arose as to whether or not Lady Sale had or had not evinced a strong prepossession in favour of Akbar Khan over Shah Shuja. Her reaction to the charge while she was still Akbar's prisoner illustrated the same blunt toughness that must have made her a trial to the authorities in Calcutta.

> Let the Affghans have the Ameer Dost Mohammed Khan back, if they like. He and his family are only an expense to us in India; we can restore them, and make friends with him. Let us first show the Affghans that we can both conquer them, and revenge the foul murder of our troops; but do not let us dishonor the British name by sneaking out of the country, like whipped Pariah dogs.[56]

Whatever honour there was left to be snatched from the disaster was being won at the hands of General Pollock's Army of Retribution. Dost Mohammed was allowed to pass quietly out of India and reached Lahore early in 1843. As to the justice of ever having dethroned him in the first pace in favour of Shah Shuja, Lady Sale would say nothing about it. 'Let our Governors-General and Commanders-in-Chief look to that; whilst I knit socks for my grandchildren: but I have been a soldier's wife too long to sit down tamely, whilst our honour is tarnished in the sight and opinion of savages.'[57]

The Sales reached India in December 1842, and then took leave. They arrived in England to a triumphal welcome, were royally entertained and received by the queen at Windsor. At the end of 1844, they returned to India. A year later the First Sikh War broke out and Fighting Bob was killed at Moodki in December 1845. Florentia spent her widowhood at a small estate in the hills near Simla on a £500 pension granted her by the queen. Her daughter, Alexandrina Sturt, remarried and she and her second husband, Major Holmes, were two of the first victims of the Mutiny. By then Lady Sale herself had died in 1853 at Cape Town where she had gone for her health.[58]

Florentia Sale's response to her captivity by Akbar Khan is very close to Eliza Fay's capture at the hands of Haider Ali. Both women hated their captors—and with very good reason. Lady Sale subsequently called the Afghans 'savages' because she had seen them behaving like savages. Like Mrs Fay, however, Lady Sale coupled her hatred with respect and refused to allow her personal sufferings to lead her to a condemnation of all Indians or of Indian cultures.

The loss of Afghanistan indirectly involved another military wife, Marianne Postans. Unlike Florentia Sale, however, the work she was to share with her husband was not military so much as scholarly. She had married Thomas Postans in London in 1833 when she was twenty-two and he was twenty-five years old, and had then accompanied him to Bombay where he was an officer in the Bombay Native Infantry. Well-educated like her husband, she took an interest in history, literature, music, and religion, and she was as certain as anyone that Britain did have an obligation to improve India economically and socially.

She returned briefly to England and then, early in 1840, she rejoined her husband who, after a short posting to Poona, had been ordered to Cutch. 'Few persons can leave Bombay without regret', she wrote.[59] The 'island-skirted harbor' filled with boats whose lateen sails 'skim like sea-birds on the surface of the deep', and the 'wooden summits of Elephanta'[60] had become familiar, loved. From the lushness of Bombay, Mrs Postans sailed across the Gulf of Cutch to a 'long line of coast [which] is a mere burning solitude'.[61] 'There is nothing very pleasing or picturesque about the country of Sindh,' she would say.[62]

The Postans' first posting was to Karachi, then a small, ugly fishing village in the sterile, flat desert. Following the loss of Afghanistan, Sind assumed a vital role in the defense of western India. About a year after the fall of Kabul, General Charles Napier who knew nothing of India, its customs, religion, or tribal politics, defeated an Indian army at Miani, and Sind was annexed in March 1843.[63] Happily for Marianne, one of her husband's assignments was to investigate the possibilities for improving agriculture and commerce in the area. He was also assigned to obtain copies of the ancient Asokan inscriptions at Girnar in Junagarh. Like Florentia Sale, she became a full partner in her husband's work, believing that a knowledge of agriculture and commerce would do more to render the Kutchis 'reflecting and rational beings' than a frontal attack on their religious practices.[64]

Despite the dangers of travelling in a forbidding landscape among hostile populations, Mrs Postans enjoyed the years she spent in western India. With Thomas, she explored upper Sind and Baluchistan, lived in Shikarpoor, an important commercial centre, and Sukkur, travelled down the Indus, travelled overland by camel and horse across landscapes that were desolate, bleak, and in temperatures that went from 111° Fahrenheit during the day to bitter cold at night. What she experienced in the next four years became the material for two books published in 1839, *Cutch; or Random Sketches Taken during a Residence in One of the Northern Provinces of Western India*, illustrated with her own drawings, and *Western India in 1838*, done in collaboration with her husband.

While Thomas wrote learned papers on the inscriptions and on the possibilities of commerce on the Indus, Marianne's lively narrative conveyed her own excitement at their discoveries, and at the people she was encountering. The travel literature of the early nineteenth century contains several descriptions of the festival of Holi, but it might be safe to say that no one so vibrantly captured the sheer, uninhibited gaiety of the feast as she did.

> ... the Hindoos are a peculiarly social people, delighting in raillery, and easily excited to gaiety and mirth. An Asiatic crowd unites a greater variety of picturesque effects than any other in the world, and the most perfect harmony and good-nature prevail among its members. The older persons gossip, and exchange jests on each other, not deficient in wit; and the younger parties stroll about, with their arms encircling each others' necks, exchanging the most gentle and endearing epithets, as they laugh and chat, on whatever may be the object of attraction unassailed by temptations to intemperance, its brutalizing effects never shade the pastimes of these inoffensive people; good-nature supplies the place of the constable's baton, and every one is merry himself, without seeking his advantages at the price of a neighbour's inconvenience. The scene is one of amiable courtesy...[65]

She had little use for Sind's despotic amirs who had brought poverty and oppression to their subjects,[66] but she liked the people who were not cheerful but then, she thought, there was no reason why they should have been. Rather, they were grave and sad, simple, even courteous, quiet, and uncomplaining. 'But they live—only to labour, and to die.'[67] She found the aristocratic classes of men remarkable for dignity and grace, 'commonly tall and stout' and they expressed themselves fluently and well in Persian.[68] Because she was unable to visit upper-class women, she could only rely on the testimony of others for reports of the great beauty of Sind women. She visited the alligator tank at the shrine of a Sindhi saint, Mangho, whom she called Peer Mungar.[69] Instead of finding Indian music harsh or dissonant, as many Westerners might, like Elizabeth Plowden, she studied it carefully and realized that Indian musical texts predate the Greeks. She described *sangita*, literally a concert, which combines song, percussion, and dancing,[70] discussed ragas, and Indian musical instruments. Unlike the Eden sisters or Florentia Sale, she was familiar with Hindustani and Cutchi, and apparently knew enough Sindhi to discuss with the wife of a farmer in Sind how often she changed and washed her clothes.[71] So well did she know Persian that she understood the intricacies of Persian poetry and described the eight categories of Persian verse.[72]

The Postans sailed home to England in October 1842, about a month after Florentia Sale was released from captivity. Two years later, they returned to India, to Marianne's beloved Bombay. It was there, in 1846, that Thomas died. The physician attending him, William Young, a widower of nearly sixty, provided Marianne with a new life and with the child she had never had, Young's baby granddaughter, Mary Anne, whom she adopted and named as her own heiress. She then accompanied her new husband, as she had Thomas Postans, to his postings in India, and then to the Crimean War in 1854. Eventually, the family retired to Somerset where Marianne lived until her death in 1897. By then, India itself had changed and she must often have recalled the apprehension she herself had expressed half a century earlier when she had written, 'In possessing ourselves of the country, we have excited feelings of revenge and retribution and have established a blood feud, that will not easily be satiated'.[73]

Lena Login was the granddaughter of Charles Campbell who, after fighting in the Battle of Culloden, escaped to Portugal where he married a niece of the Bishop of Oporto and then fled to Brazil where his children, including Lena's father, John, were born. Eventually, Charles Campbell was persuaded to leave his exile and he returned to Scotland, made his submission to the king, and the family returned to the ancestral home in Strathbraan where Lena was born and raised. Following the death of her parents, her eldest brother, also named Charles, invited Lena and her sister Maggie to join him in the Northwest Provinces. It was in Lucknow in 1842 that she met and married her husband, Dr John Login, the Resident Surgeon at the Court of Oudh.

John Login would serve under two successive kings of Oudh, first Mohammed Ali and then the notorious Wajid Ali of Mutiny renown.[74] It was in the *zenana* that Lady Login would find opportunities to assist her husband. Instead of finding it dull or its occupants pitiable as many of her countrywomen did, Lady Login discovered that

> many of these Princesses were women of great intelligence as well as high lineage, and we used to discuss all sorts of subjects, though not often religious matters, unless they specially questioned me, for my husband had a great dislike to any attempt to teach Christianity except with the husband's permission; but their curiosity was great concerning European clothes and customs.[75]

No physician was permitted to examine a female patient except through the purdah. A hole would be cut in the curtain through which the woman would thrust her tongue or her hand. Lena's help in making a diagnosis and in administering the remedies to female patients was invaluable. In one case, the life of a daughter of the prime minister of Oudh had been given up. When Login examined her, he found that her skin was encrusted with a hard shell, formed by the plastering on of ointments. He prescribed a warm bath for the child and the begums were horrified. They only consented to it if the 'memsahib' would attend and see it carried out herself. So Lady Login and her ayah arrived in the zenana with warm water, towels, scented soap, and sponges. The little girl's life was spared, and her grateful parents presented the Login children with a lovely chariot shaped like a peacock.[76]

Login left Lucknow in 1848 to do field service in the Second Sikh War. Following the war, Henry Lawrence recommended him to Lord Dalhousie as the guardian of the young maharajah, Duleep Singh, Ranjit Singh's heir. Lady Login found that neither Sikh nor English custom barred her from the court, for the Sikhs who had followed Duleep into exile

> vied with each other in showing me the greatest courtesy and deference. Many were the interesting conversations I had with them, comparing and discussing the differences between Eastern and Western manners

and ideas. How endless were their questions about all I had seen, and done, while home in England! And I, on my part, had much to learn from them on various matters.[77]

Duleep Singh turned out to be unworthy of his father. He was silly, arrogant, empty-headed, and utterly selfish. When he decided to become a Christian, however, it was Lady Login who suggested that Ganges water be used at the baptism.[78] Duleep Singh came to London, to the Court of St. James, about 1851, where his 'candor and straightforwardness' initially made him a favourite of Queen Victoria and Prince Albert. His indolence and tactlessness, however, soon made him rather unpopular, and with the outbreak of the Mutiny, especially, popular feeling ran very strongly against him. Through it all, and after her husband's death, Lady Login continued to guard the boy as much as was possible and to make excuses for his behaviour. She realized that the loss of his kingdom and particularly the confiscation of the Koh-i-Noor diamond, the symbol of Sikh sovereignty, rankled in Duleep's otherwise empty head. Her concern for Duleep Singh was as genuine as her affection for the Oudh begums. Unfortunately, unlike the begums, he probably was not worth it.

In the seventeenth century, the argument had been made that it might be a good thing for a wife to accompany her husband—or sisters to accompany their brother—to India, that it was 'fitting for the quiet of his mind and the good of his soul'. Neither then, nor certainly in the nineteenth century, had many women been content to play that simple role. Women such as the ones discussed here clearly would be full partners in whatever work the Company would be about in India.

* * *

It is easy to feel a certain repugnance for the great men of pre-Mutiny India. Wellesley, Bentinck, Dalhousie, Auckland, the Lawrences are a bit remote and cold, some of them even shallow. But the empire was not only theirs; it also belonged to the soldiers and clerks—and to the women—who lived and suffered and grew or withered in India. What mattered in the long run was not how much work one accomplished in India or how thoroughly one knew Indian languages or whether one had a taste for curry or hookahs or how much of India one saw or the amount of information one gleaned—or failed to glean. Rather, it was the philosophical and psychological framework through which one perceived India. If Indians were merely subjects and therefore weak and depraved, then India indeed became a land of exile—and of chits and ranks, and dull dinner parties, and Simla. If, on the other hand, Britain's presence in India had happened because of a series of historical accidents and Indian habits and tastes were simply different, then India could be a fascinating adventure. The empire in India was an established fact. What one did with one's own individual empire, whether one regarded it as a responsibility or as an opportunity to extend one's own spiritual and intellectual being, was a matter of choice whether one was a man or a woman.

notes

1 Patrick Macrory, ed., *Military Memoirs of Lady Sale* (London: Longmans, Green and Co., Ltd., 1969), 159.

2 Elizabeth Longford, *Queen Victoria: Born to Succeed* (New York: Harper & Row, 1964), 284.

3 Violet Dickinson, ed., *Miss Eden's Letters* (London: Macmillan and Co., Ltd., 1919), 245.

4 James Morris, *Heaven's Command* (London: Faber and Faber, Ltd., 1973), 19.

5 Emily Eden, *Up the Country*, 2 vols (London: Richard Bentley, 1866), II, 177.

6 See his introduction to Fanny (Parlby) Parkes, *Begums, Thugs and White Mughals* (London: Sickle Moon Books, 2002), v.

7 Dickinson, *Miss Eden's Letters*, 273.

8 Ibid., 265.

9 Ibid., 293.

10 Eden, *Up the Country*, I, 18.

11 W.O. refers to William Godolphin Osborne, Auckland's nephew and military secretary; F. is Emily's sister Fanny, G. is George, Lord Auckland, and the doctor, Drummond, is scolding either John Colvin, Auckland's private secretary or a Captain Cunningham, an aide de camp. The X and Z sneezing at each other are unidentifiable members of the party. Ibid., II, 176.

12 Ibid., II, 82.

13 Ibid., II, 96–7.

14 Ibid., I, 10.

15 Ibid., II, 148–9, 183.

16 Dickinson, ed., *Miss Eden's Letters*, 299.

17 Eden, *Up the Country*, I, 89.

18 Ibid., 26.

19 Ibid., I, 271.

20 Ibid., II, 2.

21 Ibid., I, 299.

22 Ibid., I, 284.

23 Ibid., II, 20. Khurruck Singh did succeed his father at the latter's death in 1839 only to be deposed and possibly poisoned by his son less than a year later. Following a series of palace coups and assassinations, Khurruck's half-brother, Duleep, attained the throne in 1843. Duleep would be the last of the independent Sikh rulers of the Punjab. He would be deposed in 1849 and spend the rest of his life as a British dependent.

24 Ibid., II, 29–30.

25 Ibid., I, 26.

26 Ibid., II, 214.

27 Ibid., I, 138–9.

28 Cited in Janet Dunbar, *Golden Interlude* (London: John Murray, 1955), 78.

29 Dickinson, ed., *Miss Eden's Letters*, 347.

30 Ibid., 343.

31 Quoted in Dunbar, *Golden Interlude*, 221.

32 George Macdonald Fraser, *Flashman* (New York: New American Library, 1970), 135, 161; idem., *Flashman and the Mountain of Light* (New York: Alfred A. Knopf, 1991), 27–8.

33 Florentia Sale, *A Journal of the Disasters in Affghanistan, 1841–2* (London: John Murray, 1843), 12.

34 Ibid., 38.

35 Ibid.

36 Edward Thompson and G.T. Book Garratt, *Rise and Fulfillment of British Rule in India* (Allahabad: Central Book Depot, 1962), 346.

37 Sale, *Journal*, 83.

38 Ibid., 181.

39 Ibid., 198.

40 Morris, *Heaven's Command*, 108.

41 Sale, *Journal*, 228.

42 Ibid., 231.

43 Ibid., 236. 'Sirdar' literally means leader, commander, or officer.

44 Ibid., 237–8.

45 Ibid., 237.

46 Ibid., 242.

47 Sale, *Journal*, 245.

48 Ibid., 285.

49 Ibid., 287.

50 Ibid., 289.

51 Ibid., 404.

52 Ibid., 407.

53 Ibid., 405.

54 Ibid., 342.

55 Ibid., 408.

56 Ibid., 401.

57 Ibid., 401.

58 Macrory, ed., *Military Memoirs*, 158–9.

59 Marianne Postans, *Cutch; or Random Sketches, Taken during a Residence in One of the Northern Provinces of Western India; Integrated with Legends and Traditions* (London: Smith, Elder, and Co., 1839), 3.

60 Ibid., 1–2.

61 Ibid., 8.

62 Marianne Postans, *Travels, Tales and Encounters in Sindh and Balochistan, 1840–1843* (Oxford: Oxford University Press, 2003), 33.

63 Napier's victory was famously underappreciated by the new humour magazine *Punch*, which carried a cartoon of Napier striding across the bloody battlefield of Miani over the caption 'Peccavi'—'I have sinned[Sind].'

64 Postans, *Cutch*, 255–6.

65 Postans, *Western India in 1838*, 2 vols (London: Saunders and Otley, 1839), II, 190–3.

66 Ibid., *Travels, Tales and Encounters*, 69.

67 Ibid., 13 and 23.

68 Ibid., 32.

69 Ibid., 54ff.

70 Postans, *Cutch*, 180ff.

71 Ibid., 33.

72 Ibid., 203ff. The most familiar of these are the *ghazel*, a favourite of the poet Hafez, the *qasideh*, a long poem in monorhyme similar to an ode, the four-line *ruba'i*, popularized by Omar Khayyam in his famous *Ruba'iat*, the two-line *biet* or couplet, and the one-line *misrah*.

73 Ibid., 36.

74 E. Dalhousie Login, *Lady Login's Recollections* (London: Smith, Elder & Co., 1916), 44.

75 Ibid., 39.

76 Ibid., 42–3.

77 Ibid., 90.

78 Ibid., 97.

afterword

IN THE AFTERMATH OF THE 1857 MUTINY, British women were usually characterized either as victims or, by dint of simply surviving, as heroines. Thus, in a sense, the two-faceted characterization of their roles in 1615 as either encumbrances or as spiritual supports, was maintained into the late nineteenth and early twentieth centuries, where they would either be the memsahibs of Rudyard Kipling's fiction or the seemingly colourless and emotionless missionaries and philanthropists that indeed many of them were.

The British women who came out to India in those two and half centuries occupied many complex worlds and, thus, it is as difficult to compartmentalize them as it is their male counterparts. Some, but not all of them, fit the stereotypical 'memsahib'. Some, but not all of them, were vastly curious about India; others were bored by it. Some were heroic, others tiresome. Sometimes, they could be what Sir Thomas Roe had feared they would be, just plain nuisances, while many others really did exist in India as emotional or spiritual supports to the men they accompanied.

The Indian experience, whether it was with the Company as a powerful merchandising entity or as the administrator of a nation occupied by millions of peoples half a world away, was always multifaceted, incredibly complex, and complicated. From its very beginnings, the Company in India had represented not only responsibilities and burdens, but also fantastic opportunities for its servants and for their wives, sisters, and daughters to enrich themselves socially, economically, and often intellectually. If, in the process of 'feathering their nests'—however the nest might be defined—the Company's or the Crown's interests could be served, so much the better.

In the end, it is the woman who began the debate about the role of women in India that comes to mind, Anne Keeling, who, in her determination to be a part of her husband's enterprise, had given an indication that women in India would be all that the Company hoped and feared they would be. And perhaps something else. The woman who stowed away on her husband's ship in 1615 gives the impression that she meant to be neither an encumbrance nor a spiritual support. She meant to share every part of William's adventure. Moreover, William Keeling meant that his wife should do just that, that she would be his full partner.

And many of Anne Keeling's successors mirror her determination. If men could profit from the Indian trade, so could a Mrs Hudson, a tavern keeper like Mrs Deningo Ash, an Anne Foquet, or an Ursula O'Neale. If men could invest in Indian stock, so could Mary Barwell and if they could take bribes or engage in illicit trade, so could the Mary Weltdens and Katherine Nicks. If the men of the Orientalist Society could engage India sympathetically, an Emma Roberts or a Maria Graham could popularize their work. If men would map India and study her geography, botany, zoology, history, and arts, women could sketch and paint India's landscapes and people. If men could learn India's languages to administer India or to proselytize, a Marianne Postans could learn them to understand her people. If men could smoke hookahs and cheroots and attend nautches, so could many women with as much delight, or as little, as men. If intimate relations with Indians were available to a David Ochterlony or a James Kirkpatrick, Phebe Gibbes could imagine the intimacy between an English woman and an Indian man that Mrs Meer Hassan Ali made fact. And while officials in Calcutta and London worried about zenanas and sati, Margaret Cooke Wilson worked to give Indian women and girls the skills they needed to break the bonds of purdah.

On the other hand, for every Fanny Parkes who relished India, there was at least one, and perhaps scores, of other women like

Madeline Wallace-Dunlop who scorned her. And while Julia Maitland was embarrassed by the treatment accorded an elderly Brahmin, there were others who thought that 'the less one sees of them the better'.

Having an empire cannot be light work for anyone. While empire may be resented by the ruled, it always produces burdens for the rulers as well. While the Company had been simply a trading entity, the natural chasm between England and India was bridged frequently and deeply, but most often only by men. Empire, especially beginning with the reforms of Wellesley, made it more difficult to bridge that chasm. Many men did continue to do so, however, as the stories of people like Richard Burton, for instance, or Colonel William Gardner who married a Moghul princess illustrate.

Empire also presents opportunities, however. As often as the Company had given women a chance to improve their personal economic and social lot in the seventeenth and eighteenth centuries, it was not until the nineteenth century that they were able to engage India on their own. Like their male contemporaries, many spurned the opportunity. Others seized it. Like Anne Keeling earlier, whatever India's official relationship to Britain was to be, there were many, many women who were determined to be fully a part of that relationship.

bibliography

primary sources

Ali, Mrs Meer Hassan. *Observations on the Mussulmauns of India: Descriptive of Their Manners, Customs, Habits and Religious Opinions, Made during a Twelve Years' Residence in Their Immediate Society.* 2 vols. London: Parbury, Allen, and Co., 1832.

Anderson, Philip. *The English in Western India; Being the Early History of the Factory at Surat, of Bombay, and the Subordinate Factories on the Western Coast from the Earliest Period until the Commencement of the Eighteenth Century* London: Smith, Elder and Co., 1856, 2nd ed.

Ashmore, Harriette. *Narrative of a Three Month's March in India; and a Residence in the Dooab. By the Wife of an Officer in the 16th Foot.* London: R. Hastings, 1841.

Asiatic Journal and Monthly Miscellany. London: William H. Allen & Co., 1829–1845.

Asiatick Miscellany. Calcutta: Printed by Daniel Stuart, 1785.

Atkinson, Captain George F. *Curry and Rice on Forty Plates,* 3rd ed. London: Day and Son, Ltd., 1860.

Bellew, John Francis. *Memoirs of a Griffin.* 2 vols. London: William H. Allen and Co., 1843.

Bengal Gazette or Calcutta General Advertiser. Calcutta: 1780–1782.

Bolts, William. *Considerations on Indian Affairs Particularly Respecting the Present State of Bengal and Its Dependencies,* 2nd ed. London: Printed for J. Almon, 1772.

Brown, Samuel Sneade. *Home Letters Written from India between the Years 1828 and 1841*. London: Printed for Private Circulation by C.F. Roworth, Lane, 1878.

Bruce, John. *Annals of the Honourable East India Company, from their Establishment by the Charter of Queen Elizabeth. 1600, to the Union of the London and English East India Companies, 1707–8.* 3 vols. London: Black, Parry, and Kingsbury, 1810 (Republished at Farnborough: Gregg Press Limited, 1968).

Burton, Richard. *Goa and the Blue Mountains*. London: Richard Bentley, 1851.

Butler, Robert. *Narrative of the Life and Travels of Serjeant B.* London: Knight and Lacey, 1823.

Buyers, Reverend William. *Letters on India, with Special Reference to the Spread of Christianity*. London: John Snow, 1840.

Calcutta Gazette.

Calcutta Magazine and Monthly Register.

Callcott, Lady Maria [Graham]. *Journal of a Residence in India*. Edinburgh: Printed for Archibald Constable and Company, 1812.

———. *Letters on India*. London: Longman, 1814.

Coley, James. *Journal of the Sutlej Campaign of 1845–46*. London: Smith, Elder & Co., 1856.

d'Arblay, Madame. *Diary and Letters of Frances Burney*. Edited by Sarah Chauncey Woolsey. 2 vols. Boston: Roberts Brothers, 1880.

Dickens, Charles. *A Child's History of England and Miscellaneous Pieces*. Boston: Estes and Lauriat, 1880.

Dow, Alexander. *The History of Hindostan, Translated from the Persian of Mohammed Kasim Ferishta*. 3 vols. London: Printed for J. Walker and eight others, 1812.

Duberly, Frances Isabella. *Campaigning Experiences in Rajpootana and Central India, during the Suppression of the Mutiny, 1857–58*. London: Smith, Elder, & Co., 1859.

Eden, Emily. *Up the Country*. 2 vols. London: Richard Bentley, 1866.

Elphinstone, Mountstuart. *The Rise of the British Power in the East*. London: John Murray, Albemarle Street, 1887.

Elwood, Anne Katharine. *Narrative of a Journey Overland from England, by the Continent of Europe, Egypt, and the Red Sea, to India; including a Residence There, and Voyage Home , in the Years 1825, 26, 27, and 28.* 2 vols. London: Henry Colburn and Richard Bentley, 1830.

Falkland, Viscountess Amelia Cary, *Chow-Chow: Being Selections from a Journal Kept in India, Egypt, and Syria.* 2 vols. London: Hurst and Blackett, 1857.

Fay, Eliza. *Original Letters from India*. Edited by E.M. Forster. London: Hogarth Press, 1986.

Fenton, Bessie. *Journal of Mrs. Fenton*. London: Edward Arnold, 1901.

Forbes, James, *Oriental Memoirs*. 4 vols. London: White, Cochrane and Co., 1813.

Foster, Sir William, ed. *Early Travels in India, 1583–1619*. London, Humphrey Milford, Oxford University Press, 1921.

———. *The Embassy of Sir Tomas Roe to the Court of the Great Mogul, 1615–1619, as Narrated in His Journal and Correspondence*. 2 vols. London: Printed for the Hakluyt Society, 1926.

———. *A New Account of the East Indies by Alexander Hamilton*. 2 vols. London: The Argonaut Press, 1930.

Francis, Philip. *The Francis Letters*. Edited by Beata Francis, and Eliza Keary. 2 vols. London: Hutchinson and Co., 1901.

Fryer, John. *A New Account of East India and Persia Being Nine Years' Travels, 1672–1681*. Edited by William Crooke. 3 vols. London: Printed for the Hakluyt Society, 1909.

Gibbes, Phebe [Goldborne, Sophia]. *Hartly House, Calcutta*. Calcutta: Thacker, Spink and Co., 1908 (Reprinted from the 1789 edition).

Graham, Maria. [See Callcott, Lady Maria.]

Grant, Robert. *A Sketch of the History of the East India Company*. London: Printed for Black, Parry and Co., 1813.

Grier, Sydney, ed. *The Letters of Warren Hastings to His Wife.*. Edinburgh and London: William Blackwood and Sons, 1905.

Hamilton, Eliza. *Translations of the Letters of a Hindoo Rajah, Written Previous to and During the Period of His Residence in England: To Which Is Prefixed, a Preliminary Dissertation on the History, Religion, and Manners of the Hindoos*, 2 vols. Boston: Wells and Lilly, 1819.

Heber, Reginald. *Narrative of a Journey through the Upper Provinces of India, from Calcutta to Bombay,1823–1825*. London: John Murray, 1828.

Hickey, William. *Memoirs of William Hickey*. 4 vols, 8th ed. Edited by Alfred Spencer, New York: Alfred A. Knopf, 1921.

House of Commons, *Parliamentary Papers*, 'Papers Relating to East India Officers', Vol. VIII (1812–13).

———. 'Free Schools in India', Vol. LX (1831–32).

Jacquemont, Victor. *Letters from India*. 2 vols. London: Edward Churton, 1834.

Kindersley, Mrs Jemima. *Letters from the Island of Teneriffe, Brazil, the Cape of Good Hope and the East Indies*. London: Printed for J. Nourse, 1777.

Lang, John. *Wanderings in India*. London: Routledge, Warner and Routledge, 1861.

Latham, Robert and Matthews, William, eds. *Diary of Samuel Pepys*. 11 vols. Berkeley and Los Angeles: University of California Press, 1983.

Lawrence, John and Woodiwiss, Audrey, eds. *The Journals of Honoria Lawrence*. London: Hodder and Stoughton, 1980.

Leonowens, Anna Hariette Crawford. *Life and Travel in India: Being the Recollections of a Journey before the Days of Railroads*. Philadelphia: Porter and Coates, 1884.

Login, E. Dalhousie. *Lady Login's Recollections*. London: Smith, Elder & Co., 1916.

Love, Henry Davison. *Vestiges of Old Madras, 1640–1800*. 3 vols. Indian Records Series. London: John Murray, 1913.

Lushington, Lady Henrietta [Mrs Stephen]. *The Sea Spirit and Other Poems*. London: John W. Parker, 1850.

MacDonald, John. *Memoirs of an Eighteenth Century Footman (1175–1779)*. With an introduction by John Beresford. London: George Routledge & Sons Ltd, 1927.

Mackenzie, Helen [Mrs Colin]. *Life in the Mission, the Camp and the Zenana: or Six Years in India*. 2 vols. London: Richard Bentley, 1854 (2nd ed.).

Mackintosh, William. *Remarks on a Tour through the Different Countries of Europe, Asia and Africa*, 2 vols. Dublin: Printed by J. Jones, 1786.

Maitland, Julia Charlotte. *Letters from Madras, during the Years 1836–39, by a Lady*. London: John Murray, 1846.

Markham, Clements R., C.B., F.R.S., ed. 'The Journals of Captain William Hawkins', in *The Hawkins' Voyages during the Reigns of Henry VIII, Queen Elizabeth and James I*. London: Printed for the Hakluyt Society, 1878.

Marryat, Florence. *'Gup': Sketches of Anglo-Indian Life and Character*. London: Richard Bentley, 1868.

Military Memoirs of Lady Sale. Edited by Patrick Macrory. London: Longmans, Green and Co., Ltd., 1969.

Mullens, Hannah Catherine. *Faith and Victory: A Story of the Progress of Christianity in Bengal*. London: James Nisbet and Co., 1865.

Mundy, Godfrey Charles. *Journal of a Tour in India*. London: John Murray, 1858.

Nugent, Maria. *Lady Nugent's Journal*. Edited by Frank Crandall. London: Adam & Charles Black for the Institute of Jamaica, 1907.

Orme, Robert. *Historical Fragments of the Mogul Empire, and the Morattoes, and of the English Concerns in Indostan, from the year MDCLIX*. Edited by J.P. Guha. New Delhi: Associated Publishing House, 1974.

———. *History of the Military Transactions of the British Nation in Indostan from the Year MDCCXLV*, 2nd ed. London: Printed for John Nourse, 1775.

Ovington, John. *A Voyage to Surat in the Year 1689*. Edited by H.G. Rawlinson. London: Humphrey Milford, Oxford University Press, 1929.

Parkes (Parlby), Fanny. *Begums, Thugs and White Mughals*. London: Sickle Moon Press, 2002.

Parkes (Parlby), Fanny. *Wanderings of a Pilgrim in Search of the Picturesque, during Four and Twenty Years in the East.* 2 vols. London: P. Richardson, 1850.

Postans, Marianne. *Cutch; or Random Sketches Taken during a Residence in One of the Northern Provinces of Western India; Interspersed with Legends and Traditions.* London: Smith, Elder, and Co., 1839.

Postans, Marianne. *Travels, Tales and Encounters in Sindh and Balochistan, 1840–1843.* Oxford: Oxford University Press, 2003.

———. *Western India in 1838.* 2 vols. London: Saunders and Otley, 1839.

Rawdon, Francis, Marquess of Hastings. *Private Journal of the Marquess of Hastings.* Allahabad: The Panini Office, 1907.

Roberts, Emma. *Scenes and Characterisitcs of Hindostan, with Sketches of Anglo-Indian Society.* 3 vols. London: W.H. Allen & Co., 1835.

———. *Hindostan: Its Landscapes, Palaces, Temples, Tombs; The Shores of the Red Sea; and the Sublime and Romantic Scenery of the Himalaya Mountains.* Delhi: Oriental Publishers, 1972.

Sainsbury, Ethel Bruce. *A Calendar of the Court Minutes, etc., of the East India Company, 1635–1639.* Oxford: Clarendon Press, 1907.

———. *A Calendar of the Court Minutes, etc., of the East India Company, 1640–1643.* Oxford: Clarendon Press, 1909.

———. *A Calendar of the Court Minutes, etc., of the East India Company, 1644–1649.* Oxford: Clarendon Press, 1912.

———. *A Calendar of the Court Minutes, etc., of the East India Company, 1650–1654.* Oxford: Clarendon Press, 1913.

———. *A Calendar of the Court Minutes, etc., of the East India Company, 1655–1659.* Oxford: Clarendon Press, 1916.

———. *A Calendar of the Court Minutes, etc., of the East India Company, 1660–1663.* Oxford: Clarendon Press, 1922.

———. *A Calendar of the Court Minutes, etc., of the East India Company, 1664–1667.* Oxford: Clarendon Press, 1925.

———. *A Calendar of the Court Minutes, etc., of the East India Company, 1668–1670.* Oxford: Clarendon Press, 1929.

———. *A Calendar of the Court Minutes, etc., of the East India Company, 1671–1673.* Oxford: Clarendon Press, 1932.

———. *A Calendar of the Court Minutes, etc., of the East India Company, 1674–1676.* Oxford: Clarendon Press, 1935.

———. *A Calendar of the Court Minutes, etc., of the East India Company, 1677–1679.* Oxford: Clarendon Press, 1938.

Sale, Lady Florentia. *Journal of the Disasters in Affghanistan, 1841–2.* London: John Murray, 1843.

Sargent, Reverend John, ed. *Life and Letters of the Reverend Henry Martyn.* London: Seeley, Jackson and Halliday, 1862.

Sellon, Edward. *Annotations on the Sacred Writings of the Hindues.* New edition. London: Printed for Private Circulation, 1902.

Sherwood, Mary Martha. *The Life and Times of Mrs. Sherwood (1775–1851) from the Diaries of Captain and Mrs. Sherwood.* Edited by F.J. Harvey Darton. London: Wells Gardner & Co., 1910.

Shore, Frederick John. *Notes on Indian Affairs.* 2 vols. London: John Parker, 1837.

Sleeman, Lieutenant Colonel William Henry. *Rambles and Recollections of an Indian Official.* 2 vols. London: J. Hatchard and Son, 1844.

[Smart, Jane]. *A Letter from a Lady at Madrass to Her Friends in London: Giving an Account of a Visit Made by the Governor of That Place, with His Lady and Others, to the Nabob (Prime Minister to the Great Mogul) and His Lady, &c., in Which Their Persons, and Amazing Richness of Dress, are Particularly Described.* London: Printed for and sold by H. Piers, Bookseller, Chancery-Lane in Holborn, 1743.

Smith, Elizabeth Elton. *East India Sketch Book: By a Lady.* 2 vols. London: Richard Bentley, 1833.

Starke, Mariana. *The Widow of Malabar.* London: Printed for William Lane, 1791.

Stocqueler, J.H. *The Handbook of British India.* London: William H. Allen and Co., 1854.

Strachen, Michael and Penrose Boies, eds. *The East India Company Journals of Captain William Keeling and Master Thomas Bonner, 1615–1617.* Minneapolis: University of Minnesota Press, 1971.

Tennant, Reverend William. *Indian Recreations.* 3 vols, 2nd ed. London: G. Steward, 1804 and Edinburgh: Edinburgh University Press, 1808.

Tucker, Sarah, *South Indian Sketches.* London: Smith, Elder and Co., 1856.

Twining, Thomas. *Travels in India a Hundred Years Ago.* London: James R. Osgood, McIlvaine & Co., 1893.

Twenty-four Plates Illustrative of Hindoo and European Manners in Bengal. Drawn on the Stone by A. Colin from Sketches by Mrs. Belnos. Calcutta: Riddhi-India, 1979.

Tytler, Harriet. *An Englishwoman in India: The Memoirs of Harriet Tytler, 1828–1858.* Edited by Anthony Sattin. New York and Oxford: University Press, 1986.

Wallace-Dunlop, Madeleine. *The Timely Retreat; or a Year in Bengal before the Mutinies.* 2 vols, 2nd ed. London: Richard Bentley, 1858.

Weitbrecht, Mary Edwards [Martha]. *Missionary Sketches in North India with References to Recent Events.* London: James Nisbet and Col, 1858.

———. *Women of India and Christian Work in the Zenana.* London: James Nisbet & Co., 1875.

Williamson, Captain Thomas. *The East India Vade-Mecum or Complete Guide to Gentlemen Intended for the Civil, Military, or Naval Service of the Hon. East India Company.* 2 vols. London: Printed for Black, Parry, and Kingsbury, 1810.

Yule, Colonel Henry, ed. *The Diary of William Hedges., Esq. during His Agency in Bengal; as well as on His Voyage Out and Return Overland (1681–1687).* 3 vols. London: Printed for the Hakluyt Society, 1887–89.

secondary sources

Arasaratnam, Sinnappah. *Merchants, Companies and Commerce on the Coromandel Coast, 1650–1740.* Delhi: Oxford University Press, 1986.

Archer, Mildred. *Company Drawings in the India Office Library.* London: Her Majesty's Stationery Office, 1972.

———. *Indian Popular Painting in the India Office Library.* London: Her Majesty's Stationery Office, 1977.

Ashton, John. *Social Life in the Reign of Queen Anne.* London: Chatto & Windus, 1925.

Babu, S. *Merchants of Politics: East India Company and Dawn of the Raj.* New Delhi: Dominant Publishers and Distributors, 2006.

Ballantyne, Tony. *Orientalism and Race: Aryanism in the British Empire.* Houndsmills, Basingstoke, Hampshire and New York: Palgrave, 2002.

Ballhatchet, Kenneth. *Race, Sex and Class under the Raj: Imperial Attitudes and Policies and Their Critics, 1793–1905.* New York: St. Martin's Press, 1980.

Barr, Patt. *The Memsahibs: The Women of Victorian India.* London: Secker and Warburg, 1976.

Basch, Francoise. *Relative Creatures.* London: Allen Lane, Division of Penguin Books, Ltd., 1974.

Basham, A.L. 'Sophia and the "Bramin"'. In *East India Company Studies. Papers Presented to Professor Sir Cyril Philips,* eds Kenneth Ballhatchet and John Harrison. Hong Kong: Asian Research Service, 1986.

Bearce, Geroge Donham. *British Attitudes toward India, 1784–1858.* London: Oxford University Press, 1961.

Bickers, Robert A. *Empire Made Me: An Englishman Adrift in Shanghai.* New York: Columbia University Press. 2003.

Biddulph, John. *The Pirates of Malabar and an Englishwoman in India Two Hundred Years Ago.* London: Smith, Elder & Co., 1907.

Blease, Walter. *The Emancipation of English Women.* London: Constable & Company, Ltd., 1920.

Blechynden, Kathleen. *Calcutta Past and Present.* London: W. Thacker & Co., 1905.

Botsford, Jay Barrett. *English Society in the Eighteenth Century.* New York: The Macmillan Company, 1924.

Bowen, H.V., Lincoln, Margarette and Rigby, Nigel, eds. *The Worlds of the East India Company.* Woodbridge, Suffolk: The Boydell Press, 2002.

Bradshaw, John. *Sir Thomas Munro and the British Settlement of Madras Presidency.* Oxford: Clarendon Press, 1894.

Briggs, Asa. *The Age of Improvement.* London: Longmans, Green and Co., 1959.

Brittain, Vera. *Lady into Woman.* New York: Macmillan, 1953.

Brown, Hilton. *The Sahibs.* London: William Hodge & Company, Ltd., 1948.

Bryant, Arthur. *The Age of Elegance, 1812–1822.* New York: Harper & Brothers, 1950.

Buck, Edward J. *Simla Past and Present.* Bombay: The Times Press, 1925.

Burton, Antoinette. *Burdens of History.* Chapel Hill: University of North Carolina Press, 1994.

Busteed, Henry. *Echoes of Old Calcutta.* 4th ed. London: W. Thacker & Co., 1908.

Calder-Marshall, Arthur. *The Grand Century of the Lady.* London: Gordon & Cremonesi, 1976.

Cannadine, David. *Ornamentalism: How the British Saw Their Empire.* New York: Oxford University Press, 2001.

Cannon, Garland. *Oriental Jones.* New York: Asia Publishing House, 1964.

Carey, S. Pearce. *William Carey.* London: Hodder and Stoughton, 1923.

Carey, William H. *The Good Old Days of Honorable John Company: Being Curious Reminiscences during the Rule of the East India Company from 1600 to 1858.* 2 vols. Calcutta: R. Cambray & Co., 1906.

Chailley, Joseph. *Administrative Problems of British India.* London: Macmillan, 1910.

Chatterjee, Amal. *Representations of India, 1740–1840: The Creation of India in the Colonial Imagination.* New York: St. Martin's Press, Inc. 1998.

Chaudhuri, Nupur and Margaret Strobel. *Western Women and Imperialism.* Bloomington: Indiana University Press, 1992.

Colley, Linda. *Captives: Britain, Empire and the World, 1600–1850.* London: Jonathan Cape, 2002.

———. *The Ordeal of Elizabeth Marsh: A Woman in World History.* New York: Pantheon Books, 2007.

Dalrymple, William. *The Last Mughal: The Fall of a Dynasty—Delhi, 1857.* New York: Vintage Books, 2006.

———. *White Mughuls. Love and Betrayal in Eighteenth-Century India.* New York: Penguin Books, 2004.

Das Gupta, J.N. *India in the Seventeenth Century as Depicted by European Travelers.* Calcutta: University of Calcutta, 1916.

Daunton, Martin and Rick Halpern, eds. *Empire and Others: British Encounters with Indigenous Peoples, 1600–1850*. London: UCL Press, 1999.

Davies, A. Mervyn. *Strange Destiny. A Biography of Warren Hastings*. New York: G.P. Putnam's Sons, 1935.

Dewar, Douglas. *In the Days of the Company*. London: W. Thacker & Co., 1920.

Dickinson, Violet, ed. *Miss Eden's Letters*. London: Macmillan, 1919.

Diver, Maud. *Honoria Lawrence*. Boston: Houghton Mifflin Company, 1936.

———. *An Englishwoman in India*. London: William Blackwood & Sons, 1909.

Dodwell, H.H., ed. *The Cambridge History of the British Empire British India*. Vol. IV. New York: Macmillan, 1929.

Dolan, Brian. *Exploring European Frontiers: British Travellers in the Age of Enlightenment*. New York: St. Martin's Press, Inc., 2000.

———. *Ladies of the Grand Tour*. New York: Harper Collins, 2001.

Dunbar, Janet. *Golden Interlude*. London: John Murray, 1955.

———, ed. *Tigers, Durbars and Kings: Fanny Eden's Indian Journals, 1837–1838*. London: John Murray, 1988.

East India Company Studies. Papers Presented to Professor Sir Cyril Philips. Edited by Kenneth B Ballhatchet and John Harrison. Hong Kong: Asian Research Service, 1986.

Dyson, Ketaki Kushari. *A Various Universe: A Study of the Journals and Memoirs of British Men and Women in the Indian Subcontinent, 1765–1856*. Delhi: Oxford University Press, 1978.

Edwardes, Michael. *Bound to Exile: The Victorians in India*. London: Sidgwick and Jackson, 1969.

Edwardes, Stephen Meredyth, ed. *The Gazeteer of Bombay City and Island*. 3 vols. Bombay: The Times Press, 1909.

Embree, Ainslie. *Charles Grant and British Rule in India*. London: George Allen and Unwin, Ltd., 1962.

———. 'Tradition and Modernization in India: Synthesis or Encapsulation?' Presented at the International Symposium on Science and Society in South Asia, Rockefeller University, 5 May 1966.

Fawcett, Sir Charles, ed. *The English Factories in India: The Western Presidency, 1670–1677*. New series. Oxford: Clarendon Press, 1936.

———, ed. *The English Factories in India: Bombay, Surat, and the Western Coast, 1678–1684*. New Series. Oxford: Clarendon Press, 1954.

Franklin, Michael J., ed. *Romantic Representations of British India*. London and New York: Routledge, 2006.

Fraser, George Macdonald. *Flashman*. New York: World Publishing Co., 1969.

———. *Flashman and the Mountain of Light*. New York: Alfred A. Knopf, 1991.

Furber, Holden. *John Company at Work*. Cambridge: Harvard University Press, 1948.

Gardner, Brian. *The East India Company*. New York: Barnes and Noble, 1971.

Ghosal, Akshoy Kumar. *Civil Service in India under the East India Company*. Calcutta: University of Calcutta, 1944.

Ghose, Indira, ed. *Memsahibs Abroad. Women Travellers in Colonial India*. Delhi: Oxford University Press, 1998.

Ghosh, Durba. *Sex and the Family in Colonial India: The Making of Empire*. Cambridge and New York: Cambridge University Press, 2006.

Ghosh, Suresh Chandra. *The Social Condition of the British Community in Bengal. 1757–1800*. Leiden: E.J. Brill, 1970.

Greenberger, Allen J. *British Image of India*. New York: Oxford University Press, 1969.

Hall, Catherine, ed. *Cultures of Empire: A Reader—Colonizers in Britain and the Empire in the Nineteenth and Twentieth Centuries*. Manchester: University Press, 2000.

Hall, Catherine and Sonya Rose, eds. *At Home with the Empire*. Cambridge: University Press, 2006.

Hawes, Christopher J. *Poor Relations: The Making of a Eurasian Community in British India, 1773–1833*. Richmond, Surrey: Curzon Press, 1996.

Herbert, N.M., ed. *A History of the County of Gloucester*, vol. xi. In *The Victoria History of the Counties of England* edited by R.B. Pugh. London: Oxford University Press, 1976.

Hibbert, Christopher. *The Great Mutiny: India 1857*. New York: Viking Penguin, 1978.

Hutchins, Francis. *The Illusion of Permanence*. Princeton, New Jersey: Princeton University Press, 1967.

Hyam, Ronald. *Empire and Sexuality*. Manchester: University Press, 1991.

Ingham, Kenneth. *Reformers in India, 1793–1833*. Cambridge: University Press, 1956.

Jasanoff, Maya. *Edge of Empire. Lives, Culture, and Conquest in the East, 1750–1850*. New York: Alfred A. Knopf, 2005.

Keay, John. *The Honourable Company: A History of the English East India Company*. New York: Macmillan, 1991.

Kincaid, Dennis. *British Social Life in India, 1608–1937*. London: George Routledge and Sons, Ltd., 1938 (reprint 1939).

Levine, Philippa. *Gender and Empire*. New York: Oxford University Press, 2004.

Llewellyn-Jones, Rosie. *Engaging Scoundrels: True Tales of Old Lucknow*. New Delhi: Oxford University Press, 2000.

Longford, Elizabeth. *Queen Victoria: Born to Succeed*. New York: Harper & Row, 1964.

Macaulay, Thomas Babington. *Minute on Indian Education.* Available at
http://www.mssu.edu/projectsouthasia/history/primarydocs/education/
Macaulay001.htm

Mahajan, Jagmohan. *The Grand Indian Tour: Travels and Sketches of Emily
Eden.* New Delhi: Manohar, 1996.

Marshall, P[eter] J. *Bengal: The British Bridgehead—Eastern India 1740–
1828.* Vol. II, Part 2 in New Cambridge History of India, Gordon
Johnson, general editor. Cambridge: University Press, 1987.

Martin, Giles. *Nathaniel's Nutmeg.* New York: Penguin, 1999.

Mason, Philip. *A Matter of Honour.* London: Jonathan Cape, 1974.

McMillan, Margaret. *Women of the Raj.* London: Thames and Hudson,
1988.

Metcalf, Barbara D. and Thomas R Metcalf. *A Concise History of Modern
India.* 2nd ed. Cambridge: University Press, 2006.

Metcalf, Thomas R. *An Imperial Vision: Indian Architecture and Britain's Raj.*
Berkeley: University of California Press, 1988.

Mills, Sara. *Gender and Colonial Space.* Manchester: University Press, 2005.

Morris, James. *Heaven's Command.* London: Faber and Faber, Ltd., 1973.

Naidis, Mark. 'British Attitudes Toward the Anglo-Indians', *South Atlantic
Quarterly,* 62 (Summer 1963), 407.

———. 'Evolution of the Sahib', *The Historian,* XIX, no. 4 (August 1957),
425.

Nechtman, Tillman W. 'Nabobinas: Luxury, Gender, and the Sexual Politics
of British Imperialism in India in the Late Eighteenth Century', *Journal
of Women's History,* 18, no. 4 (Winter 2006), 8–30.

———. *Nabobs: Empire and Identity in Eighteenth-Century Britain.* Cambridge:
University Press, 2010.

Nightingale, Pamela. *Fortune and Integrity: A Study of Moral Attitudes in the
Indian Diary of George Paterson, 1769–1774.* Delhi: Oxford University
Press, 1985.

O'Faolain, Julia and Lauro Marines, eds. *Not in God's Image.* New York:
Harper & Row, 1975.

O'Keefe, Timothy John. *British Attitudes toward India and the Dependent
Empire, 1857–1874.* South Bend: Notre Dame University Press, 1968.

Pearson, R. *Eastern Interlude.* Calcutta: Thacker, Spink, & Co., 1954.

Pedersen, Susan. 'Introduction: Claims to Belong', *Journal of British Studies,*
40, no. 4 (October 2001), 447.

Penny, Reverend Frank. *The Church in Madras: Being the History of the
Ecclesiastical and Missionary Action of the East India Company in the
Presidency of Madras in the Seventeenth and Eighteenth Centuries.* 2 vols.
London: Smith, Elder, & Co., 1904.

Penrose, Boies. *Travel and Discovery in the Renaissance, 1420–1620.* New York: Atheneum, 1971.

Porter, Bernard. *The Absent-Minded Imperialists: Empire, Society, and Culture in Britain.* Oxford: University Press, 2004.

Procida, Mary. *Married to the Empire: Gender, Politics and Imperialism in India, 1883–1947* Manchester: University Press, 2002.

———. 'Good Sports and Right Sorts: Guns, Gender, and Imperialism in British India', *Journal of British Studies,* 40, no. 4 (October 2001), 454.

Raza, Rosemary. *In Their Own Words.* New Delhi: Oxford University Press, 2006.

Rice, Edward. *Sir Richard Burton.* New York: Charles Scribner's Sons, 1990.

Sen, Indrani. *Woman and Empire.* Hyderabad: Orient Longman Limited, 2002.

Sen, Indrani, ed. *Memsahib's Writings. Colonial Narratives on Indian Women.* Hyderabad: Orient Longman Private Limited, 2008.

Singh, O.P. *Surat and Its Trade in the Second Half of the 17th Century.* Delhi: University of Delhi Press, 1975.

Smith, Hilda, ed. *Women Writers and the Early Modern British Political Tradition.* Cambridge: University Press, 1998.

Spear, Percival. *The Nabobs.* London: Oxford University Press, 1963.

Spry, Henry. *Modern India.* 2 vols. London: Whittaker and Co., 1837.

Stone, Lawrence. *The Family, Sex and Marriage in England, 1500–1800.* New York: Harper & Row, 1977.

Sykes, Laura. *Calcutta through British Eyes, 1690–1990.* Madras: Oxford University Press, 1992.

Tague, Ingrid. 'Love, Honor, and Obedience: Fashionable Women and the Discourse of Marriage in the Early Eighteenth Century', *Journal of British Studies,* 40, no. 4 (October 2001), 76.

Thompson, Edward and G.T. Book Garratt. *Rise and Fulfillment of British Rule in India.* Allahabad: Central Book Depot, 1962.

Trautman, Thomas. 'The Missionary and the Orientalist'. In *Ancient to Modern: Religion, Power, and Community in India,* edited by Ishita Bannerjee Dube and Saurabh Dube. New Delhi: Oxford University Press, 2008.

Turberville, A.S. *English Men and Manners in the Eighteenth Century.* Oxford: Clarendon Press, 1926.

Wheeler, J. Talboys, ed. *Annals of the Madras Presidency.* 3 vols. Delhi: B.R. Publishing Corporation, 1985.

———, ed. *Early Travels in India (16th & 17th Centuries).* Delhi: Deep Publications, 1974.

Wilbur, Marguerite. *The East India Company and the British Empire in the Far East.* New York: Richard R. Smith, 1945.

Wild, Anthony. *The East India Company: Trade and Conquest from 1600.* New York: Lyons Press, 2000.

Willett, C. and Cunnington, Phillis. *The History of Underclothes.* New York: Dover Publications, Inc., 1992.

Willson, Beckles. *Ledger and Sword or the Honourable Company of Merchants of England Trading to the East Indies, 1599–1874.* 2 vols. London, New York and Bombay: Longmans, Green, 1903.

Wilson, Charles R., ed. *The Early Annals of the English in Bengal, Being the Bengal Public Consultations for the First Half of the Eighteenth Century.*. 3 vols. London: Thacker & Co., 1900.

Wilson, Kathleen, ed. *A New Imperial History: Culture, Identity, and Modernity in Britain and the Empire, 1660–1840.* New York: Cambridge University Press, 2004.

Woodruff, Philip. *The Men Who Ruled India.* 2 vols, *The Founders* and *The Guardians.* New York: Schocken Books, 1964.

Wright, Arnold. *Early English Adventurers in the East.* London: Andrew Melrose, Ltd., 1917.

Wright, Arnold and William L. Sclater. *Sterne's Eliza.* London: William Heinemann, 1922.

Yarwood, Doreen. *English Costume.* London: B.T. Batsford, Ltd., 1953.

Yule, Colonel Henry and A.C. Burnell. *Hobson-Jobson: A Glossary of Coloquial Anglo-Indian Words, Phrases, and of Kindred Terms, Etymological Historical, Geographical and Discursive.* Edited by William Crooke. London: Routledge and Kegan Paul, 1968.

from the india office library

Europeans in India, Vol. 25, OIOC.

Factory Records. Original Correspondence.

India Office Records. *Ecclesiastical Returns. 1698-1968.*

List of passengers to India in EIC Letter Books. 1626–1753. E/3/84–111.

Marriages at Fort St. George, Madras. 1680–1815 'FEP' (Exeter, 1907).

Wills, administrations, probates, inventories & estates. 1618–1725, 1704–1783. G/40/23.and L/AG/34/40.

index

St John's Church, 106, 110, 218
St Mary's Church, 45, 52, 54n18, 78
Sale, Florentia, 230–1, 237–44, 246
sangita, 246
Sankskrit/Sanskritic, 130, 131, 169, 190, 196, 197
San Thomé, 41, 42, 44, 45,
sati, 127, 136, 140, 170, 176, 177–9, 196, 227n
Second Sikh War, 247
Second Voyage, 4, 6
'setting up', 106–7
Shakespeare, William, 4, 32
Shaista Khan, 28, 31, 37
Shah Abbas, 10
Shah Alam, 99
Shah Jehan, 9see also Khurrum, Prince), 59
Shah Reza, 87–8,
Shah Shuja, 238–9, 243
Sheikh Zain al-Din, 132
Sherley, Robert, 10, 18–20
Sherwood, Mary, 181–2, 185, 199, 201–3, 206
Shivaji, 59–60, 65, 166
Shore, Sir John, 100, 130, 179, 218
Shuja ad-Daula, 133
Simla, 234
Sind, 245
Sleeman, Colonel William, 176, 186n1, 218, 227
Smart, Jane, 88–9, 93, 95, 133, 137
Smith, Elizabeth Elton, 224
Smith, Sir Thomas, 3, 8, 11
Sooknay Roy, 125
Spice Islands, 4, 14, 41
Spurin, Agnes, 34
Steele, Frances (Webbe) 18–23, 90, 92, 137–8
Steele, Richard, 18–22

Surat, 4–5, 7, 13–15, 17–19, 25, 29, 32, 41, 43, 53n4, 57–8, 60, 64, 66, 212
Swally (Sually) Hole, 13, 16, 53n4

Taj Mahal,15, 169, 221
Talleyrand, Charles Maurice de, 113
tarofe, 222
Taverns, 76, 145
Ten Commandments, xii, 58–9, 67
Tennant, Reverend William, 183, 186, 193, 211, 216
Tent Club, 122
Third Voyage, 4–5, 9, 14
Thuggee, 176, 178, 186n1
Timms, Biddy. *See* Meer Hassan Ali, Mrs
Tipu Sultan, xv, 161, 181
Tolfrrey, Stackhouse, 150–1
Towerson, Gabriel, 16, 22
Towerson, Mrs, 16, 18–23
Tutchin, Samuel, 44
Twelfth Voyage, 5, 9, 11
Tytler, Harriet, 8, 164–5, 198

United Company of Merchants, 6

Victoria, Queen, 230–1, 248

Wallace-Dunlop, Madeline, 217, 220, 255
Walsh, Master Charles, 44
Ward, William, 190
Warner, Reverend Patrick, 46–7, 61, 186
Weitbrecht, Martha, xii, 191, 197
Wellesley, Richard, xv, 100, 181, 248
Weltden, Anthony, 75

about the author

JOAN MICKELSON GAUGHAN is an independent scholar based in Manchester, Michigan, USA. She served in the Peace Corps in Iran and was professor of history at Washtenaw Community College in Ann Arbor, Michigan (1968–2002). She is a member of the British Scholar Society and has presented papers at the Midwestern Branch of the North American Conference of British Studies. Her publications include *Milestones in Western Civilization* (3 vols, 1998) and seven articles in *Victorian Encyclopedia* (1988).